MW00332845

ADVANCE PRAISE

Annette Libeskind Berkovits' *Aftermath* is a gorgeous bouquet of a book, chronicling her family's journey from Soviet Kyrgyzstan to Poland in the wake of World War II and the Holocaust, their subsequent sojourn in Israel and, finally, their gamble on building a new life for themselves in the United States. It is both a touching coming-of-age memoir and an inspirational immigrant story, an absolute pleasure to read.

—Andrew Nagorski; an award-winning author and journalist who spent more than three decades as a foreign correspondent and editor for Newsweek. Former Vice President and director of public policy for the East-West Institute, an international affairs think tank. Author of *Hitlerland: American Eyewitnesses to the Nazi Rise to Power*, 2012; *The Nazi Hunters*, 2016; and *1941: The Year Germany Lost the War*

Aftermath is a delightful memoir that draws you in with its lively, child's-eye perspective. Spanning three continents, the book vividly depicts the constrictions of post-war Poland, the vibrant energy and material rigors of the young state of Israel, and the expansiveness of the post-war American dream. Berkovits is sensitive to what it feels like to carry the burdens of history on the slim shoulders of childhood; to the dislocation and identity confusion of the immigrant experience; and to the ways in which a child absorbs parental trauma. Most of all, the book is a joyful celebration of the adaptability and resilience of childhood.

—Rabbi Rena Blumenthal, psychologist in New York City and Jerusalem; author of *The Book of Israela*; Former Assistant Director of the Office of Religious & Spiritual Life and Advisor to Jewish Students at Vassar College and Board member of the Reconstructionist Rabbinical Association

In her charming and inspiring memoir, Annette Libeskind Berkovits, manages to combine terror, deprivation, desperation, hope, romance, and humor into an artful story of wandering, love, loss, and ultimately triumph. Berkovits' personal journey from Kyrgyzstan in Central Asia, to Poland, to Kibbutz Gvat, then Tel Aviv and finally New York, mirrors the awesome and awful saga of 20th century Jews. Berkovits draws the reader deeply into her sad, wounded, but loving family, even as she presents the full range of the modern Jewish experience from tragic loss to redemption and healing.

—Rabbi Phil Graubart is the Judaica Director at the San Diego Jewish Academy. He is an author of ten books, the latest being *Women and God*

Aftermath is an enthralling coming-of-age memoir recounting the hardships and challenges facing a young girl's family in the years following the Holocaust. Searching for a place to call home, they move from a valley in Kyrgyzstan to the streets of war-torn Poland and then to a kibbutz in Israel, a land of dazzling contrasts. The children quickly learn Hebrew and relax into the communal lifestyle of the kibbutz, but life is not easy for the parents. The mother, a talented seamstress, has little interest in farming and, more importantly, the father, not speaking Hebrew, cannot find a job in Israel. What to do? Go to America, 'the Golden Land.'

With characters you genuinely care about, exotic locales, and edge-of-your-seat tension, *Aftermath* is the best memoir I've read in years.

—Barbara Donsky, EdD; International Best-Selling author of *Missing Mother* and *Veronica's Grave: A Daughter's Memoir*

Aftermath by Annette Libeskind Berkovits is one of those necessary books that provides a rare account of the lives of Holocaust survivors after the war. Most survivors did not repatriate, but the Libeskind family did for some post war years. It poignantly depicts how this Jewish family negotiated the residual antisemitism in Poland as it tried to re-establish itself. An impossible feat, the family then followed the heart-rending nomadic path of so many survivors, moving from place to place until almost out of exhaustion, they settled in the U.S.

The book is the tender and disturbing coming-of age memoir of the author as she is wrenched from one place to another and repeatedly finds herself having to learn a new language and the ways of yet another culture. It is also a little-treated story of gender in this population, as the family deals with the post-war reduced status of the father and his support of the author's younger brother, who would grow up to be the renowned architect Daniel Libeskind. This book is a sequel to her family Holocaust memoir, *In the Unlikeliest of Places*, which is an unusual depiction of Jewish survival in the Soviet Union and has been translated into Polish. *Aftermath* is Berkovits' fifth book. *The Corset Maker*, her fourth book, a historical novel was released in March 2022.

—Ellen G. Friedman, PhD. Professor of English and Women's & Gender Studies, The College of New Jersey; Coordinator of the Holocaust and Genocide Studies Program; author of *The Seven, a Family Holocaust Story*

Aftermath is the remarkable memoir of two resourceful children and their parents as the they emerge from the losses of the Holocaust. In cinematic, unsentimental language, Berkovits places us at the scenes of the crimes: "In our family alone, at least sixty people had been exterminated: aunts, uncles, cousins and my maternal grandmother." But she also depicts personal victories, such as her classroom walkout with four Jewish girls to protest being shamed in school during Christian prayers in Poland or getting into one of the most selective public high schools in America without taking the required entrance exam.

Aftermath is both a personal and universal immigrant survival story of striving for the American Dream, but with an important subplot. Before feminism was a glimmer in Gloria Steinem's eye, there were girls and women like Berkovits and her mother. Gritty, intelligent, iron-willed survivors who, against all odds, made the best of the worst possible situations, stitching together a new American life.

—Alan Sharavsky; Author of *Boarding School Bastard, A Memoir: Life in an Orphanage for Fatherless Boys*

As a non-native speaker of English I was amazed (and a little jealous) of Annette Berkovits' linguistic ability when I read her memoir, *Aftermath*. She not so much *learned* languages as *absorbed* them. Growing up speaking Polish, she quickly became fluent in Hebrew when her Holocaust survivor parents were finally able to obtain exit visas and moved to Israel in 1957. When a couple of years later the family moved again, this time to New York, when Berkovits was 16, she only knew two things about America: the Statue of Liberty and Coca-Cola. Yet she quickly mastered enough English to gain access to one of New York City's most prestigious high schools, skipping the mandatory entrance exam and graduating with honors.

Many immigrants, especially young people, will relate to Berkovits' story: the feeling of loss and the urge to return to the place where one had matured. Her yearning for Israel became so strong in New York she even dreamt of stowing away on a ship to return. Israel had become her home—the place where she left many of her closest friends. But soon after Annette graduated college the miasma of the Holocaust she'd carried from childhood began to lift as she embraced her American life with new dreams.

—Benno Groeneveld, retired U.S. correspondent for Dutch and Belgian media

AFTERMATH

COMING OF AGE ON THREE CONTINENTS
A MEMOIR

ANNETTE LIBESKIND BERKOVITS

ISBN 9789493276413 (ebook)

ISBN 9789493276390 (paperback)

ISBN 9789493276406 (hardcover)

Publisher: Amsterdam Publishers, The Netherlands

info@amsterdampublishers.com

Cover image by Rachel Libeskind. Photo: Anetka age 6, Poland 1949

Aftermath is part of the series **Holocaust Survivor True Stories WWII**

Disclaimer. The author made every effort to recreate events, locales and conversations from her memories. However, she asks readers to understand that memory can be fallible and apologizes for any misstatements of fact. In order to maintain anonymity, in some instances names of individuals, identifying characteristics, and physical properties of residences may have been changed.

AUTHOR'S NOTE

Whenever I come across former Israeli Prime Minister Golda Meir's quote: *"You'll never find a better sparring partner than adversity,"* I smile and think that my life's experiences have made me into quite the pugilist. But I did not come into this realization fully until my adult years or perhaps not even till my old age.

My childhood filled with the shadows of the Holocaust did not seem strange to me. It was the life I led. I had nothing with which to compare it. Ensconced in our small, but cozy apartment, protected from the courtyard bullies in Łódź, Poland, and doted over by our nanny, I felt happy. As I grew into school age, I did notice that unlike most of my classmates we had no family around us: no grandmothers, or grandfathers, no aunts, no uncles. It was then that I began asking questions. And the answers, though puzzling, didn't truly register the scope of the family tragedy, the enormous losses, the depth of my parents' pain.

It wasn't until in my later years that I looked back with the perspective of history and time and began thinking about the career choices I made in my life, my likes, my dislikes, and my choice of my life partner and friends. It all added up to one clear image: I was shaped by the aftermath of the Holocaust.

What impact does it have on a child to hear time and again, "Shh... the walls have ears," followed by whispers; darkened rooms with shades drawn where Mama is weeping; stares and insults from strangers and neighbors; holidays and birthdays observed with no extended family? The precise answer is unknown to me even now, except that I adapted, developed thicker skin, grew a protective shield for self-preservation, then put on a smile and moved forward to meet the world on my own terms.

The cuts of antisemitism in Poland which manifested in myriad subtle and overt ways did not simply slide off my back. Perhaps at the time the incidents took place I submerged them deeply so I could function as a "normal" child, but they eventually emerged in adulthood. This may be why I am super sensitive to antisemitic dog whistles; why I cannot abide anyone questioning my or anyone's Jewishness, or vicious attacks on Israel despite my deep reservations about some of its policies.

The most optimistic thing I can relate—but only in retrospect— is that children are blessed by a miraculous ability to adapt, survive, and thrive. And that ability is strengthened if they grow up surrounded by love and encouragement within the nuclear family. Both my brother and I had plenty of those requisite supports. Perhaps more than any other factor, our parents' love, and respect for one another account for our successes in our personal and professional lives.

I dedicate this book to both of them:

Dora Blaustein Libeskind
and Nachman Libeskind

*"Do you not see how necessary a World of Pains
and troubles is to school
an intelligence and make it a soul?"*

—John Keats

"Life is not easy for any of us. But what of that? We must have perseverance and above all confidence in ourselves. We must believe that we are gifted for something and that this thing must be attained."

—Marie Curie: Physicist and Chemist who was awarded the Nobel Prize twice for her work in radioactivity

PART 1
RED

1

I spent the first three years of my life unaware of the disaster that had befallen my family. My most vivid recollection of that period is standing in my crib under fragrant trees whose boughs hung so low I was able to reach the peaches that hung on them and imprint each with a tiny nick of my two teeth. My fingers still remember their fuzzy skin, softer than my camel hair blanket.

The world was drenched in red; the fiery orange red of poppy fields, the blood red of the flags, the flickering red embers glowing in the center of the huge yurt where we slept. Like the Uzbeks who shared their home with us, my parents and I lay like spokes of a wheel covered by thick wool rugs, warming our feet near the central fire pit.

Long before I remade myself into the all-American image of Annette Funicello, the Disney Mouseketeer, I was Anetka, a little girl living in one of the remotest corners of the world.

The town of my birth, Kyzyl Kiya, was nestled in the fertile Fergana Valley of Kyrgyzstan, Central Asia. In millennia past it was a welcome rest stop along the Silk Road for traders and their camel caravans laden with exotic cargo: Persian rugs, yak wool, silk, cinnabar, and the rare spices and flavors of the Orient.

By the 1940s the only remnant of those heady times, when a Babel of languages passed through, was the raggedy mix of Eastern European refugees thwarted on their southward journey by impassable mountain ranges. The snowcapped Pamir Mountains, part of the formidable Tien Shan range, towered to heights of over 24,000 feet, but the valley in their shadow seemed hospitable enough to my parents, Nachman and Dora Libeskind.

It was my most carefree time yet the bleakest of all for my parents. Living hand to mouth and counting the days until it was possible for us to return to Poland, Nachman and Dora couldn't afford much beyond the barest necessities. I had no toys to speak of but that did not mean that I went without amusements. The portraits of the Party's Central Committee luminaries that hung in my father's office, at the brick factory, were my earliest playthings. Father would point at the portraits, and I would call out their names. With each additional one I recognized, Father would clap his hands and laugh as if I were the smartest child in the world. Soon I was able to identify each and every one of them as Father pointed, sometimes in order, sometimes at random when he wanted to increase the challenge of the game. I stored them in memory under what must have been my first concept of the alphabet. The "K's": Krupskaya (Lenin's wife); Kalinin, Kaganovich, Khrushchev; the "M's": Malenkov, Mikoyan, Molotov; and Stalin, in a category all by himself.

Exhausted by their efforts to survive the Second World War in the Soviet Union, my parents waited for the aftershocks of the war to subside before embarking on the 1200-mile return trip to Poland. Rumors circulating through refugee networks had reached them that returning Jewish survivors were harassed and robbed, that hundreds were killed in pogroms in dozens of Polish cities and villages. There were even rumors about the concentration camps, but few people believed them. My parents knew the journey back would be long and arduous, but the hope that they would return to the lives they left behind kept their spirits aloft even when their empty stomachs issued angry growls.

Early spring 1946 brought news that the refugees could, at last, attempt the westward journey to Poland if they were lucky enough to find space on the infrequent freight trains.

Instead of its usual cargo, the cattle train my parents caught was now stuffed with wretched, weary humanity. People had forgotten their prewar habits, comforts, and manners. They pushed and shoved to squeeze into the packed trains, dragging in their odd-shaped bundles, and smells of sweat mixed with the unpleasant scents of meager food provisions, food that had to last through a trip everyone knew would likely last for weeks.

Father often spoke about the greeting we received from the guards at the Polish border. He would tell the story calmly, but with a distant look in his eyes as if he were trying to see himself and Mama in that train, listening to the voices outside, hoping for a sympathetic welcome.

As our train pulled into the station, my parents overheard a conversation. "Look at that," said one young guard to the older one, "squeezed in like cattle." He pointed at our boxcar. "Who are these miserable people?"

"Jews," answered the older one with disgust.

"I thought they got them all."

"Nah, Hitler didn't finish the job."

Father wanted desperately to get to Łódź, his native city, because he had heard through the refugee grapevine that his sister, Rosa, was living in Łódź. He had not yet learned her story of survival. His hurry had much to do with the fact that Mama was about to give birth. She was nine months pregnant and Father hoped that his sister would provide us with temporary shelter.

At last, the cattle train screeched to a stop as if its heart had given out. Disoriented human cargo spilled onto the tiny platform. Clusters of returning refugees and their bedraggled belongings crowded the little train station, just inside the Polish border. Now they would have to muster all their strength and luck to squeeze onto the packed passenger trains that they hoped would arrive before they lost their last vestiges of energy. These trains would take them back to the towns and villages they had left seven years before. Beyond the station, a field in early spring glory, emerald green, gave the impression that nothing had changed.

At the station, Father gave Mama a scrap of fabric, torn from a yellowing sheet on which his sister's address was written in his bold, block letters.

"Look, Dora, they'll never let me aboard a passenger train with this sack," he said. He held a large burlap sack of salt, our only possession of any value.

"Take this address and Anetka and get to Rosa's apartment as soon as possible. Tell her you are my wife. She'll take care of you until I get there. I know she will."

Mama dreaded Łódź, our destination. A native of fashionable Warsaw, she had never been to Łódź and knew its reputation as a grim industrial town. She closed her eyes for a moment and tried to imagine how it might look now, after six years of Nazi occupation, but the image was a blank.

She made a feeble effort to resist the journey. "But how will I know your sister?"

"Just go to the address I gave you. Rosa is a good woman. You'll like her."

Mother was too exhausted to argue.

We stood among throngs at the station, where I amused myself by listening to the sounds; I couldn't see much because of the phalanxes of bodies in every direction. The hissing and clanging of the trains as they came to a stop, the whistles of the conductors and the huffing and puffing of the steam escaping from the engines held my attention. The dripping of the condensing steam trickling off their glistening black bodies made them seem like immense sweating beasts. I stood on my tiptoes and stretched my neck, then crouched down to look under their belly. Many trains passed, but they were destined for cities where we knew no one. At last, our train pulled into the station. Father tried to board with Mama and me, but the conductor yelled at him and made him get off.

Alone, Mama and I pushed our way through the packed, narrow corridors: suitcases bursting at the seams and wrapped with tape, or twine; wicker baskets and bundles tied in cloth; instrument cases, and crutches that stuck out at awkward angles. Mama was lucky. Except for her enormous belly, I was her only baggage. We made our way to a car full of silent passengers. A woman moved over to give Mama a seat. I made myself comfortable in her lap wrapping my body around the big ball in her stomach. I was falling asleep when a sudden movement woke me. "Don't be frightened, Anetka," she said softly "it's only the baby." The rhythmic motion of the wheels lulled me back to sleep. I woke up as we were disembarking and rubbed my eyes.

"Mama, I am thirsty."

"Not now, Anetka. We will get you something to drink when we find your Auntie Rosa."

We exited the train platform and emerged on a wide street crisscrossed by tram tracks. The tall gray buildings looked nothing like the low brick home I had known. I was confused by the unfamiliar surroundings. "I want to drink now." I began to cry.

"Come on, give me your hand and let's walk. It's getting late." The wartime curfew was still in effect. People quickened their pace to be sure they were in their homes on time. Mama asked a passerby how to get to the address she was looking for.

"Oh, it's a long way from here, lady. I hope you have the

strength to walk." He saw her emaciated frame and the circles under her eyes.

"Thank you," she said and tugged at my hand.

After a few blocks I piped up, "Mama, I am tired. Carry me."

"Anetka, try to walk a little more, we have to get off the streets very soon." Father had told her that he'd heard people were arrested after curfew. It was getting darker.

I started to cry again. "Mama, Mama, I can't walk any more. My feet hurt." She picked me up and I held on to her neck, still whimpering. Her silence transmitted to me a kind of nameless anxiety. She continued to walk for blocks, putting me down and stopping only once to remove her shoe and wince at the blister on her heel. The streets were empty now. Mama's footsteps reverberated on the pavement.

At last, we arrived at the address. It was a gray building made darker by the evening shadows upon its pockmarked surface. Mother started to climb the dirty staircase, stopping often to adjust me on her belly and sighing. A stale smell of cabbage permeated the air. It wasn't pleasant, but it reminded me how hungry I was and made me fuss again. We arrived on the fifth floor. Mother rang the bell.

A disheveled, gray-haired woman opened the door a crack. "What do you want?"

"Excuse me, I am looking for my sister-in-law, Rosa Libeskind. Does she live here?"

The woman opened the door a bit wider and warmed slightly, giving me a toothless grin. I was frightened by her and clutched mother more tightly. "I am sorry to tell you this, lady, but *Pani* Rosa moved out, left for Germany this morning."

"Excuse me?" Mama said, not comprehending.

"I think she's on her way to the Displaced Persons camp. She said something about looking for her family." After a moment, when my mother just stared at her, the woman shut the door and we could hear the clicking of her many locks.

Mama trudged downstairs slowly, and I clung to her neck. She stood at the building's entrance pressing me to her chest. She had no money and no idea where to go. Venturing out on the street was dangerous. I must have sensed the tension in her body because I lifted my head off her shoulder and looked at her face.

"Don't cry, Mama," I said, "let's look for Auntie in another house."

"Don't worry, Anetka, we will look for someone to help us and we will get you a drink soon."

Mother continued walking, but I could tell she was getting tired because our pace slowed down with each block. We came to an imposing building with a guard booth at the side. Mother approached the booth, and a figure emerged out of the narrow door. It looked like a monumental statue, tall and thick bodied. The large bosom was the only indication she was a female. Her very stance, the rifle slung over her shoulder and her long military coat with epaulets said, "Keep out."

She addressed mother in Russian in a deep, stern voice. "Comrade, why are you out at this time? Don't you know about the curfew?"

Mother understood the guard and explained that we had nowhere to go for the night.

The giant woman fixed her gaze on Mother's belly. "I could get in trouble for this, but come in." She gestured for us to come into her tiny guard booth and said, "You can spend the night on my cot. I have to stand outside. My commander doesn't like it if I sit inside while on night duty."

Mother's whole body exhaled. "I will never forget your kindness. Thank you, I bless you," she said in her limited Russian.

The cabin was tiny; our three bodies filled it almost completely. Before she went outside, the guard pointed to the narrow metal cot. "Here, you can squeeze in with your little girl and rest till I'm off duty when the sun comes up." She put a dented kettle on the little pot-bellied stove in the corner and said, "You can make yourself a cup of tea."

The last thing I remember of that night is Mother tucking in the scratchy gray wool blanket around me. I fell into a child's juicy sleep even before the tea was ready.

———————

In the morning, the guard escorted Mother and me to the shelter for Jewish refugees returning to the city. Father still hadn't arrived. We were assigned a cot in a huge room that housed dozens of women. That afternoon Mother gave birth to Daniel in the shelter infirmary.

Father arrived in Łódź one day later without the sack of salt. The conductor did not allow him to bring it aboard the teeming train. Father left it leaning against the station house, a treasure waiting to be found by someone luckier than he. One could tell by the fallen slope of his shoulders that he was distraught. Surely, having a new son was a blessing, but without a job or a home it was impossible to imagine what kind of a life was awaiting them. He had nothing but the clothing on his back and a sore shoulder from lugging the sack. Where would he house his family? That thought more than anything else blotted out everything in front of him. He could not even appreciate the sight of his beloved city. And the notion that he had abandoned Mama to give birth in a shelter full of strangers gnawed at his gut and filled him with remorse. Would she ever forgive him?

2

My first home in Łódź could have been fun if my brother Daniel didn't scream around the clock. Mama brought him from the infirmary with a severe ear infection. There was no medical care to be had for refugees like us. We were lucky that my father's school friend, Janek, and his wife, Surcia, took us in to share their one room on the third floor of a tenement on Więckowskiego Street.

I liked Janek because he played with me and invented constant amusements for me when Mama was occupied with the baby. Sometimes he let me run in the long hallway outside the room where I could hear the noises of other residents, but when I couldn't stand the stench, I'd say, holding my nose, "Come, Janek, it smells here like the baby's diaper, let's go back inside." The eight families on that floor shared one toilet.

Father was out every day looking for work. Janek, who had a job, would lend a jacket when Father went out to see potential employers. Janek was even shorter than my father, so Father's arms stuck out of the sleeves like a scarecrow's.

Surcia couldn't help take care of me because she worked on the other side of town and came home late each night, but Janek was my best friend. On some days, he would take me to his nearby place of work at lunchtime. I would skip home with a full belly and chirp to Mother happily, "Mama, I ate Janek's meat, it was yummy."

"And what did Janek eat?" she would ask.

"He ate the soup."

"Janek, you shouldn't have. That soup is nothing but water. You are getting skinnier every day," she chided him.

"Just for a little while, until Nachman gets a job," he would say with his crooked smile and rub his head so his hair stood up and made me laugh.

As soon as Mama stopped nursing Daniel and could leave him for a day with a neighbor, she insisted on going to Warsaw to look for her family. "Look Dora, we have heard about the devastation of Warsaw," my father said.

"I don't care. If I don't find anyone, at least I can look at the house where I lived," she said quietly.

"All right, we will go then," my father said. "But, Dora, I want you to be prepared. You know what happened to my family."

"Mama, Mama, can I go too?" I jumped up and down.

"Come here, Anetka." She hugged me tight but didn't answer. "Let's not wake up Daniel."

I slept curled up across my parents' knees almost the entire journey from Łódź to Warsaw. In contrast to my first experience on a train, our compartment was strangely empty and did not provide much amusement. I was eager to exit the train as soon as it stopped. We arrived in late morning. The November day was cloudy and gray. On the platform I held on to Mama and Father's hands on each side of me. They swung me and I squealed expecting more fun and games but Father said, "Dora, I am going to search the survivor registers at the Central Jewish Committee. I will also try the Local Council. Maybe they have something. Why don't you take Anetka and walk over to your old neighborhood?"

"Good, it looks like rain, let's get this done," Mama said, and buttoned up my coat. "Let's go, Anetka," and we left the train station.

The city's air smelled of dust. It was eerily silent, nothing like the noisy streets of Łódź. Whole streets lay in ruins. Not a single building remained intact. Partial skeletons of buildings stood on some blocks and openings of what once were windows stared at us like eyeless skulls. A lone mangy dog sniffed among the piles of rubble. I tugged at Mama's hand. "Can I pet him?" She didn't answer. We walked some more and I kept asking, "Are we there yet?" Finally, we came to a stop at a heap of rubble that beckoned me to climb, but even then, I knew that I shouldn't do something so frivolous. Instead, I took hold of Mama's hand and clutched it tightly.

"This was my house once," Mama said, shaking her head, but her voice sounded thick and strange. She was silent for a long while. Her wide-eyed look coupled with the pallor of her face frightened me. I wrapped my arms around her leg. Somehow that unleashed a flood of tears and deep sobs shook her chest. That was one of the rare times I saw Mama crying. My parents were totally silent on our return trip. It was only later that I learned they hadn't found Mama's mother or her four youngest sisters on any of the survivor registers.

Less than a year after our Warsaw trip I got sick. Mama tried to feed me various concoctions of milk, butter and sugar or eggs when she could get them, but I wasn't hungry in the least. At night I'd wake up crying and hot. She'd kiss my forehead and say,

"Nachman, Anetka has fever again, I need a wet cloth to sponge her."

"We have got to get her to a doctor," my father would say. "What do you think is wrong, Dora?"

"Let's not discuss this now," she'd say as she replaced my soaking wet nightie.

When they managed to scrape up enough money for a doctor, the diagnosis was the one they had dreaded: a tuberculosis infection. Immediately, I was whisked away 100 miles (160 km) northeast of Łódź to a sanatorium in Otwock to regain my health.

―――――――――

The little window in the locked door seemed so far away, way, way at the end of an endless table. Except for me and the matron in the white coat, there was no one there. My feet dangled; I couldn't reach the floor. I was transfixed by the little window in the door, hoping that Daddy's face would appear in it as it did on some days.

"Pick up your spoon and eat your porridge," boomed the disembodied voice coming from the white coat. "If you don't eat it now, you'll get it for dinner and then it'll be even colder." I squeezed my lips shut. I was not hungry. If Mama had made me *gogl mogl* with warm milk, honey, and cinnamon I would have drunk it. But Mama was nowhere to be seen. She was home taking care of baby Daniel.

Each day I wished with all my might for Daddy to come to the window and for the lady in the white coat to let him in. I knew just what I'd do. I'd jump off the chair and run to him. He'd pick me up and I'd snuggle in his neck inhaling the starch on his shirt. And I wouldn't let go.

"You'll never get better if you don't eat." I heard the white-coated lady say time and again. "All the other children have eaten and gone to play, except for you. You are always the last." But she didn't know I was playing too. I pushed the bowl away, put my face down on the table, and then popped up to see if Daddy was at the window. If I did it enough times maybe he'd appear. It was so quiet I could listen for his footsteps coming down the long green corridor. Mostly I heard nothing except distant sounds of the radio. Finally, I'd start to cough and cough until I couldn't catch my breath. Then the white-coated lady would come over and pat my back saying softly, "It's okay, you will be fine."

Several months after my infection subsided, I was sent away again. It was too soon for me to return home because of the risk that Daniel might yet be exposed to the disease. This time it was Torun, a city 93 miles (150 km) north of Łódź where Mania, my mother's cousin, lived. She had survived a harrowing six years of the war hidden in an attic and was ecstatic when she discovered Mama was alive. Mania and her husband Henio, a decorated officer in the Polish military, were young and childless at the time and eagerly welcomed a lively five-year-old, but to me they were total strangers.

After a while I responded to their attention, but I missed my parents. When I cried, Henio hoisted me up and let me touch the colorful medals and ribbons on his uniform. "Tell me the names of the colors," he'd ask and I'd proudly name them. Since neither my parents nor my new custodians had a car or a phone, the separation seemed permanent.

To ease my discomfort, they took me for walks along the Vistula. I swung as they held my hands and lifted me up in the air. Sometimes Henio let me throw tiny pebbles into the water so I could watch the ripples. But they won me over completely one Saturday when they took me to a puppet theater, a place even more special than the river.

When I returned home about seven months after I was banished, Mama was so thrilled to have me back that she gave me a huge sleeping doll that was nearly my height. I didn't know at the time that she'd spent a month's budget on it and that it was an incredible feat to find, as there were no functional toy stores. She had gotten it through one of her customers. By then Mama had opened a tiny corsetry workshop across the street from our apartment. The skill in designing and sewing women's undergarments she'd developed as a young woman in prewar Warsaw would be our major source of income.

Alas, I rejected the striking doll completely. Her long black hair, a frozen smile, and cold blue eyes that rolled back with a click frightened me. I cried until it was stashed in the chifforobe and later given away.

3

Mama grew up in an Orthodox family in Warsaw. She was one of eleven children and never got over the scant attention she received from her mother, who could barely keep up with household chores and the sewing of piecework she took in to augment her husband's miserable earnings. Both of my mother's parents could trace their lineage to the great rabbis of Europe in Hamburg, Germany and Padua, Italy. Mama often told me that her home was deeply steeped in arcane Orthodox Jewish traditions and rituals. As she reached her teenage years she found the strictly religious environment of her home stifling. She became strongly drawn to secular literature, the most forbidden fruit in her household. The more she read, the more she yearned to know the world outside the constricting borders of her home.

After her father died, Mama left home to live on her own though she was only eighteen. This was a most unusual and much frowned-upon decision. In the 1920s, young women just didn't live on their own. But conventions never fazed my mother. She joined forces with her friend and the two opened a corset shop of their own on Ulica Marszalkowska, one of Warsaw's most elegant streets. The shop prospered. Her skillful fingers and an eye for design allowed her to support her widowed mother and the four younger siblings still at home.

Mama had an interest in different political theories. Though university education was out of reach, she read a lot. She befriended Zionists, socialists, anarchists and communists to get a deeper understanding of the people who subscribed to these different world views. But being a fiercely independent spirit, she forged her own philosophy on life.

When she was in her mid-twenties, Mama became very influenced by the writings of Lion Feuchtwanger, a German-Jewish author and philosopher who was one of the first to expose the dangers of the Nazi Party as it was ascending to power. His books, which were subsequently burned by the Nazis, sensitized her to the dangers that loomed ahead for Jews. These writings prompted Mama to leave for Palestine in the mid-1930s. She wanted to see for herself how Jews worked to tame the wild land to reclaim it as their ancestral home. And her two older sisters Esther and Chava had already settled there.

Never afraid of a challenge, she set out on the arduous journey to the Middle East armed only with her curiosity and a longing for her sisters. The journey was full of surprises. She loved seeing sunburned Jews rolling up their sleeves to work the land. They seemed an altogether different species from her black-coated Hasidic relatives back in Poland, swaying day after day over prayer books in dark *shtibls*. In Palestine, light and sun and sweat were the order of the day.

Soon, however, Mama became troubled by what she saw. Jewish vigilantes roamed the dry, inhospitable land scaring old Arabs off the lands that had been in Arab hands for at least several generations. Her mind told her it was ancient Jewish land, but her heart asked: What of the people that live here now? The fate of the Arabs and Jews vying for the same small scrap of land bothered her. She could not resolve the conflict raging within her.

In the summer of 1939, however, other concerns filled her mind. Her widowed mother, back in Warsaw, fell seriously ill and needed help: four of Mama's youngest sisters still lived at home. Mama returned to Poland only weeks before the German Luftwaffe launched its air strikes against Warsaw, Łódź, and Krakow on September 1, 1939. The twenty-nine-year-old Dora tucked her questions about Palestine away deep at the back of her brain; the brutal war blotted out all that came before. Her life would change in ways she could not imagine.

In 1946, when we returned to Poland from Kyrgyzstan, it was Mama's second return to the country of her birth under depressing circumstances. After she learned that the Nazis had killed her mother and four youngest sisters along with her aunts, uncles, cousins and dozens of friends, her heart was broken forever. Sleepless nights left Mama with black circles under her eyes. She was melancholic much of the time. I knew because even when she smiled, it was as if by accident. A smile, like a momentary flash of sun on a cloudy day, would leave her looking vaguely surprised.

Mama didn't talk much about the war, but she was often in a dark mood, or retreated to the bedroom where she kept the shades drawn. At times like these, Father told us to be quiet. I hated when she got like this because her withdrawal always reminded me of the trip to Warsaw when Mama stood and cried in front of the pile of rubble.

Shortly after our arrival in Łódź, Mama rented a small corner of a shop belonging to a tailor across the street from the apartment we shared with Janek and Surcia. There, she started her brassiere and corset shop working on a borrowed sewing machine. Made-to-measure undergarments were highly sought after by women tired of the privations of war. Within a year her business prospered enough so she could rent a little shop where she set up her workshop and a fitting room for her customers. It was then that we moved to our own apartment on Piotrkowska Street.

With the help of a prewar friend Father found a clerical job. He was so competent that in just a few years he was promoted to Division Head of the city's largest textile manufacturing and export firm—Centrala Textylna. After years of exile my parents' life began to assume a more normal shape. But the post-traumatic stress and losses sustained in those bitter years lay just below the surface. Mama did not have Father's inborn optimism. There was anger in her that she tried to smother. What was the use? She couldn't bring any of them back. Father must have had as much pain for his lost family, but he managed to disguise it with his singing and cheerful exterior.

By the time I was six I was back home from my exile in Torun. Most days, I felt lucky to have a little brother. Daniel and I shared the one bedroom in the apartment with our parents, but since all the furniture, the beds, and the huge mahogany chifforobe were arranged around the perimeter of the room, we kids could use the floor at the center as our play space.

We didn't have a lot of toys until Jack, Father's friend from America, began to send packages. He was a fellow gulag inmate who attributed his survival to Father's help and wanted to express his gratitude. Jack's packages were always great sensations when they arrived. We would rush to the post office to pick up the brown boxes with the big letters spelling out M-A-C-Y-S. Covered in exotic-looking multicolored stamps and with our address elaborately underlined and printed in Jack's large flowery hand, they became messages from a land of plenty that beckoned seductively.

After a lengthy interrogation by the postal officials about the contents and value of the coveted American packages that we, of course, had no way of determining, we would hurry home, to open them with great pomp and ceremony. Daniel was the only child in our neighborhood with a wind-up train whose tracks formed a large figure eight. I was the proud keeper of a mechanical monkey that climbed a palm tree to bring down coconuts hidden under green plastic fronds—heavy little metal balls whose weight and smooth surface felt like a treasure each time I collected them in my hand.

I also liked playing blocks with Daniel. Sometimes he annoyed me because he'd knock down the castle we'd built, and we'd have to rebuild it. But he was funny, and I liked the way he laughed showing a mouthful of teeth like tiny pearls.

4

We had a steady procession of housekeepers and nannies named Marysia living in our home, young women from the countryside, illiterate and unaccustomed to city living. Some were frightened of the electric lights, having known only candlelight in their villages, others were terrified of traffic. They were superstitious, tongue-tied and withdrawn. Mama hired them to take care of Daniel and me and to help with household chores while she worked long hours in her shop. After a while most of them blended into one.

But one Marysia stood out like a shining gem. She, too, came from the countryside, but she was an exceedingly self-possessed, articulate, and self-taught young woman. She had a beautiful face with luminous large brown eyes shaded by long lashes, a high forehead, and long hair piled artfully on top of her head. Marysia had a physical deformity that made her an outcast in her own large family. She had a hunched back, a result of a fall from a tree as a young child.

Our apartment consisted of only three rooms: a living room that doubled as a dining room at meal times, elegant with its tall white tile stove that reached the ceiling, a large bedroom and a kitchen.

There was no bathroom in the conventional sense. There was a cramped dark space at the end of a long hallway, illuminated by a single light bulb, that housed the toilet with a rusty pull chain emanating from a water tank near the ceiling. A nail with squares of old newsprint we used for toilet paper was the only other convenience. We had to walk down the hallway to the kitchen to wash our hands. When our family's finances improved, a bathtub was installed in the kitchen, but when not in use it was covered by a board to create a work counter. Before the tub was installed, we bathed weekly in a deep metal washbasin in priority order since hot water was a scarce commodity: Mama first, then Daniel and me, and finally Father, by which time the water was tepid and had a ring of soap scum around it. Our nanny always slept on a cot in the kitchen. It wasn't the most convenient, or luxurious arrangement, but it worked. I never saw her wash, but she was always clean and neat in her starched white apron.

We all adored this Marysia. I think that initially she might have preferred to take her meals in the kitchen, but Father always insisted that she join us at our dinner table. After a short time she became an integral member of our family.

Marysia's deformity caused her anguish, but it seemed that her own suffering made her unusually sensitive to that of others. When Mama endured terrible toothaches, Marysia would prepare endless remedies she learned from her mountain folk to soothe Mother's pain. Whenever I had a cold, I shuddered in anticipation of a house call by our doctor who would invariably prescribe *banki*, or cupping. He would open his dreaded black bag and set up three or four dozen small glass cups on a tray, dabbing alcohol along their rims while I lay on my belly convulsed with fear, clutching Marysia's hand.

The doctor would then take a lit match to each cup, creating a vacuum, and attach it to my bare back. The cups made a sucking sound like hot leeches as they adhered to my skin. With each passing moment, the flesh moved deeper into the cup and brought the blood closer to the surface. Each breath made the glass assembly on my back tinkle. Marysia held my hand throughout the ordeal, or stroked my hair cooing, "It'll be just another minute and you will be all new again, and able to ride your bicycle in the park." Her soothing voice reminded me that the brown circles of slightly charred skin covering my back would eventually disappear. But when it occurred to me that her back would never recover, I stopped my histrionics and waited submissively for the pop that accompanied the removal of each glass. I knew that the frequent cupping sessions were my parents' way of trying to keep my lungs clear.

From her first day in our home, Marysia played with us. She took us to the park and knitted matching multicolored sweaters and berets for Daniel and me. Best of all, she sang in a lovely operatic soprano. Raised in the backwaters of the Silesian Mountains, she was deeply Catholic, and the only songs she knew were Christian hymns.

Even as a young girl I couldn't fall asleep without her songs. I would plead with her to sing about angels. "Oh, Anetka, it's late!" but she'd relent. "All right, just one." And would croon softly as she tucked me in under my embroidered down duvet. Soon, I floated off to sleep accompanied by baby Jesus and the archangels. She sounded like the enchanted nightingale I knew from stories. Daniel was almost always asleep by then and I loved knowing that she sang just for me.

Sometimes late at night I would hear her murmuring and ask the next morning, "Were you saying your prayers?"

"Yes, I do pray a lot, don't I?"

"What did you pray for, Marysia?" I often asked.

Sometimes she said she had prayed for a mild winter so her family's crops wouldn't freeze. Once she said she had prayed for Mama's teeth to stop hurting.

Then one day I worked up the courage to ask her the question that had been on my mind all along. "Do you ever pray for your hunched back to get better?"

"Oh, Anetka!" She hugged me. "If that is what the Lord wanted, so be it. You have to accept His judgment," she said calmly.

I was horrified that God was so unkind. I wanted to hear nothing more. I never asked what she prayed for after that.

After school, I always rushed to finish my homework so I could follow Marysia around and observe her perform her duties, which seemed full of mystery. On days Daniel went to play with his friends, I could tag along with her to observe the laundry ritual. I loved watching her scrub dirty shirt collars on a metal washboard and boil the underwear in a huge kettle bubbling on the coal stove. Clouds of steam rose from the kettle fogging the windows and creating a perfect surface for my finger designs. Pungent smell of laundry soap permeated the kitchen and tickled my nostrils.

The most exciting part came when Marysia took the clean laundry up to the attic of our building to hang it on lines that stretched the entire width of the dark space right up to the cobweb-filled corners. It was a scary place that made me want to hold on to her skirt, but I was brave. She would hand me a bag of wooden laundry clothespins and say, "Make yourself useful, hand these to me." Each time I handed Marysia a laundry pin I glanced into the darkened corners watching for whatever menace lurked in them, gulping back my fear and moving just a bit closer to her.

Another part of the washday ritual was taking the dry bed sheets, pillowcases and tablecloths to the *magiel*—a huge roller with a hand crank that pressed the linens into smooth, stiff sheets. Operated by a gnarled old woman who carried on the business at the front room of her ground-floor apartment, the *magiel* held a

31

different kind of fascination. This was the only apartment in the building that I visited in the eight years we lived there.

Though I never had to buy anything by myself, or for myself, I liked accompanying Marysia on her daily trips to the market. I was mortified in the courtyard because on those occasions the insults were addressed to her instead of me: "You and your hump belong in the circus!" a foul-mouthed pimply boy yelled. His younger brother, the one with a perpetually snotty nose, roared, "They won't even need a camel."

Marysia held my hand and kept walking without looking at them and when we finally emerged onto the street unscathed, at least in the physical sense, she would say, "Don't pay them any attention; they are ignorant." It was her signal that I could relax the tight grip on her hand and let out my breath. Marysia always impressed me with her bravery. I was glad we were allies, though in those moments I felt more sharply the sense of isolation from our neighbors. Both of us offended them in ways I couldn't grasp.

5

When people said I was the spitting image of my father, my chest puffed out with pride. The only difference between us was that I didn't have his light cornflower-blue eyes. Mine are green. We did share a small mischievous nose, fair complexion, and fine, light-brown hair. My high cheekbones were more like my mother's, but the overall effect made it clear I was more of a Libeskind than a Blaustein.

When I was still in grade school I realized I wasn't doing my father justice calling him *Tata*—Dad, in Polish. He was special. He deserved a special name to match, to differentiate him from all the other fathers. I tried out various Polish variations and diminutives for Father: *Ojciec, Tata, Tatuś*. I didn't like any of them. They weren't sufficiently distinctive and did nothing to reflect his lighthearted, playful personality. Ultimately, I came up with *Tatinek* and shortened it to *Tinek*. It stuck. From there on, Daniel and I, even Mama, called him Tinek.

Tinek had always been an extremely outgoing person. He could manage to strike up a conversation with a lamppost and afterward say he found something interesting in the exchange.

Although openly Jewish, Tinek had more luck befriending Poles than Mama. Maybe it was because he looked like a Pole, or maybe he just had more opportunities to interact having been employed in an organization with hundreds of Poles. Most of his friends after the war were his fellow employees. Mama always worked alone and though her clientele was Polish, except for Maria, she never managed to develop more than a business relationship with them. She was introverted. Any free time, which was rare, she spent reading and listening to classical music.

Some of my friends' fathers went wild when they huddled near the radio and listened to the impassioned voice of the announcer relating soccer game scores, others couldn't wait for vacations to dip their fishing rods into cool Silesian lakes. Others, I am sure, loved nothing more than to cozy up in their overstuffed easy chair with a glass of vodka. None of these pleasures held one iota of excitement for my father. No, not just excitement, they failed to arouse even the faintest interest. His passion was music.

Because he grew up in a family so poor that he and his siblings slept two to a bed, he couldn't even imagine acquiring an instrument larger than a tiny harmonica. Instead, he sang and whistled hundreds of tunes turning his lips and throat into musical instruments. When he wasn't singing, he was listening to music on our floor model console radio whose wooden cabinet Marysia polished weekly to a honey-colored glow. Even then, I could see him tapping his fingers and feet to the music, waggling his whole body. He swam amid the notes as comfortably as a fish.

I asked him once, "Tinek, don't you ever feel too unhappy to sing?"

"No! That's how Jews *find* happiness, how they keep sadness at bay." Seeing the puzzlement on my face, he added, "Really, that's what we did in the gulags and when we were starving in Kyrgyzstan. The singing assuaged our hunger."

For Tinek singing was like breathing. He sang or whistled constantly. We were lucky that he had a wonderfully resonant voice and remembered lyrics to every song he had ever known. When he was in his twenties Tinek was part of an acting group, The Ararat Yiddish Revue Company, in Łódź. Though he could not make a living performing and his theatrical career was very short lived, he retained the ability to see life as performance and the everyday scenes that others took for granted were his stage.

Mostly he sang Yiddish songs whose words I didn't understand, but whose melodies were the most soothing sounds in the world. I didn't need to understand their words to know that they were our history, our roots. Sometimes he sang Russian songs and those made me think of the red poppy fields of my early years. Mother did not share his musical talent but she was always asking him to sing specific songs out of his extensive repertoire. He was her crooner, always glad to oblige.

Tinek often said he wanted at least one of his kids to play an instrument, something he had never gotten a chance to do. Hiring a music teacher for both of us was too expensive. One day, he hit on what he thought was a very clever idea. After dinner, he called Daniel and me over to the table and said, "Kids, I want to give you a kind of a test."

"A test? What kind of a test?" From the start, I didn't like the sound of it.

"Oh, but it will be fun, you will see in a minute," Tinek said.

The velvet curtains muffled the courtyard sounds in the living room and the quiet made me extra nervous. Daniel had a huge grin on his face. "Can I go first?" he asked.

"Wait a minute, I will tell you how it works," Tinek replied. "In the first part, I will tap out a rhythm on the table and ask you to repeat it. It may be a little complicated, but don't worry. Do your best. Ready?" He started tapping with his knuckles on the table.

What made it more challenging is that the pattern was not a replica of some familiar tune and that the taps varied in their intensity. Each was a totally random sequence. There were many variations on the pattern of taps. Ta-da-da-da-TA-TA-da. DA-DA-da-da-Ta-TA-TA-Ta-Ta-DA.

Daniel and I took turns trying to repeat them as best we could. Discomfort grew in the pit of my stomach. Daniel kept saying, "Dad, when can we do the next part?"

After repeating the tapping portion of the test, Father said cheerfully, "Now, you are ready for the next part. I will sing several notes and you try to repeat each one correctly and in the exact same order." Again, Daniel went first. I went after him, but this time with a feeling that I had made some mistakes.

At the end of the test Father issued the verdict. "It looks to me that Daniel has more musical aptitude. We will sign him up for music lessons." Tinek must have noticed my crestfallen expression and said, adding insult to injury, "When Daniel learns how to play, he will teach you."

Not long after, my father brought in a large black case and told Daniel to open it. We both came running over.

"What is it, Dad?" Daniel asked, his eyes and mouth wide open.

"It's your piano in a box," Father said.

I had never seen such a tiny piano and couldn't wait for Daniel to figure out how to unsnap the silver closures. We both gasped when the case opened. The gleaming red body and silver trim of the accordion were dazzling. Daniel could barely lift it and Dad helped him get the straps over his shoulders. The instrument covered him from his chin to his knees.

It wasn't long after my conversation with Marysia about her prayers that I decided to ask my father the big question that had been simmering in my brain. Marysia was out picking Daniel up from his music lesson, so Dad and I were alone. "Tinek, do you believe in God?"

He looked at me very intently focusing his blue eyes on mine and remained silent for a moment. "Sit here next to me and I will tell you."

I didn't know why he made such a big deal of my question. "Tinek, just tell me. Yes, or no?"

He patted the sofa next to him motioning for me to sit. Then he started slowly, "Let's assume for a moment that there is a God—an all seeing, all powerful being. If such a God could turn away from the murder of innocent people, then I don't want to know him; certainly not to honor him."

I looked at him but didn't say anything. I had to think about what he'd said. A moment later I followed up, "Do you mean people like your brothers and sister and Mama's mom and her little sisters?"

"Exactly!" He looked sad and put his arm around my shoulders. His eyes looked shiny and I thought they were filling with tears. "But not just our family. There were millions like them."

"Millions?" I couldn't imagine it. We had only studied numbers up to thousands in math.

After a moment he added, "Anyone with some understanding of science can see that the concept of God makes no sense."

"Why do people pray to a God that doesn't exist?"

"It was an idea invented by humans long ago to give people hope, to allay their fear of death, and to have them believe that things will be better in the afterlife."

"Will they be?"

Tinek sighed, "I only care about this life."

"Me too," I said, but knew I'd still think about this when I went to sleep. I felt as if he entrusted me with a great, important secret. I must have looked more solemn than he expected because he said, "Anetka, do you understand?"

"I think I do, but can you still be a Jew if you don't believe in God?"

"Who says you can't? Of course, you can." I felt relieved and he added, "This is something you just need to know for now, but you will really understand it when you get older."

Those words stayed with me long after our conversation. I turned them over in my mind again and again. So you can be a Jew and not believe in God? In the end, I had to agree. Tinek was never wrong, except maybe when he chose Daniel to get the music lessons. Yes, Tinek was right. He was a Jew *and* an atheist. I now knew that if someone had asked him "What are you?" he would identify himself without a moment's hesitation, "I am a Jew." I decided I would do the same.

———————

Despite my conviction that we were Jewish, sometimes I ran into situations that confused me. Most often it happened on our rare trips to Warsaw to visit Mama's cousin Mania. I had warm feelings for her and Henio dating back to the time they had taken care of me in Torun. By now they lived in the capital and had two children: Arthur and Basia.

We used to visit them during the winter holidays. To my and Daniel's delight, but to my parents' dismay, they had a huge Christmas tree in the living room. Mania's home became synonymous with the pungent aroma of the pine tree that permeated their entire apartment. I remember how I couldn't take my eyes off the delicate ornaments, or the sparkling silver star at the apex of the tree.

One year, as soon as we arrived, Arthur and Basia ran around the tree pointing to the boxes of gifts beneath it.

"Do you have such a big tree?" Basia squealed.

"No, we are Jewish," I said, wrinkling my brow.

"So are we," Arthur chimed in.

"It's not about religion, Nachman," Mania said to my father seeing the look on his face.

"What is it about then?" he asked.

Looking away from him, Mania replied, "Just the scent of the forest and light to brighten up the winter."

6

During the mid-40s and 50s there was no organization more feared or more powerful in Poland than the UB, the Ministry of Public Security—the secret police. More than 30,000 of its employees were installed in every community to serve as a listening post for the faintest signs of political opposition. Everyone was considered a suspect under the UB's lidless gaze. To maintain its grip, the communist government depended on neighbor denouncing neighbor. Within a decade more than 300,000 people were arrested and 9,000 executed for alleged anti-government activities.

In our home conversations were usually whispered, especially if they related to money, to our friends or neighbors, or things about our plans for the future, to anything of importance. "*Sha, sha,*" Mama usually cautioned with a finger to her lips and a look of concern on her crinkled forehead. "Even the walls have ears."

It wasn't until much later that I understood the reason for the secrecy. In communist Poland any neighbor could have been a spy and even the most innocent remark could have landed my parents in jail, or subjected them to relentless scrutiny and endless questioning by the authorities. As uncomfortable as such a life must have been for my parents, we kids felt a part of our own little secret society, taking comfort in our togetherness and a shared sense of purpose; us against unfriendly neighbors and a hostile city. In Poland we were keenly aware that we were Jewish, like none of our neighbors. That meant that many of our relatives were killed during the war, that my parents spoke Yiddish, but only at home, and that Israel was where some of my mother's relatives lived. It also meant that our neighbors thought we had horns and lice on our heads, and piles of money under our mattresses. At least this is what I surmised from the frequent derogatory comments thrown our way.

Mama's shop was on Jaracza Street, not too far from the oldest theater in Łódź. Most of its female stars were her clients. My mama's corsets and brassieres were known to be the finest in the city. Women lined up to have custom-made undergarments not only because there were none to buy, but because hers would make women's figures as graceful as Venus de Milo's. They waited months to get an appointment for their fittings because Mama had just one pair of hands and no helpers. She could barely keep up with the orders though she kept long hours at her shop, designing, cutting, and sitting hunched over her sewing machine.

Bolts of peach and white and pink damask lined the shelves. Boxes of lace, ribbons, hooks and eyelets were stacked high. I often stared curiously toward the fitting corner where elegant women of all sizes disappeared behind the velvet green curtain to get advice on how best to sculpt their flesh with my mama's creations, lacy brassieres and solid corsets supported by whalebone ribs and tied with laces to minimize girth.

Mama's was one of the few private businesses in the city, a rarity under Poland's communist system. While not explicitly forbidden, such private enterprises were seen as a threat to the government's control. Anyone with the temerity to own a business faced the constant danger of intimidation by tax inspectors. I overheard many of the stories she whispered to Tinek late at night when she thought I was asleep.

Tax goons would appear unannounced in her shop more often than some of her best customers. The element of surprise was meant to help them uncover a crime against the state. They'd interrogate her as if she were a criminal. They always presumed guilt and hissed at her questions I did not understand. "Did you understate your income? Do you keep two sets of books? Who are your customers? Did you pay all the taxes on time? Did you bribe any officials?" They demanded the information in hostile, accusatory tones, jabbing a finger into the air with each question.

When I asked Tinek for an explanation, all he told me was that other shop owners were terrified of visits by these officials, but not my mama. She fought them with every ounce of the anger perpetually simmering in her bowels. Her olive cheeks flamed, but she was not cowed. "Aren't you ashamed to be rummaging among women's undergarments?" she asked coolly as the goons pushed her merchandise around. "What do you think you will find? Do you think I have hidden gold?" Her cheeky retorts could have easily gotten her arrested, but she shamed even the most hardened bureaucrats.

Tinek's workday was quite different from Mama's. As division director at Centrala Textylna, the largest textile distributor in Poland, he had an impressive office, a personal secretary, thirty clerks in a secretarial pool and a fleet of chauffeur-driven cars at his disposal. Father's job didn't pay well; after all, it was a government post in a Soviet bloc country. Mama was the one whose shop brought in far more money, but not the prestige of Tinek's position. It was her earnings that allowed us to hire household help and take annual vacations in the Tatra Mountains, or to rent summer cottages in forested, rural villages.

Each year as June approached I itched to get to the country. This was a time when I had Mama to myself because each summer Marysia went back home to help out on her family's farm. Father stayed in the city and joined us only on weekends. We would pack big bundles and travel to Kolumna by train. I stared at forests and endless farms along the way. Cows dotted the countryside. Small figures in the distance pulled plows like beasts of burden. They fascinated me as they flickered before my eyes like a string of images on a roll of film.

"Who are these people?" I asked.

"They are peasants," Mama replied. From her tone I could tell it was not something to choose as a future profession.

The closer we got to our destination the more excited I became. I was immersed in the memory of past summers' lazy days spent picking berries and mushrooms in cool, verdant forests, stepping with our bare feet on the carpet of pine needles that always beckoned with a mystical power.

The year I turned nine, Mama's closest friend, Maria Nowak, visited us in our rented cottage. It was only we kids, Mama and Maria. After a long day of berry picking, weaving flower wreaths, and making jam we were all soundly asleep in country-style beds piled with thick straw mattresses and down quilts. The only sound in the cottage bedroom was even breaths and ticking of the grandfather clock.

Before dawn, several local hoodlums stumbling home from a night of drinking banged on our closed shutters yelling, "Open up, you stinking Jews, open up or else we'll break down your door." The women awoke from deep sleep disoriented. The banging became louder as if something other than a fist were used. I sat up in bed rubbing my eyes, not comprehending. Daniel, in the bed across from mine, began whimpering though he still looked asleep. Mama reached for her robe.

Maria jumped out of bed in her long pink nightgown and exclaimed, "*Jezus, Maria!* Now I'll die because of these damn Jews!" She ran to the door in her stocking feet.

"Stop!" Mama ordered Maria. "Don't dare open it." Mama's voice sounded sharp like the edge of a knife.

"Oh, Dora, I'm sorry... I was just... I don't know what came over me," Maria mumbled, standing near the door with her hand across her mouth.

Mama didn't reply. The pounding on the wooden shutters and hoarse alcohol suffused curses continued. Mama sat sideways on my bed, hugged me and said, "Shh, go back to sleep, Anetka. It's just a bad dream." She fluffed my duvet, then walked over to Daniel's bed, tucked him in and went back to her bed.

I couldn't tell just how long the drunken shouting and banging lasted. I lay in bed clutching my pillow, listening to the voices outside growing fainter, until it was again only the ticking of the clock. The only even sound of breathing belonged to Daniel.

When the sun came up Mama asked Maria to leave. She never spoke to her again and my enthusiasm for the serene summers in the country evaporated. The incident peeled away the thin veneer of politeness that had smoothed over a deep wound between postwar Jews and Poles.

I learned to be cautious when befriending Polish girls.

Despite her painful disappointment with Maria, Mama showed kindness to our downstairs neighbors. The Podobyczkos were a family in constant distress. Too many of them were cramped in the small apartment, and Mrs. Podobyczko was totally exhausted by her husband's regular drunken rages and the physical abuse that followed. When he was sober, Mr. Podobyczko was a gentle man with perpetually bloodshot eyes and the kind of dejected stance of someone who is not in control of his life. His shoulders were stooped, his clothes baggy and wrinkled. He looked helpless. But when he was drunk he was maniacal. His face contorted and spittle foamed at the corners of his mouth making him look like a mad dog.

On more than one occasion, while in the midst of a drunken harangue he would grab the ax that stood in the corner of their kitchen and chase Mrs. Podobyczko, whose anguished screams pierced the walls of their apartment and escaped into the courtyard. She always managed to run upstairs and bang on our door frantically, pleading for Mama to help. Mama would open and run downstairs speaking to Mr. Podobyczko calmly, but very sternly.

"You must stop right now! Just look at yourself. Aren't you ashamed of your behavior?"

For some strange reason she was the only one to whom he would respond. Instantly, he would turn maudlin, grab a hold of Mama's hand and kiss it as he slobbered and blubbered. "*Pani Dora*, I am so sorry. Please forgive me."

"It's your wife you have to apologize to, not me. Now go to sleep!" She would take his elbow and lead him to bed whereupon he would collapse in a heap and start snoring.

Mrs. Podobyczko always shook her head in disbelief as if Mama had just performed witchcraft and couldn't find enough words to thank her. "*Pani Dora, dziękuje, dziękuje*, you are an angel, I will pray for your soul in church."

7

On March 5, 1953, radio stations broadcast funereal music from morning until an uneasy nightfall. At first, I didn't know what was happening except that my parents, eating breakfast in the living room, spoke in hushed tones. The strangely uplifting sound of their voices was in such contrast to the somber music in the background.

I sat up in bed and listened. After a while I heard the deep voice of the radio announcer say, "Today we lost the father of our nation, Joseph Vissarionovich Stalin." I was stunned and just barely began to comprehend the sorrowful music. Our great leader, the man they called "man of steel" had died. In school we had just been studying what a brave man he was, how he brought freedom to his and our nation and to millions of workers in Eastern Europe and Central Asia. We read a book with beautiful illustrations about his childhood in Georgia. I felt so bad about how poor he was growing up, the only surviving child of a boot maker and a washerwoman; how he nearly died of smallpox when he was a small boy. And now he was gone.

A deep sense of grief settled in my chest. I had never personally known anyone who died. Death—it was such a frightening thought.

I was about to put my fingers in my ears so I wouldn't hear any more, but Mama came into the bedroom. "School is on as usual. Stop daydreaming and get dressed, Anetka."

"But, Mama, today..." I tried to tell her I was sure school would be cancelled.

"Hurry up, it's getting really late," she said, and went over to Daniel's bed to wake him up.

I dressed in my school uniform with the black pinafore and my red Young Pioneers necktie. (Want to or not, we all had to belong.) Then Mama tied big red bows in my braids. I still thought it was strange to act as if it were a normal day, and as it turned out there was nothing usual about it.

As I walked out on the street I saw that all the shops had framed photos of Stalin in their windows with black crepe stretched across the corner of the frame, or black crepe framing the entire window. Some had a single red rose lying in front of the portrait. A grainy gray haze hung over the city and over the faces of the few inhabitants who ventured out.

Wind whistled through silent gray streets. Piles of melting, soot-covered snow lay like dying behemoths near the curbs. The sky matched the color of smoke that emerged from the many smokestacks of our city. Even the weather mourns the passing of our leader, I thought.

Upon entering the school, it became immediately clear that there would be no regular classes. The children were in a subdued mood, too, with none of the usual running and laughter in the hallways. We gathered in the auditorium. Our principal made a speech about the leader we had lost and how all of us were now orphaned. His eyes glistened as he spoke and his bald head seemed shinier just for the occasion.

A funeral march followed on the loudspeakers. As the music reached a crescendo I, along with many classmates, dissolved into tears. The chorus of crying girls was as impressive as the patriotic songs directed from stage by the music teacher. We were dismissed for the day and walked home in silence holding hands with our best girlfriends, stopping at the storefronts to see which had a bigger Stalin portrait. Now there seemed to be more people out on the streets. They gathered in small groups and whispered. Their faces and those of my parents and teachers made me think that something big was about to happen, but I couldn't tell if it was a good thing or not.

The next morning at breakfast, my father said, "Why do you look so sad?"

I was rubbing my eyes, which still stung from the previous day's crying. "Don't you know why?" I asked surprised.

"If it is Stalin's death, don't waste your tears."

I looked at him as if he had gone mad, my eyes so wide I thought my eyeballs might fall out of their sockets.

"Yes, I know," he said. "I know what you have been learning in school. Now, let me tell you the truth," he said lowering his voice to a near whisper. "Stalin was an enemy of the Jews and didn't much care for working people either, especially not the ones in Poland." Then Tinek made me swear I wouldn't tell any of this to my friends. "It can be very dangerous for our family if people find out what I told you."

Still wide-eyed, I nodded. I kept nodding even after my response registered because everything inside of me was churning. So his death was not such a tragedy, after all? I have been duped!

The world was suddenly askew. I went to bed with a terrible stomachache even though I could hardly eat supper. I started wondering what was true and what was a lie of the things I had been learning in school.

8

Anyone looking in on my fourth-grade class in Łódź would have seen the usual: three dozen girls in black pinafores, ruffled at the shoulders, worn over neat white blouses with round baby collars. But a sharp-eyed visitor would have noticed something new: a wooden cross adorned with a bleeding Jesus now hung over the blackboard. Not long after Stalin's death the Catholic church began to flex its muscle. For the time being, though communism was still the law of the land, undercurrents of change had already permeated my public school.

I was the one seated at the desk closest to the front of the classroom. By now my parents stopped calling me Anetka and used a more grown-up variant of the name—Ania. I was one of several Ania's in my class. I was a good student and beamed at my parents' approval of my high grades and despaired if I received anything less than perfect scores on my quizzes because both of them would look at me as if I had shamed them.

On closer inspection, a visitor to my class would notice that three of the girls had black braids, so much in contrast to the blonde and chestnut tresses of their classmates. Those were my three

Jewish girlfriends: another Ania, Ala and Slawka. Though I looked more like my Polish classmates, after school I played mostly with my Jewish friends because their mothers invited me over. I liked Elżbieta, one of my Polish classmates, very much, but her mother never invited me, nor allowed her to come to my house.

A few weeks after the crosses were hung, the teacher announced that we would have a new way of starting our school day. Instead of the usual announcements from the Principal's office, the day would start with prayers. Prayers? I panicked. I didn't know any real ones. Would we get grades on this? I wondered but was too embarrassed to ask.

I didn't mind the cross because it made me think of Marysia's hymns, but the prayer idea was a whole different thing. I already knew two things: Jews like us do not believe in God and do not pray. And, anyway, prayers are useless because I had once made up a prayer for Marysia's hump to go away and it didn't. That evening I told my parents about the cross and the prayer announcement. When I went to bed I overheard them.

"Isn't it strange that the communist authorities would permit such a thing?" Mama whispered to Father.

"You know, for the Poles, Christ always wins over government bureaucrats. Why are you surprised?"

"I sure hope they won't force the Jewish children to participate in the morning prayers," she replied.

"Don't be so sure."

The next morning, my class stood up briskly and said in a chorus, "Good morning, *Pani* Maria," when the teacher entered the classroom. She replied, "Good morning, girls." Then she added, "You may as well stand. We will say our prayers now."

I blanched and glanced over to Ala and Slawka who sat nearest me and were directly in my view. They seemed as confused. The teacher must have noticed me looking from Ala to Slawka and back again because she said, "Is anything wrong, Ania?"

"Well," I hesitated. "We Jewish girls don't know the prayers." I thought I had no option but to appoint myself the spokesperson for all four of us, though I wasn't sure if all of us were as unfamiliar with prayers as I was.

Many girls tittered, irritating the teacher more than my statement. "Girls!" she said in a high-pitched voice registering her annoyance with her tone.

At first, I thought she was addressing her irritation to those that were still snickering. Then she said, thrusting her finger toward me, "We can settle this easily. Ania, you and your Jewish friends can just stay seated and put your head on the desk while the rest of us say our prayers." Then, in a more appeasing tone, she added, "It won't take too long."

The way she said, "*Jewish friends*" sounded mean and made me uncomfortable. I didn't like being singled out that way. What made it especially upsetting was that I really liked my teacher and never expected her to act so, so... different. Was she an impostor?

I don't know what got into the usually obedient me. It was as if all my blood suddenly shot up into my temples and my fists clenched of their own volition. My breaths started sounding quick and loud even to me. I motioned with a small gesture of my hand for my friends to follow me and we marched defiantly out of the classroom to the dismayed stares of the teacher and the rest of the class. I was scared and a hot flush blossomed on my face as if I had been slapped. My palms were moist and my mind raced. How would I explain such behavior to my parents? Wasn't I the good girl, who never got into any trouble, the one who sat right in front of the teacher and who never called out without raising her hand?

We found ourselves in the silence of the hallway, and the knowledge that no one was allowed out of the classroom without permission made us nervous like rabbits facing a hunter. Ala, Ania and Slawka looked at me.

I suppose I started this, so I have to supply the way forward, I thought. "Let's go to the Principal's office. We will tell Mr. Sobinski that this is not fair."

The others looked skeptical. "But kids are not allowed in his section of the building. His secretary won't let us in," said Ala.

Her doubt only egged me on. "Let's go, come with me, or you can stay here and get into trouble by yourselves," I said. "Who is coming?"

They all followed. We crept down the curving staircase with its marble stairs and polished banister, trying to make our footsteps as quiet as possible. On the main floor I turned left and headed toward the office that all of us dreaded. I knocked softly on the shiny oak door, but when I heard no reply, I put my hand on the brass handle and pressed it down cautiously. My heart was pounding, but I had to go through with it. I didn't want to lose face with my friends and I certainly didn't want to stay in the classroom while the rest of the girls prayed and stared at us as though we had three heads.

The door yielded, and we entered the small office where the secretary usually sat. She was not at her desk. I was glad, but even more nervous about continuing into Mr. Sobinski's office unannounced. Something inside my chest pushed me forward. I opened the door and Mr. Sobinski stood up from his chair, looking very surprised. I turned to see if my girlfriends were still behind me. They were so quiet I thought they didn't have the guts to go in with me, but they were there.

Mr. Sobinski said, "What are you girls doing here? Why aren't you in class?" His eyes were two large question marks. This gave me the opening I needed and I launched into a breathless explanation.

Mr. Sobinski rubbed his chin. The bright overhead light made his bald head shiny. "I see. I see." That was all he said at first and looked as if I had given him a difficult quiz. He put his hands on his hips and stood in the middle of his office. He looked more like a lost boy than the severe man we usually saw conferring with parents or teachers.

"I have an idea," he said in a moment, looking not the least bit angry. "You have my permission to stay out in the hall during prayers. No one will bother you."

Victorious, I said, "Thank you." Suspecting that Mr. Sobinski's unusual state of consternation wouldn't last too much longer, I led my small band of protesters to the upstairs hallways.

From that day on, our classmates looked at us enviously as we left to play in the school corridors while they prayed. Each day we pushed the limits. We roamed the halls peeking into unoccupied labs and peered into the nurse's station. We explored the geography classroom and spun the big globe. We slid down the polished banister. We were free.

My euphoric feeling of having triumphed lasted only a few weeks. One day, when I was getting tired of our hallway escapades, I realized that I didn't feel as comfortable in my heretofore beloved classroom and that my ocean of love for my teacher had petered out to a small, muddy puddle.

9

Situated on the main street of Łódź, our small apartment was our refuge. Its tall windows, covered by green velvet drapes, muffled sounds, and buffered us from the noisy courtyard below. By the time my family moved in, time and war had all but erased the building's status as a century-old bourgeois edifice on the most presentable Łódź street. The building's long, narrow courtyard terminated near our entrance. At our end of the courtyard stood a metal frame on which diligent housewives beat the rugs with plaited wooden *trzepaczkas*. On sunny mornings the energetic thuds on the rugs would produce cloudlets of gray dust, rising to mingle with the pollution that always hung over the city.

At the opposite end of the courtyard, a longish tunnel-like exit, a *brama*, opened to the street letting in light and a prospect of escaping the claustrophobia-inducing courtyard, devoid of trees or grass. Inside the *brama* hung a list of tenants on which our distinctly Jewish name stood out as much as a flower would among cobblestones. One dirty staircase on each side of the *brama* led to the street-facing apartments, whereas our section of the building was sheltered from the noise of the city, if not the shouts of children playing in the courtyard and the yelling of their mothers who used open windows as a way to communicate dinnertime, displeasure, or gossip.

Nothing escaped the malicious rumor mill of the courtyard where sounds reverberated and carried all the way to the top floors. There were women who spent their days propped on their elbows at the open windows, observing—who and why? It was hard to tell. For some it was a form of amusement in the pre-television days of the early 50s; for others, gaining the currency of "news" about their neighbors, the more titillating the better, was an entrée to a social network. It is to this courtyard my thoughts always return when Poland knocks on my psyche.

Despite our more than satisfactory material conditions in Łódź, our lives were circumscribed by Polish society. Many Poles absorbed the Nazi characterization of the Jewish look—hooked nose with a big hump, beady black eyes, faces that could scare children. It was a lie that seeped like poison into many encounters between my parents and their Polish neighbors and acquaintances in Łódź. I remember the many times when Mama and I would run into acquaintances in the street or in a store who would smile and pinch my cheeks complimenting mother cheerfully on my looks saying, "You must be so proud. Your Ania is so pretty, she doesn't look Jewish at all!"

I was always puzzled by those "compliments" and embarrassed by them on my mother's behalf. I didn't look much like my mother. She had dark hair that matched her dark eyes, olive skin and a classic nose. Were the compliments meant to please her, or to tell her, however politely and indirectly, that she was different, someone who didn't belong? I thought my mother was beautiful and the comments about my looks, meant to be pleasing, always made me cross.

The rejection by most Poles was as clear and painful as it was subtle. My friend Elżbieta's mother never seemed to run out of excuses why her daughter couldn't come to my house after school.

My mother's otherwise perfectly pleasant clients never chatted with her the way I heard people bantering with the Polish baker next door to my mother's shop, or the dressmaker down the block. No neighbor ever said hello, or even knocked on our door to borrow a cup of sugar. Sometimes it felt as if we were suspended in a vacuum.

Though Jews and Poles did not socialize before the war, for the most part, there was cool civility between them. After the war, an impenetrable wall, with bitterness the cement between its ugly bricks, stood between the two groups. I think now that each time a Jew looked at a Pole of a certain age, a nagging question always lurked at the very edge of consciousness: did this person sell out my mother, or sister, or uncle to the Nazis?

How could they not think it? Of the quarter of a million Jews in our city before the war, fewer than 900 remained. In our family alone, at least sixty people had been exterminated: aunts, uncles, cousins and my maternal grandmother. Some died of starvation in the Łódź and Warsaw ghettos, others were burned in the ovens of Auschwitz, and others still were gassed on trucks heading toward Chelmno.

We were the only Jews in our building of about 100 families. And we stood out in other ways too, making us great fodder for the ceaseless rumor mill. My parents' relative economic success gave the building's gossips plenty of material with which to pass time. Teenagers hung out in the courtyard like fixtures and, likely, emboldened by the gossip, showered us with a litany of insults so common that we almost got used to them. "Get out of here, go to Palestine, you stinking Jew!" or, "Hey Jew, how many dollars have you hidden under your mattress?" When they were feeling less mean, the insults were scaled down to, "How did you get so fat, porky?" To which our parents taught us to reply, "By the time the fat man gets skinny, the skinny one will drop dead." That was a retort we would pull out of our meager arsenal only when someone our size hurled the insult.

To judge from the epithets yelled at us in the courtyard I knew that we did not belong to the Polish nation, but I couldn't figure out where we did belong. When they said, "Go to Palestine," in their annoying singsong, the words left a stinging sensation in my eyes. I hardly knew where this Palestine was, but, in their menacing voices, it sure didn't sound like a good place.

Daniel and I were most afraid of the older bullies. But one day, we hatched a plan to silence their taunts. Our parents hadn't yet returned from work and Marysia must have stepped out to do some shopping. We were home alone. It was spring. Though no trees, or even grass, were visible in our barren courtyard, we knew the weather had changed. Even with our white tiled chimney turned off, the apartment felt stifling. The usual taunts rose to our open second floor window. After a while we couldn't hear all the words, but the *Żydzi! Żydzi! Żydzi!* (Jews! Jews! Jews!) reverberated through the apartment.

"Do you hear them?" Daniel asked.

"You think I'm deaf?" I replied, anger rising in my throat.

"Maybe we should shut the windows."

"No, it's too hot!" I said, but immediately an idea sprung to my head. I remembered that Marysia had left a cauldron of hot water on the stove. She had been planning to boil the laundry in it. I wasn't sure it was still hot, but it would do. "Come with me," I instructed eight-year-old Daniel to join me in the kitchen. "Want to help me shut them up?" I wrapped a towel around each handle of the cauldron. "Grab one handle!"

"But it's so heavy," he protested as he lifted it with me trying to balance the other side.

I told him the idea.

"Wow, Ania," he was duly impressed.

"Remember, only on the count of three."

With great effort not to spill its contents, we lifted the cauldron off the stove and carried it carefully to the open window in the living room.

I stuck my head out for a moment. Our tormentors leaned nonchalantly against the wall right beneath our windows. We waited a moment. When they uttered their next chant, I counted off quietly, "One, two, three."

We hoisted the cauldron and dumped its contents on their heads. We heard their screams. Then, we ran to hide in the bedroom behind the tall mahogany chifforobe because we thought they would come to kill us. Squeezed in and sneezing from the dust we stayed there until we could no longer stand our uncomfortable position and heard no alarming sounds. We were stunned by our own audacity, but we felt victorious. For a while the taunts stopped, but our fear in crossing the courtyard grew.

10

Ever since her incarceration in the Siberian gulag and a bout with typhus, Mama's health was fragile. She suffered from stomach ulcers and swollen glands that the doctors were unable to diagnose. Her teeth, badly affected by starvation and lack of dental care in the Soviet Union, were a perpetual source of pain. She became so familiar with oral maladies that she could diagnose an abscessed tooth as easily as a cold.

One Tuesday as we came home from school, Mama, rather than Marysia, greeted us at the door. "I closed the shop for the afternoon. I have an important appointment," she said, reaching for her coat. Mama did not look happy and she never closed her shop except for summer vacations.

"But where is Marysia?" I asked.

"It's her day off."

"You are leaving us alone?" I asked, because this was highly unusual; Marysia's usual day off was Sunday.

"Ania, you are eleven. You can stay by yourself for a few hours and watch your brother."

"Where are you going, Mama?" Daniel asked.

"I have to see the dentist and I'm late, so let me run now, but there's one thing you two must remember. Do not open the coal bin in the boiler."

"But, why, Mama?" I asked. "What if it needs more coal?"

"Never mind, just do what I asked, please, children."

She looked exasperated and filled with a nervous kind of energy. I could hear her locking the door and calling out, "I will be back soon." Most days, Marysia, or Tinek were there to supervise and to make sure we did our homework and that Daniel practiced on his accordion, but now we were alone.

As soon as we heard Mama's footsteps descending the steps, we looked at one another trying to decide what the other was thinking. "Daniel, you better go practice," I tried to sound like the adult.

"Why are you bossing me around?"

I could tell my order was not terribly persuasive. "No, I have a better idea," I said when Daniel made no move toward the accordion case. "Let's play with the mechanical monkey."

Daniel's eyes lit up. We both loved this toy.

We played in the living room until we became bored. "Do you hear the hissing coming from the kitchen," Daniel asked.

"No."

A moment later I decided we should go into the kitchen to investigate. We marched down the narrow corridor that led to it. As soon as we opened the door, a wave of cold air hit us. The kitchen was always freezing unless Marysia was cooking and had the oven on.

The hot water boiler stood in the corner of the kitchen. This is where our bath water was heated so long as the fire bin at the lower part of the boiler was filled with shiny, irregular chunks of black coal.

"Ania, open the door so we can see if there's enough coal. I hate cold bath water," Daniel said in a tone that belied his meager eight years of experience with ablutions. I was dubious and didn't want to disobey Mama's order. I vacillated momentarily and reached for the handle to the small metal door behind which a fire burned.

"Mama will be really angry. We are not supposed to open it," I said, almost as if to reiterate a formality. After another split second of hesitation, I said, "Let me just check."

I pulled the door open.

A puff of hot air shot out. "Ooh, it feels nice and warm," Daniel said, rubbing his pudgy hands together. We squatted in front of the open door, peering in, fascinated by the contents of the fire bin. The coals glowed orange and sizzled.

"It does look as if the fire is dying down," I pronounced the verdict.

"Well, shouldn't we add some coal?"

I dipped an old metal scoop into the coal bucket nearby, lifted it full of black pieces then dumped them into the belly of the boiler. The flames licked at the coals and burst into red tongues that danced and swayed. We could not take our eyes off the fiery display. It was forbidden fruit we just had to taste. This was much more fun than the mechanical monkey or practicing on the accordion. As the coals burned down, Daniel egged me on to add more and then more again.

After a while, we lost track of time. The sky turned navy blue and I said, "We better go back to the living room and start doing homework before Mama comes home." With that, I closed the fire bin door. We walked out of the kitchen hastily as if the guilt at disobeying Mama's instruction had already lapped at our conscience.

As we rummaged in our school bags for the homework books, a loud boom shattered the silence. We stood for a moment frozen, facing one another wide-eyed and terrified.

"What was that?" Daniel asked.

"I... I don't know. I think the sound came from the kitchen."

We tiptoed out into the darkened hallway moving forward cautiously. A few steps and we began to understand the extent of our crime. Water was seeping out from underneath the kitchen door. "Ouch! It's hot," Daniel screamed first, looking down at his wet socks.

"Let's go back to the living room," I said and grabbed Daniel's hand. "I think the boiler may have exploded."

Tears formed in my eyes, but I tried to hold them back and take charge of the situation. "Come on, we must get out of here." I pulled Daniel behind me, stepping gingerly over the quickly growing waves of hot water. But the jangling of keys in the door told us Mama was back. I knew there would be hell to pay for the fireworks display that had captivated us.

Mama opened the door and flipped on the light switch in the hallway. "Nachman, what happened here?" she exclaimed, a handkerchief pressed to her mouth. He was right behind her. They returned together from the dentist's office. Tinek hoisted up his pant legs and waded toward the kitchen. The extent of the disaster lay before him: the torn belly of the boiler, the steam filled room, the swirls of water covering the kitchen floor.

He cursed as he reached for a mop and a bucket. "How did this happen?"

"Please, Nachman, please," Mama mumbled, "I can't deal with this. Not today."

She stood in a puddle of water with the handkerchief still plastered against her mouth surveying the mess. She looked lost, pained, and exhausted. That was when I noticed a thin trickle of blood on the side of Mama's chin. I ran toward her and wrapped my arms around her waist.

"Tinek, what happened to Mama?" I asked, even more frightened about her strange condition than about the spanking I was expecting.

"The dentist pulled out most of her teeth. She is in a lot of pain. Leave her alone and let her go to bed."

"But why? Why did he do it?" By now, my silent sobs erupted into audible crying. Daniel made himself scarce.

"Her teeth rotted in Russia," Tinek said. "Now you come and help me mop up the water. Be a good girl."

This is how I knew there would be no spanking, not that I'd ever gotten one. Mama's condition was worse than any punishment. Later that night I heard Tinek whispering to Mama, "We are so lucky the children weren't injured in the explosion. They could have been badly burned, or worse..."

That evening, I lay in bed shaken; my eyes swollen from crying and my nose so stuffed I could hardly breathe. My duvet felt hot and I shifted this way and that unable to sleep. Remorse and shame flooded my entire body. I wanted to call for Marysia but felt I didn't deserve her singing that night. I swore to myself that I would not disobey my parents again, not if it meant they could lose more people they loved.

11

Just as his promotion to a Regional director was about to be announced, the boss strolled into Tinek's office with his thumbs stuck behind his red suspenders and hesitated at the door. He shut the door behind him and announced, "Nachman, now that your position will be more important, your name will be printed on a large sign outside your door, alongside your new title."

"Thank you. I am glad to hear that," Tinek flashed a broad grin of satisfaction; the promotion was overdue. He motioned for his boss to sit, but the man stood near the door as if he worried Tinek would bite him.

"Nachman," his boss cleared his throat noisily and paused then spit it out, "We can't have such a Jewish sounding name appear so publicly. I'll come right to the point: We'd like you to change it to one with a more Polish ring to it."

A minute later, he added, sounding vaguely apologetic, "You know how it is these days..."

Tinek's face fell. He drilled his gaze into the boss, "No, it's not just these days. This is nothing new. I hate to disappoint you, but I will not change my name."

"Sleep on it," the boss said, turned on his heel and walked out of the office after an awkward moment of silence.

"I don't need to sleep on it. I know the answer," Tinek mumbled to himself as the door was closing.

I remember how angry Tinek was when he told Mama about it that evening.

"Not in a million years would I change my name. They can keep their job!"

Mama was supportive. "Next time ask your boss how he'd like to give up his name, his father's name and his grandfather's name."

"I'll just keep doing my very best for my division. There's no arguing with good performance... or with antisemites."

In the end the promotion went through several months later. My father's name was printed in large bold letters on the sign, along with his new title, and the administration never repeated the request for a name change.

My father's refusal to change his name could have put his job at risk. Many Jews changed their names and erased centuries of forefathers. But my father would never compromise his dignity. His total faith in himself and the rightness of his beliefs sustained him through the war and in the difficult years that followed. He was a man of no doubts. This is what appealed to my young self so much. There was never any wishy-washy equivocating. He always had direct and straightforward answers. Some may have thought it a flaw that he did not allow himself to be anguished by doubts, but to him it was a badge of courage.

In May of 1955 the Warsaw Pact was signed. In between the triumphant military marches on the radio, there was constant chatter about how much safer our country would be from aggression now that we were under the large protective umbrella of the Soviet Union and its allies. I didn't understand most of the discussions, but the very idea that war was less likely made me happy.

Sometimes radio commentators said that America was armed to the teeth, but it didn't square with what my father was saying in the privacy of our living room. He mentioned America more often than in the past, but only in hushed tones. Come to think of it, he said the word "America" with a kind of longing in his voice, the reverent, languid way you would utter the name of a long lost love. He listened for any scrap of news about America, but the Polish press reported only negative information, like the arrest of Rosa Parks who refused to give up her bus seat to a white person. My father was very upset by this. It didn't fit with his positive view of the country.

His sister, also named Rosa, lived in America and that, no doubt, was one of its attractions. Rosa was his only remaining sibling and an Auschwitz survivor. He spoke of her beautiful singing voice and how she cared for him after my grandmother died. That was still before the war. He said, "I would give anything to see my sister again."

"Why can't we go there?" I asked.

"We don't have a visa to leave Poland."

I didn't know anything about visas but I could tell by his raised eyebrows and the index finger across his lips that I shouldn't be asking.

It was Tinek's secret longing for America that fueled my interest in a country that was always painted as evil and imperialistic by the Polish regime. I looked for books about America in the library but could find none. I read my parents' magazines when they were not at home. One day I came across an article in the Polish popular weekly, *Przekrój* (Cross-section), about American teenagers.

It said American girls were spoiled and more concerned with external appearance than with anything else, but there was something fascinating about it that made me want to read on. It all sounded so improbable, almost like science fiction. Those girls wore makeup and some kind of special pants called "pedal pushers" and drove their own cars! My God, they even drank Coca-Cola, a drink that seemed to me as exotic as liquor on some remote island and yet, forbidden, like an illicit drug.

Far from making me repulsed, which seemed to be the intent of the article, America became more mysterious and New York hovered in my mind more like a fairy tale than a real city where real people lived and kids went to school. I wondered if I might ever have a chance to see this otherworldly city, but then I quickly remembered that in our country we are supposed to be disgusted with the capitalist swine that populate New York.

I knew that I could not aspire to the glamor of American girls I'd read about in the magazine, but I vowed that I'd look my best for my thirteenth birthday. We had been planning a party at our home for all of my friends and even invited some of Daniel's buddies. Marysia would bake a big cake and Tinek would buy new records.

I begged Mama to buy me the beautiful blue velvet dress I'd seen in the dressmaker's shop window.

"Well, doesn't it look a bit too grown up?" she asked.

"What do you mean?" I asked pretending not to understand.

"The neckline is kind of low."

"Mama! I'll be thirteen," I squeezed the words through my teeth.

She laughed and I could see her features soften.

I thought I'd won, but she came back at me.

"In that case, I will make you a training bra—your first one! It will be my pleasure."

"What?" I exclaimed indignantly. I was mortified and would never admit I could see her point.

"My friends will laugh at me," I protested.

She smiled. "How will they know what's under your dress? It will be our secret."

I felt splendid in the knee length velvet dress on the day of my party. Its midnight blue was a color I imagined would be worn only by a royal. I spun around in front of the chifforobe mirror and admired how the soft skirt flared.

On this day Mama allowed me to wear my hair loose, instead of braided. She brushed it for a long time to a chestnut sheen. I'd often wondered about my mother's preoccupation with my hair. Perhaps it was because hers had been thinning. She made a face each time she looked in the mirror. Father said that her pregnancy with me while she was starving in Russia during the war had sapped some vital minerals and caused it.

For my birthday Tinek and Mama gave me my first ever piece of jewelry, a rope-like golden bracelet. "She looks so grown up," Tinek said when he saw me all dressed up. Mama winked at me. I was glad she didn't tell him. Tinek helped me close the clasp of the bracelet and I asked, "Is it real gold?"

"Do you like it?"

"Of course, I do!"

"Then it doesn't matter. Does it?"

I felt sorry I'd asked such a stupid question.

The party went off without a hitch. We played games and everyone got along. I wished the day wouldn't end.

It wasn't until a few weeks later that I became truly grown up. The red stain in my underwear horrified me, but I'd been expecting it. I stared as it spread to a large pink oval. I knew that it and that darn training bra were part of the same ugly manifestations of womanhood. My friends and I had explored this subject and obsessed about it. Ala had mentioned that hair would soon begin to grow in parts of my body that never had it. How disgusting! I could not imagine that any more than hair growing on my nose or the palm of my hand.

12

In the mid-fifties, 50,000 Jews fled their Polish towns fearing that strict exit visa restrictions would be rapidly reimposed. They knew that the "thaw" that followed Stalin's death in 1953 would not last long and they were right. Periodically, the government announced a loosening of exit visa restrictions and then slammed the doors shut just as people gave up their jobs and sold off their possessions. This is why in the spring of 1957, seven months after my thirteenth birthday, my parents started packing up our belongings in a hurry. This had been the third time they were given permission to leave Poland and this time they vowed to get out before it was revoked.

Great big wooden crates appeared in our apartment one morning taking up all the living room and bedroom space. There was scarcely any room to move around. These crates whose raw, unfinished wood paralleled our emotions, swallowed our possessions one by one in their cavernous depths.

In went the fluffy down quilts and pillows, the hand-embroidered linens, my mother's fabrics and notions for corset and brassiere making, bicycles, china, rugs, even two motorcycles my parents bought hoping to sell them for cash in Israel. The only items that did not go into the shipping crates were three pieces of jewelry that my mother sewed into the lining of my coat: her gold ring and necklace and my father's gold watch.

Mama instructed me repeatedly, "Ania, don't forget that we have entrusted something special to you. You must promise to be careful not to call attention to yourself, or to your coat."

"Did you understand what Mother told you, Ania?" Tinek wanted to be sure I was clear about this.

"When do I start being careful?"

"When the border agents come aboard the train to interview us," Father clarified.

"Why do they need to interview us?"

"Oh, Ania, just do what we ask and be courteous when the agents enter our train car, OK?"

"When will that be?" I asked with growing panic in my voice.

"When our train crosses the Polish border," Mama answered quickly and watching my face, seemed to give Tinek a signal with her hand to stop talking about this. She could tell now that the admonitions were only making me anxious. I was so terrified that in one false move I could spill the beans and get us all arrested.

After a couple of weeks of packing, our voices echoed through the empty rooms. Much the same scene was repeated in the homes of all my friends who were also leaving Poland for good; Ania, Ala and Slawka—we all scattered around the world like leaves in a fierce storm.

When we left Poland, my parents trusted Marysia to settle our bank affairs because our departure was so rushed that they couldn't do it themselves. We parted with Marysia at the train station with more hugging and crying than if we were close relatives. But there were no relatives to see us off, so I cannot be certain.

I wasn't exactly sure how to feel about leaving Poland. We left in such a hurry that I didn't have time to contemplate the consequences of permanently abandoning the land of my forefathers. Yet I was not especially ruffled by our departure. My parents and I left the Soviet Union when I wasn't quite three, but somehow, I felt more Russian than Polish. Maybe it was because of the beautiful Russian songs that my father sang in his resonant voice, or the stories my mother told about the impossibly high, snow covered peaks of Kyrgyzstan, or that my first words were Russian. Maybe without grandparents, or any family living in our city, I had not developed the kind of ties that bind one to a place. I knew only one thing: I didn't like leaving my friends and our beloved Marysia behind.

Marysia had always treated me as if I were a princess and she my lady-in-waiting. I knew I'd miss her the most, and not just because of the things she did for me, but her genuine warmth and empathy. She both understood me and spoiled me, catering to me long after I should have learned to do things for myself. It used to irritate my mother no end when I would lift my leg and ask Marysia to tie my shoes. "You are old enough to do it yourself, Ania. You are eleven years old."

"Oh, *Pani* Dora, let her be a child. Childhood is too short."

I remembered how I glowered at Mama and said, "See, Marysia doesn't mind."

I knew there would never be another Marysia.

After the hustle and bustle of boarding the Venice-bound train, we took our seats and each of us was momentarily silent. I wondered what my parents were thinking about. Was Tinek remembering his childhood among friends and family scattered on so many streets of Łódź? Was Mama wishing she had just one more chance to see the Warsaw of her youth, cosmopolitan and vibrant? And Daniel? He was probably all too happy to miss his daily accordion practice.

PHOTOS

Anetka age 6, Poland 1949

Dora and Nachman Libeskind found shelter with a
Muslim family in Kyrgyzstan

Libeskind family shortly after arrival from
Kyrgyzstan. Daniel 3 mos. old; Anetka 2 years
and 11 mos

Dora in the doorway of her corset shop on
Jaracza St. #1in Łodź, Poland

Anetka age 8 (fourth from right) with
her classmates

Ania age 9 and Daniel age 6

Daniel age 10, Polanica Zdrój, Poland

Ania on summer vacation wearing the magical
sun hat that could be folded into a small circle to
fit in a pocket

Dora's license to operate her shop from the
Chamber of Crafts. Bottom line reads: license is
cancelled upon two months arrears in payment
of dues

PART 2
BLUE

1

Here it is, Venice, looming before me like a giant theater set! After twenty-one hours on the train from Łódź, with a stop in Vienna, finally, the eternal city is so close I can almost touch it. We've boarded a small ship of Greek registry near sunset. I have never seen a large body of water like this. And I've never been on a ship! Its gentle swaying is disconcerting. It matches my nauseating sense of dislocation, but I am fascinated by everything I see and hear.

The sky glows red with the intensity of hot iron. Charcoal clouds on the horizon herald the approach of evening as small lights twinkle in the distance. A cauldron of humanity—passengers from foreign lands, sailors, peddlers, and beggars are milling about the pier. The fishy smell of the sea, the whistles of the ships in the harbor, the salty air, the cacophony of languages and cries of the gulls assault my senses as surely as the idea of our sudden departure from Poland.

All the mixed-up emotions are still churning in my stomach when my father says, "You will have plenty of time to look around, Ania, for now we are going to settle into our cabin."

"Cabin? You mean we are sleeping on this ship? How long is this trip?"

"I am not sure, maybe a week," he says, and I stand there with my mouth open watching my brother inspecting the row of small boats hanging on the deck. "What are these for?" Daniel asks.

We descend down a narrow winding staircase to our tiny cabin below deck and stow our suitcases, then we come back up on deck. This is when I realize that we are not the only emigrants on this ship; we are part of a large group. A squat Israeli representative, in a short sleeve white shirt with sweat stains in the armpits, greets my parents and some others in Yiddish. He looks older than my father and he is hairy. Black fuzz covers his arms and more of it sticks out on his chest where the collar is wide open.

When a large group has gathered on deck, he calls out, "Shalom!" in a loud voice and when few people acknowledge him he yells loudly again, "Shalom!" Now the crowd responds, some calling out the greeting enthusiastically, others mumbling the unfamiliar word. Then the hairy man welcomes us in Polish that sounds funny to my ears. Daniel snickers. Mama says, "It has been a while since he lived in Poland. One day you will sound like that."

Why? It doesn't make any sense, I mumble to myself, but the representative's instructions in Yiddish alternating with Polish grow more detailed so I listen. He divides us into groups, giving each a color designation. People push and try to switch assignments to be with friends. After a while, people begin to speak over him and one another, asking questions, making a ruckus. It is so noisy that the man lifts a megaphone and shouts instructions on when, and where we are to report for our meals. It all seems to depend on the color of the tickets he distributed. Ours are blue.

Once the hubbub has settled down, the representative announces that on each day of this momentous voyage he will teach us some Hebrew songs. We are expected to gather on deck and sing them on our arrival in Haifa. As his speech about our new life goes on and on I grow bored and pay more attention to sailors working on the side of the deck, coiling thick rope and swabbing the deck.

One of them reminds me of the Greek statue I have seen in a picture book. He is so beautiful! He glances in my direction from time to time making the butterflies in my stomach dance. The first night he stars in my dream: he twirls me on deck under a velvet blue sky dotted with millions of blinking stars.

Next morning I'm the first one on deck, staring at the placid blue water of the Mediterranean, but every now and then I turn around quickly and scan the deck to see if the sailor has appeared. Daniel joins me before I catch sight of my dream dancer and says, "It's the blue group's time to go to breakfast." Darn! I wish we had a later time slot.

Finally, on the second day I see him in his crisp, white uniform. He smiles and says something in Greek, sending my guts aflutter again. A day or two later, I see a man in uniform with fancy braiding at the shoulder speaking to my sailor sternly. For a crazy minute I imagine he's being scolded for looking at me, but of course, I have no way of knowing. The rest of the trip he is nowhere to be seen and I feel terrible. I wish that I had at least learned his name.

"Let's go out on deck, it's stifling in this cabin," Mama says, and we clamber up the staircase bumping into passengers trying to go down. I squint into the morning sun unaccustomed to such a brilliant sky. Daniel runs to snag a small table and we settle in to continue the talk about our arrival and who might be on shore in Haifa to greet us. "I'm sure my brothers and sisters will all be there," Mama says with a confident smile. Then we get into the most hotly debated subject: Mama's youngest surviving sibling, Nechemiah.

"Don't plan on hugging him. You will embarrass him and you will be disappointed if he turns away," my father comments.

"Why, Tinek, why did you say that?" Daniel and I demand an answer to his strange assertion.

"He is a Hassid."

Mama gives Tinek a look and with a tiny nod of her head points to a nearby couple. The man is wearing a black hat. "Shh..." Mama says.

"What's a Hassid?" I whisper.

Mama moves in closer. "I came from a Hassidic family so I will explain."

And she tells us about the unusual customs of the Hassidim: their dress, special food they call kosher and how they have to use separate sets of dishes for meat and milk products. Daniel and I are fascinated and full of questions. She shushes us repeatedly.

"Do you think Nechemiah will kiss you?" I ask. "You haven't seen him in eighteen years!"

"No, Ania," Tinek says. "The most he can do is smile."

"What about a handshake?" Daniel wants to know.

"Hassidim are not allowed to touch women's hands," Tinek says.

"But why? What's wrong with that?" I am offended already.

"Never mind," Mama says. "You'll soon learn all about that."

In the evening, when we are all tucked in our four narrow berths, Mama and Tinek on the bottom, Daniel and me on top, Mama tells us about Nechemiah's miraculous survival through Auschwitz. I learn things that boggle my mind.

Because of the strict rules of their religion even fewer Hassidim survived the Nazi concentration camps then other Jews. Hassidic inmates in Auschwitz would not eat the non-kosher slop fed to the inmates and so became weakest first within their transports and selected for extermination before the others.

Now I can see why Mama can't wait to see him. The way she tenderly mentions how frail and pious he was, only seventeen when the war broke out, I know that in her mind he is still the vulnerable kid brother, twelve years her junior. Something in her voice tells me she yearns to hug him, to press him to her bosom, to revel in his victory against death. I feel sad that such an expression of emotion isn't allowed by his religion. I had no idea some Jews could be so strange!

A couple of days more and our ship nears Haifa harbor. This is the day I've been both dreading and anticipating with more excitement than I care to admit. At breakfast, the Israeli representative uses his megaphone again to overcome the din in the dining hall, "All of you, *olim chadashim,* please, finish up quickly and come up on deck. Soon you will know that it means 'new arrivals.' Leave your things in the cabins."

None of us has much appetite today. "Let's go," Mama says, pushing away her coffee cup. We get up and move toward the stairs before the crowd overtakes us. On deck, the sun is blazing as it has each day of our voyage. It is only seven and already I'm sweating. Tinek mops his brow with a handkerchief and Mama fans herself with immigration forms distributed at breakfast. Daniel is roaming the deck, inspecting coils of rope. Soon, everyone who is part of our large group is up on deck. The man lines us up, instructing the children to come forward. I push Daniel into the front row. He is eleven, but still very short.

The ship approaches the shore. The land is in view, but I can't make out anything just yet. I look around and many of our group seem tired and have confused looks on their faces as if this whole trip has been a mistake. Maybe it's the heat. Suddenly I, too, feel disoriented. Are we here already?

The man distributes song sheets and gives us a signal to begin singing the first song he taught us: *Avinu Shalom, Shalom Aleichem,* we brought peace unto you. The group breaks into song. The strange language that is not yet ours feels awkward and forced. To my ears, we are a disappointing chorus, as if the journey has sapped all our enthusiasm. As I sing I realize the tears in my eyes are more about the sailor I'll never see again than about the new land that looms in front of us, ancient and indecipherable as the words I am uttering.

Our ship sails into Haifa harbor. Everyone seems to be rushing toward the railing at once as the sailors tie up the ship to bollards on the dock. Those who have relatives here shout their names and wave frantically. "Genia! Yossl! Chana! Moishe! Here, here, look up! *Gotteniu!* Oh my God!"

At first, we can't even get to the railing, but then the gangplank is attached and I see a heavy-set man with a thick reddish beard running up on it. His arms are outstretched, his ear locks fly sideways from under his wide-brimmed black hat and a broad grin stretches across his face.

"Nechemiah!" Mother screams and bursts out crying.

He runs toward her and wraps his thick arms around her. *Dvoyrele, Dvoyrele!* He keeps repeating the Yiddish diminutive of her name. "Let me look at you!" Then *he kisses her* on each cheek.

She sobs and smiles, then she hugs him.

Tinek, Daniel and I stand to the side dumbfounded.

A delicate pink hue erupts on Mama's olive cheeks. She looks radiant. We have never seen Mama so animated.

As Nechemiah waves his arms excitedly, the front of his black frock flies open revealing a white shirt and *tzitzes,* ritual fringes hanging down the sides of his trousers. No longer the skinny yeshiva boy Mama described, Nechemiah provides us with instant and powerful evidence that love is stronger than religious dogma.

Next in line are Mama's sisters, Esther and Chava. Their tears mix with laughter. They hug Mama as if they plan to remain glued to one another in a permanent embrace. And all those cousins milling around, waiting their turn to be introduced! I don't know any of them except from Mama's telling and the photos in our album.

The tallest one must be Rami, Chava's oldest son. He is

handsome and very suntanned. The girl with shiny black hair drooping over her eyebrow and almond shaped eyes must be his sister, Ruthi. I know she's my age. Zvia, the younger sister, Daniel's age, hangs back. She looks shy and has a puzzled expression on her freckled face. A little guy, Moshele, hugs his mother's leg and tries to hide behind her skirt. He is her youngest. That's the kibbutz group, all dressed in white shirts and brown sandals.

Then there is the group of blond cousins. The boys, Yankele and Avremeleh, look to be close to my and Daniel's age and like their father, Nechemiah, have long ear locks except they are not wearing black frocks or black hats. They wear yarmulkes on their blond heads. A small girl in a frilly pink dress, Atara, has blonde curls and blue eyes. She looks just like one of the Polish girls in my class. All three of Nechemiah's children have flaxen hair, pink cheeks, and the bluest blue eyes. Their fair features prove to me the lie of the "Jewish look." Now I know for sure that my father and I are not the only Jews with light hair and blue eyes. I can't believe these are all my relatives! And I wonder if I'll learn to call the bearded man in a black frock, "Uncle."

In short order we are introduced to the others: Chava's wiry husband Benjamin and the skinny lady with a scarf wrapped around her head, Chayka, Nechemiah's asthmatic wife. The last to arrive is Mama's half-brother, Maxim, and his wife who is also Chava now, but was Katie before she converted to Judaism. Maxim, too, hugs Mama and booms his greeting. He seems bombastic, though I don't know what he is saying. I can tell he thinks he is an important man by the way he struts and shakes everyone's hand. He has a neat beard, not as profuse and untamed as Nechemiah's and I know he is not a Hassid because his head is not covered.

I can't quite absorb the fact that I'm related to all these people. It isn't just their odd clothing, or facial hair, or tans, or toes sticking out of sandals. I am fascinated by the idea that we have blood ties. We get off the ship and they are carrying our bags, talking over one another. Between the Hebrew and Yiddish flying in all directions, I'm surrounded by a gaggle of exotic birds. But as I look around the port I see some newly arrived who seem to have no one meeting them. They guard their overstuffed suitcases and wicker baskets stacked helter-skelter against the fence under a sign that says IMMIGRANTS. A young girl sleeps curled up on a suitcase.

2

Thank God for Aunt Chava and Uncle Benjamin! They have rescued us from a miserable shack in Givat Olga, the place that our group of *olim chadashim* was first taken. The government gave us a temporary place to live in the middle of nowhere, but the barrack was so depressing that we'd have had to turn around and run back to Poland! Chava and Benjamin have volunteered to host us for the first few days. "And then... what?" I whisper to Mama as we pile into Uncle's borrowed van with our suitcases and roses that Mama's sisters brought to the port.

"We will see," Mama whispers back as we stuff ourselves into the vehicle, but I am trying to figure out what that means. See what? I need to know where our home will be. A knot of anxiety begins to form in my stomach. I don't like not knowing.

Uncle Benjamin is our driver. En route to kibbutz Gvat in the Jezreel valley he is trying hard to orient us, maybe because of the bewildered looks on our faces. "Our kibbutz is less than ten miles (16 km) from Nazareth. It was Jesus' childhood home, now it's the main Israeli Arab town."

"Jesus? Arabs?" I think my head will explode.

He laughs and says, "I know, I know, I felt that way when I first came from Warsaw, no fancy cafes, just swamps and mosquitoes."

Along the road to Gvat I keep quiet trying to absorb all the newness, the people, the strange white buildings, the road that runs along the sea and trees unlike I've ever seen. "Cedars," Uncle says as he sees me staring at them. After the raucous arrival and exhausting trip to Givat Olga we are all tired. Daniel has nodded off in the rear seat. I'm up front and can see his head in the rearview mirror bouncing on Tinek's shoulder. Mama and her sister are chatting quietly. They have years to catch up on. Benjamin is the only one paying attention to me now and he narrates like a tour guide as he zips along the nearly empty road. The van bounces on the poorly paved surface and groans with the weight of the six of us.

"Why is the road so empty?" I ask.

"Few people have private vehicles here," he says.

"What are those green tarpaulin-covered trucks?"

"Oh, these belong to our military," he says proudly.

A Jewish military, our own soldiers! For some reason it makes me euphoric until Benjamin says, "In Israel women serve in the military, not just men. When you turn eighteen you'll be a soldier too."

"Me? A soldier?"

"Yes, why not?"

To dispel my apprehension, I focus on the road: hills covered with gnarled, ancient looking olive trees, stands of stately cypresses, vineyards and orange groves, blue skies, and unfamiliar sweet fragrances.

As we approach the area of the kibbutz, Chava instructs Benjamin, "Let's drive them around our place, just to give them the general idea. You know, like an introduction."

"Great. Tomorrow I'll have to return the van. First, I'll take a spin around the perimeter of the property."

Endless fields of Gvat cotton with their fuzzy puffs grace one side of the road. Then we pass fragrant orchards. I'm amazed. "There must be as many fruit trees here as in the Garden of Eden!"

Benjamin laughs. "Not quite, but we do grow apples, plums, pears, olives, oranges and grapefruit." Even from the distance I can see the bent boughs laden with what I imagine is luscious fruit. "Hey, Mama, remember when your sister came from Paris to visit us in Poland and brought us the first oranges and bananas we ever saw?"

"No oranges or bananas?" Chava sounds surprised.

"Polish stores have nothing much in them, certainly no tropical fruit," Mama says.

"Yes, of course, I should have known," Chava sighs. "Well, now you'll have plenty. And you'll discover lots of new fruits too, like sabras and guavas."

"What are those?" I've never heard of either.

"You will recognize guavas by their strange smell soon enough," she laughs. "And sabras by their prickly skin."

Benjamin now follows a narrow road adjacent to vineyards whose wooden trellises stick out of rocky slopes. And I thought grapes grew only in France! Uncle Benjamin chuckles at my amazement and smiles. "That's not all," he says. "We also grow corn, wheat, watermelon, and all kinds of vegetables." That doesn't surprise me as much, but since I had never seen them except on a plate, I am looking forward to seeing how they grow.

By now it's clear. Gvat isn't anything like the small Polish farms: a field, a cow, a man with a plow. Gvat is huge.

"It's like a country all of its own," I say.

"What?" asks Benjamin.

"Your Gvat."

"No, it is only about 4,000 dunams, but it is *our* piece of paradise," he says. I have no idea what a dunam is so he explains that it is about 1,000 acres, but that still doesn't mean anything to me. All I know is that Gvat's borders seem to go on forever, up the hills, across the main road and down into the valley as far as the eye could see.

Tinek, mostly silent during the drive, suddenly speaks up, "I can see living here."

Mama doesn't respond. Maybe she hasn't heard him.

Once we pass the stretches of Gvat fields and groves we come to an area surrounded by a chain link fence and a wide-open main gate. "This is the heart of Gvat," Chava says. "We are home."

"How many people live here?" I ask.

"We have nearly 1,000 members," she answers.

I had no idea so many people would live on one farm! This isn't anything I'd imagined.

"Are they *all* Jewish?" I ask, finding it impossible to imagine so many Jews in one place.

Now Chava and her husband both chuckle. "Yes, yes, of course."

Modest, one and two-story cinderblock buildings meander down narrow gravel paths shaded by palm trees. Oh, the palm trees! I can't get over their scaly trunks and fronds that resemble feathers of prehistoric birds. Fragrant gardens wrap around each building, their showy profusion of flowers dizzying. Most of the plants here look unfamiliar. I have never seen cacti. Some are the size of trees with spikes that make them look like dangerous animals. Only the children's houses are easily recognizable. These one-story structures have sandboxes, tricycles, animal shaped climbing equipment and all manner of toys strewn in their front yards.

On the ship, Mama told me that kibbutz kids don't live with their parents. They live in separate children's houses for different age groups. This isn't something I can comprehend. Don't they miss their parents? Who cares for them? Who feeds them?

"Well, I know we have exhausted you," Chava says. "We are almost at our building. You will have a chance to wash up, eat and rest in just a few minutes."

"Eat?" Daniel is finally awake. "Where are we? I'm starving."

"Welcome to kibbutz Gvat," Benjamin says.

Now it's Daniel's turn to be amazed as I have been during the ride. "Look at those animals!" he exclaims as we pass rows upon rows of long cowsheds, pastures where sheep graze, chicken coops, stables, and even a small zoo with camels. "And what are those?" He points to garages filled with exotic farm machinery. "And this?" Daniel spots a long channel with water in the distance. "A pool?"

"Not exactly," Benjamin says. "This is water for irrigation, but kids do swim here sometimes."

"We'll have to learn how to swim!" Daniel is excited.

All I can think is how did they ever manage to turn a desert into such a lush oasis? How carefree their lives must be. This *is* paradise, just like Benjamin said.

3

On the first morning in Gvat I wake up disoriented. Where am I? Last night's trip from Haifa seems like a dream. Exotic fruits, ancient olive trees, Jewish soldiers, and farmers. Did it really happen? I'm sleepwalking, trying to find the bathroom, but Daniel is already in it. "Hurry up!" I bang on the door, then I hear Mama calling from the balcony, "They'll be here any minute, get dressed."

"Who?"

"Your aunt and uncle," she says.

"Why didn't you wake me up?"

"You were so tired," she calls out. Her voice has none of my fatigue. It is full of sunshine.

Next thing I know there's a knock at the front door and it opens before we respond. Luckily, Daniel emerges from the bathroom with his hair wet and a surprised look on his face. I dive in, my clothes in a pile under my arm. Oh, God, I can't deal with visitors this early! Wait, *I* am the visitor. This is their apartment. We have already heard that no one ever locks the doors here. I should have known.

"*Boker Tov!*" Chava's cheery voice reminds me we are no

longer in Łódź. "No use waiting," I hear her say, "I said good morning, so you can start learning Hebrew right away." Learning a new language before breakfast? I throw water on my face and pull on my long-sleeved wool dress. It seems ill suited to this climate, but it's all I have. I crack the bathroom door open, hoping not to be seen, but no luck.

"Come here," Chava stretches her arms to me and I approach her shyly. She gives me a mama bear hug. "Anat, you will love it here," she says.

I look at her strangely, "Auntie, what did you call me?"

"Oh, I think *Anat* is the perfect Hebrew name for you. It's close to Ania, don't you think?"

Anat? It sounds strange, but I dare not voice an opinion so I keep quiet. What do I know about Hebrew names anyway? Mama watches us, and her eyes light up. "Your aunt is right, you will see," she reassures me, but that only makes me wonder.

Tinek and Benjamin are sitting on the sofa that was my bed last night. They chat in Yiddish as if they were old friends. Tinek asks him about a sister that still lives in Russia. "Any prospects of getting her out?"

Benjamin laughs. "Not now," he says. "*Nisht unter Khrushchev.*" Benjamin is lean and taller than the average Polish Jew, much taller than Tinek. He has a twinkle in his eyes and sparse graying hair.

Physically Benjamin and Chava are mismatched. On a good day she stands probably four foot eight and is nearly as wide, but she has a commanding and calming presence. Her high cheekbones and slanted eyes make her look Asian when she smiles her easy, wide grin revealing a mouthful of healthy teeth. They've come to collect all of us for breakfast.

Bright sunlight streams into the room spotlighting the pile of blankets and pillows we used and I feel badly that we have disrupted the orderly little nest that is my aunt and uncle's apartment.

"Who is hungry?" Benjamin asks.

"I am!" Daniel says.

"Next stop *cheder ochel*," Chava announces. I am very curious what it is, but I don't want to impose by asking too many questions. We have already disrupted their routine, but both have been gracious and welcoming. Chava and Benjamin slept in their friends' vacant apartment so we could use their room—one room is all they have. I know that staying at their place can't go on long.

We file out and down one short flight of stairs, exiting past the flower garden and onto a gravel path. It is only May, but the air is hot, hotter than any I have ever experienced. How hot will it get here in the summer? I don't think I'll be able to stand it.

"I wonder if they eat *naleśniki*," Daniel speculates as we walk behind our parents who are engrossed in their conversation with Chava and Benjamin.

"Nah, that's a Polish food," I say, recalling the sweet, cheesy taste.

It turns out the *cheder ochel* is the communal dining room. As soon as we enter, Chava and Benjamin's friends surround us and we are introduced as if we were long awaited dignitaries. People crowd around us and seem genuinely glad we have come.

"Welcome! Welcome! Such a beautiful family! We've heard all about you!" A cacophony of greetings in Hebrew, Polish, Russian, and Yiddish fills my ears and I feel overwhelmed at the instant familiarity. So many faces and names to remember: Itzhak, Motl, Shoshana, Malka, Itamar and some I can't even pronounce.

We settle down to breakfast and several of the people who have greeted us join us at the table; a grandmotherly woman, tanned to a crisp and wrinkled like a prune; a smiling young woman with a number tattooed on her forearm, and two men in overalls whom Benjamin introduces as his work colleagues.

Chava leads us to the long self service station: soft and hard-boiled eggs, white cheeses, yellow cheeses, yogurts, fruits, jams, breads and rolls. "We produce all of these right here on Gvat.

Everything is fresh and the eggs come from our own chickens," Chava beams. Her eyes now mere slits, her cheeks like small shiny tomatoes. How proud she is of her farm!

Suddenly all that talk about eggs brings a recent memory that makes me feel odd, not nostalgic like an old person reminiscing, but a strange feeling I can't quite define settles below my breastbone. In Poland, Marysia used to make me soft-boiled eggs with butter for breakfast that she presented with great flourish in a carved wooden eggcup. I guess that will never happen again.

Once we are introduced to the system, Daniel and I circle the long table and we spot huge bowls of salad and tomatoes. Daniel looks at me quizzically. "Ania, they eat raw vegetables in the morning!" These people *are* strange, but I say nothing. I just give him a look that says *shh*. We fill our plates with familiar foods and sit down. Chava looks over our plates puzzled. "Where are your olives? Why didn't you take any?"

"Olives?" Daniel and I asked in unison. Chava points to her plate. We had never seen these green marbles before, never mind tasting one. "*Ciociu*... they look raw," I say under my breath.

She laughs, "No, no silly, that's how they are eaten. They are ripe."

Benjamin picks out one from his plate and moves it toward me, "Here, taste it!"

I can't disappoint him. I pop it into my mouth. It is hard and bitter! I try not to grimace and twirl it in my mouth for a long while. "Don't swallow the pit," Benjamin cautions.

Our tablemates look at me expectantly as if I am about to pronounce a verdict. I will myself not to spit out the whole olive and nod, shifting it from one side of my mouth to the other. Daniel is staring at me from across the table. From the look on his face I can tell he isn't about to try one. Whew! Finally, I work it over, take it out of my mouth and put the pit on my plate.

"Want another one?" Chava asks. "I'll bring you a few on your own plate."

"*Dziękuje, Ciociu,*" Thank you, Auntie, I say in my most polite, grown-up voice. "One is enough."

Chava extols their dietary virtue, "When eggs get too expensive we eat a few olives, they are just as nutritious as eggs."

"I will have to remember that," Mama says, but neither she nor Tinek want to taste them. I hope we haven't disgraced ourselves in front of their friends.

4

Just three days after our arrival Mama and Tinek decide to move on. Sitting on the balcony at dusk, sipping tea, they chat with my aunt.

"Chava, this arrangement is such a hardship for you. It can't go on," Mama says.

"Nonsense, we can sleep in our friends' apartment a few more nights, then we will see," Chava says.

"See what? We can't stay in limbo forever," Mama says. "We have done too much of that in recent years."

"You are a good sister, Chava," Tinek says. "But I must get to Tel Aviv sooner or later to find a job. Sooner is best."

"But where will you stay? I know you can't afford a hotel." Chava's voice rises with concern.

"I think Esther will let us stay with her for a few days while we look for a sublet," Mama says.

"But her studio is smaller than our room. It's minuscule!" Chava exclaims.

"We have managed in worse situations. Don't worry, we will be fine," Mama assures her.

"At least let me keep the kids," Chava says. "They will learn Hebrew and make new friends."

And so it is. Daniel and I are left behind in Gvat, our objections notwithstanding.

Despite the nearly three-year difference between us, Daniel and I are close. Having been raised sharing one bedroom for the past eleven years, we have figured out how to get along. It isn't that sometimes he doesn't get on my nerves, but especially now, we're glad to have each other's company, maybe because both of us are odd specimens here, and maybe because we know that soon we will be separated. Like all kibbutz boys and girls we will live in separate children's houses. Like me, Daniel has been given an Israeli name. He is *Dani*, to my *Anat*, but we are still the same city kids we were when we arrived a week ago.

While we wait for placement in our respective group homes we fight boredom playing checkers in Chava's apartment and we talk about the crazy ways things are done here in Gvat.

"Have you noticed that all kids wear practically the same clothing?" I ask Daniel.

"That's no surprise," he says, sounding like a wise old man. "Here it's share and share alike. Dad told me," he says, cleverly jumping his red disc and capturing mine to make a king.

"Oh, that must be why Chava refused to accept the gifts Mama brought for our cousins. They weren't all the same."

"I wonder if they would be mad if they knew they lost out on the gifts," he muses. "I would be, for sure."

Our checkers game is over. I have lost this time. I hate it when he beats me, but I'm proud of how smart he is. "Want to play another round?" he asks eagerly. I know he wants to win three in a row.

"Wait, I want to ask you something," I stall, unsure if I want another round. "Daniel, do you remember how in Poland there was this attitude toward peasants?"

"What attitude?" He looks at me as if I'm speaking Greek.

"Never mind," I say waving my hand. He is too young to discuss what's on my mind.

"No, tell me, I want to know what you are talking about," he insists, frowning.

"Well, I had the impression that peasants were... I don't know... stupid, had no manners."

Now he is really curious about where I'm heading. "Do you think people on the kibbutz are peasants?" I ask. He looks at me as if he doesn't get it, so I clarify, "You know they work the land, milk cows..."

"No," he says as if it were obvious. "They are farmers."

"What's the difference?" I ask, not expecting an answer. He shrugs and sets up the checkerboard for a new game.

I can't stop thinking. Ever since we arrived I've been asking myself: are the people in Gvat—my family— farmers, or peasants? But something I learned in history class in Poland churns in my head. The peasants worked the land of the nobility. An image from a Polish history textbook comes to mind. Pictures of richly dressed men on horses and stooped men in rags plowing the fields; below them a caption: peasants and nobles. Here in the kibbutz people own the land and no one bosses them around. Maybe that's the difference.

Somehow, I feel better now. "Okay, let's play another round," I say.

We've been getting to know our cousins. They come over to their parents' apartment after school to get a snack and say hello. Daniel and I await them eagerly because we are going a bit stir crazy without any friends our age. Each cousin is a strange but welcome revelation. All are *sabras*, born and raised in this still new Jewish country.

Rami is a couple of years older than me. He throws shy smiles my way, but he looks at me sideways, kind of nervous, as if he has never seen a girl. The thick veins on his muscular arms fascinate me, but I try not to stare. He must be so strong! He never stays long, just grabs the snack and, poof, he's gone. Zvia and Ruthi stay longer and they chat with one another, the way I imagine sisters do; the way Daniel and I banter when we are by ourselves. Every now and then they cast glances our way, then whisper and giggle.

Zvia is Daniel's age. She's quite shy and hardly looks in his direction of her own accord, but he doesn't care. He has made friends with a few boys already. Maybe boys don't need to talk. Maybe they just grunt. I have yet to make friends.

Ruthi is the cousin who fascinates me the most. I love her exotic looks, her almond eyes, the jet-black shiny hair. She looks Asian, like her mother. Her eyes are lively and her face curious. She looks at me in a friendly way, but I think she is assessing me. Her posture impresses me the most. She holds herself straight as a candle, looking taller than she is—about my height—a regal kind of bearing.

Moshele, Chava's baby, is about seven, but he's small for his age. He has a mischievous twinkle in his dark eyes. He stays around the longest and even though I don't understand him either, his speech sounds like baby talk. Chava just can't take her eyes off him. I can tell he delights her.

For the last few nights before falling asleep, my last thought has been I have so much family here! This powerful feeling of belonging is something I just can't get over. In Poland we only had two of Mama's cousins, but they lived in Warsaw and we saw them rarely. At long last, I am not the only Jewish girl in my building and only one of half a dozen in the whole school.

I would love to speak with my Israeli cousins. I'd ask them a million questions, but the trouble is they address me in Hebrew, the only language they know. Yesterday, when Ruthi came over and said *Shalom, Anat, ma shlomech?* I had no idea what she was saying.

"*Ciociu,* Auntie," I called Chava. "Can you tell Ruthi I don't know what she is saying?"

"She knows, she knows, she is trying to ask, 'how are you?'"

"Tell her I am fine," I say, and feeling helpless and dumb, manage an inane smile.

Since we arrived, Daniel and I have been following Chava like newly adopted puppies, repeating at every turn, *Ciociu, jak się to mówi po Hebrajsku?* "Auntie, how do you say that in Hebrew?" By now even our cousins recognize our most frequent Polish phrase and chuckle whenever they hear it. Once Ruthi tried to repeat it with no success. It was my turn to laugh. So sabras can't pronounce Polish words. Ha!... so unfamiliar sounds can twist anyone's tongue.

Each night I lie in bed for hours unable to sleep. Dare I hope Ruthi will eventually embrace me in her circle? It is her acceptance I crave most because she is of my blood. I could be her sister, or a friend, but she already has a sister and more than enough friends. For now I feel like an extra thumb. I am awkward around her and the rest of my cousins, like a clumsy clown tripping on oversize shoes. They must think me a freak.

I decide to ditch my pillow. I've heard that kibbutz sabras think of it as a bourgeois frivolity, just perfect for someone soft, like me. I get out of bed and stash it in a closet, then get back in bed and gyrate uncomfortably trying to bend my elbow into a pillow.

5

I am rolling my new name on my tongue, tasting it like some strange fruit. Anat. *Anat*—doesn't quite conform to the shape of my mouth. It feels too guttural and foreign. It contorts my epiglottis. It's the third name I have been given in my thirteen years. Everyone says that I better get used to it quickly, but I wonder if *I* will change along with it. Will I become someone else, or be the same old Ania in Anat's skin?

Aunt Chava rolls up the shade. Sun pours in through the window with a blinding intensity, making me squint. The bluest sky I have ever seen squeezes in through my eyelashes. It shimmers. Its brightness is unnerving. Its unreal cerulean hue seems surreal like my presence in this place.

"Anat, get up, we have a plan for this morning. Remember?" Chava snaps me out of my disoriented state in her amusing Hebrew accented Polish. She has been away from her native Warsaw for more than two decades. I wonder if this is how I will sound at some distant time, but I am unable to imagine it.

"Anat, did you hear me?" Chava calls out from the next room.

"Yes, *Ciociu.* I am getting ready."

Anat? I try to convince myself that it is really my new name. Maybe years from now it will not feel so awkward, but for now it grates on my nerves.

The overwhelming sense of relief we first experienced when we arrived in this beautiful valley, a place whose fragrance alone could transport one to paradise and meeting the family, so loving and welcoming... well... it seems to be dissipating. We've been here two weeks! Now, I don't feel so enchanted anymore. Mama and Tinek left Daniel and me on our own! No one says for how long. Not knowing drives me crazy.

This morning I dawdle, still thinking about my odd new name, like so many other strange things I have been seeing for the last two weeks. Will anything here ever become as familiar as the home I left behind? It can't happen soon enough, for I stick out like an albino among my bronze-skinned peers, whose tanned legs flash out of their white shorts like chiseled columns.

"Anat, put your clothing in the sack I left for you," Chava calls out again.

"Do you want me to take it *all* out of my suitcase?" I have no idea why she wants me to do something so stupid.

"Yes, we have to label it all with your name."

"Why? I know it's mine." She laughs, a deep belly laugh.

I have found myself here so suddenly that sometimes I think I'll wake from this eerie dream and find myself in our cozy apartment where Marysia will be setting the table for dinner and the smell of *gołombki* will permeate the air. I am by turns resentful at being left on Gvat like a piece of abandoned farm machinery and, for a while at least, glad to be rid of my parents' rules and their Polish sensibility.

Mama and Tinek are city people, Mama especially. I want to giggle just thinking of her with a cow udder in her hand, or a bucket of manure. Not that she hasn't done farm work, but that was in the Soviet Union where she was forced to do it. So far, we've heard nothing from our parents. Letters are slow to arrive and there are no phones. Where will we be a few weeks from now? A few months? I wish I knew.

Every kibbutz member is allowed to have visitors, but after two weeks they must go to work, or leave. Our second week on Gvat is coming to an end and with it, our status as guests. The Israeli school year is now over so even the Gvat kids will be assigned jobs and so will we. Jobs? I have never worked. Well, unless schoolwork counts.

"Ania—are you ready?" Chava asks, interrupting the endless stream of questions in my head. Even she is still confused and by a slip of the tongue calls me by my Polish name, my real name. "We must get going," she says.

"But, *Ciociu*, it's so hot out. We are not used to such heat. Can we go later?"

She chuckles. "It will be even hotter in the afternoon. Anyway, it is high time for you to become familiar with the kibbutz and our ways."

I push the trundle bed closed and fold up my blanket thinking of what to say. Daniel and I are guests in Aunt and Uncle's tiny one-room apartment. I have to be careful with my words and expressions. Let's be honest: we are an inconvenience, not that Chava or Benjamin ever act as if we are, but I am just thinking of what we would have done with two extra people in our small Łódź apartment. "Where are we going?" I ask, hoping it will be a short trip. Daniel is already out with Yoni, a friend who communicates with him in hand gestures, so he will be skipping this kibbutz lesson.

"Let's first go to the laundry and the *cheder ochel*," Aunt Chava says cheerfully.

———

We leave the cool of Chava's modest apartment and walk down a winding, dusty path together. We pass palm trees that look like mythical trees I have seen only in books. Like a duckling following its mother I follow my squat aunt. To anyone looking at us we must look comical. A short, heavy-set woman wearing a strange khaki colored hat that makes her look like a mushroom is carrying a large bundle under her fleshy arm and waddling down a path with a young girl following closely behind. The girl is clearly not of this place. She is pale and quite overdressed. Beads of sweat form on her forehead and upper lip. There is an invisible rope connecting the two.

In the mild Polish summers we spent our days in ancient villages shaded by enormous leafy trees, or under the thatched roofs of rented summer cottages, hiking shady pine forests or mountain climbing in the Tatra Mountains. It was never this hot, except on the day my father brought me a magical folding sun hat from the city. Made of white gauzy material covered with tiny flowers, it had around its rim a band of flexible metal that with some dexterity could be twisted just so to make it pocket-sized when closed. Open, it was enormous and made me feel like a movie star. But here everyone wears a different type of sun hat—a ridiculous looking, olive drab thing with a short round brim.

"They call it *kova tembel*," Uncle Benjamin said as he donned his this morning.

"What does that mean, Uncle Benjamin?" I asked.

"Well, I'm not sure I should tell you," he laughed as he took a last gulp of tea from his mug and dabbed his mouth with a napkin.

"Why not?"

"It means 'stupid hat' in Hebrew. Now you know." Then he added, "Ask your aunt to get you one."

I wondered if he was teasing me, but he looked serious and stopped smiling.

"The sun is very strong here, Anat. You don't want to get sunstroke. You must cover your head, especially when you are out working."

Never! I make a silent vow. My only thought: I'll probably get a stroke from the work, not the sun. Work? Wait till they find out that I don't know how to do anything! I'll surely get kicked out. Especially now that our two weeks are up.

We enter the kibbutz laundry, Chava hands a sack of soiled clothing to the woman behind the counter and they chat. I stand there like a dummy not understanding anything. I hate not understanding what is being said. The woman hands my aunt a stack of neatly pressed shirts and pants. "See, these have our name printed on the labels," my aunt says. Already, she's starting to instruct me in the ways of the kibbutz. "Each week you will bring your laundry here and get fresh clothes."

"Oh, so that is why you wanted to label my clothes," I say feeling foolish.

She pats my back, "Don't worry, you will get used to all this."

My mind races to my bed in Łódź, where Marysia always laid out clean clothes for me each morning. I am somewhat appalled at the idea that I'll now have to take charge of my own dirty laundry. "*Ciociu*, how much does it cost?" I ask.

She laughs. The narrow slits of her almond-shaped eyes crinkle. "Nothing. We don't pay for anything here, or maybe better put; we pay with our labor."

I am wide-eyed; I still don't understand.

"Who knows, you might get assigned to work at the laundry one day," she says.

My jaw drops. All I can see is Marysia stirring the cauldron of boiling linens. They might make me do *that*?

A few minutes later, we arrive at the *cheder ochel* where Chava needs to speak with someone about her kitchen duty schedule. This time I observe it carefully. It looks like a huge restaurant, with long bare tables and plastic chairs perched on thin metal legs. The chairs make me wonder how they can support a full-grown person. The space isn't decorated in any sense of the word, but it isn't depressing. It is suffused with bright light. Three of its walls are glass. The palms swaying gently outside soften its severe look.

"This is where you'll come for your meals next week by yourself." Chava makes an unexpected announcement with a bright smile.

"Why... why by myself?"

"No, you won't eat alone! Your cousin, Ruthi, will meet you here because I'll be back at work."

"You won't be with me next week?" Even I can hear the whine in my voice, but I am distressed. "*Ciociu*, how will I communicate?"

Chava has been our translator since we arrived and I can barely say a handful of Hebrew words. No way I can patch together a sentence!

"Oh, don't worry, somehow you will manage," she says. "We were all new here once."

I won't tell my aunt about my notoriously horrid sense of direction, but I don't even remember the way from her apartment to this place. Gvat is so huge! I am shaken by her sudden declaration, frightened by another change in my status.

In a moment she adds, "We'll be moving you into the group home soon. After that you will always take meals with your friends." I panic. Moving again? I do know that kibbutz kids don't live with their parents, but with peers their age. Still, the idea is so alien I can't absorb it.

"Who lives in that group home?" I ask.

Chava laughs, "I have told you, Ruthi and her classmates."

"Are they all girls?" I ask, thinking of my school in Poland.

"No. What gave you that idea? It's boys and girls, all more or less your age."

I say nothing. I can't tell her how terrified I am to be lodged with a bunch of strangers whose language I don't speak and whose lean and bronze bodies are so unlike mine. I try to push back the thought that boys will be living in the same house, not in the same room I hope!

No, wait. Maybe I'll have my own room. Who will clean it and make up my bed? Certainly, Marysia isn't coming from Poland to do it. I feel my intestines twisting and my stomach doing summersaults. Instead of asking questions I just smile and a deep blush spreads on my cheeks.

"Are you alright, Anat? You are so quiet," Chava asks.

"Yes, *Ciociu*."

Chava stops to speak with a woman in a gauzy white shirt with beautiful embroidery while I stand there like an extra appendage and think about how I'll ever learn this odd guttural language. I've been trying to memorize Hebrew words as best I can: *cheder*- room; *ochel*- food. I can remember the sounds, but I still lack the ability to properly pronounce the "ch" sound; trying to make it, I sound as if I am choking. The same thing happens when I try to pronounce the letter *Ayn*, which is at the beginning of my new name. My aunt is always very amused by my efforts.

Their conversation now finished, Chava says, "It will be lunchtime soon." And it dawns on me that my parents left me without any money. I ask for the second time this morning, "How much do meals here cost?"

"You don't pay here either," Chava replies. "But you do have to take your turns in the kitchen, cooking, or washing dishes."

I stare at her in amazement. "But... but I don't know how to cook."

She laughs again; her eyes just tiny slits, with crinkles extending to her temples. It seems almost anything I say is a source of amusement. I know Chava isn't laughing at me, at least I don't think so, but I must seem like a creature from another planet.

"Even our kids don't cook yet. You need experience for that. You'll learn in due course, but washing dishes is nothing." All I can think of right now is that I don't want to become experienced in cooking, or dishwashing. Ever.

Just as she says this, we approach the back portion of the kitchen. Huge, long sinks line the wall. There are metal carts stacked with all manner of dirty dishes. The young women at the sinks wear stained aprons, their hands gliding in and out of the grayish soapy water like fins of some strange aquatic creatures.

This is surely turning out to be the worst day of my life. I am beginning to wonder if this is a part of some evil plan by my parents to have me grow up in a hurry. I will have to do things here that in Poland only our help had to do. I am furious with my parents for sentencing me to the kibbutz. And yet, yet... people here look so happy. Could I ever hope to feel at ease dipping my hands into a sink full of other people's greasy plates?

By now I am becoming acutely aware that the queasiness in my stomach is not only anxiety: I've missed breakfast. Presently I hear groups of people approaching the *cheder ochel* from all directions.

"Anat, now you will join us for lunch, our main meal of the day."

"Who is us?" I ask, not sure if Chava is talking about her immediate family.

"The entire kibbutz is family," she answers as if she had read my mind. "Most everyone has a lunch break now and your cousins will be joining any minute."

The big sister instinct takes over. "What about Daniel?"

"He will be coming in with cousin Zvia. He is with her group today. They will be in the same class in the fall."

Lunch? Great, so long as no one offers me olives again. I don't want to offend anyone with an ungracious refusal.

It surprises and pleases me that the family members make it a point to eat their main meal together though the kids sleep in separate group homes. I watch the people walking in. Most seem to be young, but even those who appear to be older carry themselves with an air of competence and purpose quite unlike any I have ever seen. Motioning to their friends to join their tables, they hold their heads up and wave their rough hands and wiry arms with rope-like veins. There is a feeling of solidarity here; these people have *chosen* to live, work and break bread together. They are one huge family.

Daniel walks in, just behind Zvia. A short boy next to him is gesticulating wildly trying to convey something, but Daniel has no clue. Still, he has a grin on his face and his hair seems a shade lighter from the sun. I make a mental note: he is not wearing the *kova tembel*. I wave to him, but he doesn't notice me and sits with his group. I feel left out.

People approach the long buffet tables at the back of the dining hall to load the trays with today's lunch offerings. Cautiously, I approach the tables too. There are many dishes I don't recognize, though I see that few of them are meat. "Meat is expensive and not so good for you," Chava indicates as if reading my mind. She stands right behind me in line to guide me on this adventure. There are bowls overflowing with what I now recognize as olives. They look green and unripe, but I already know they are to be eaten green. I see many salads and a lot of dairy products produced on the kibbutz. The yogurt in deep metal bowls looks smooth and creamy, but I can't picture it as the day's main meal. At home we always had soup, meat and potatoes.

Balancing my tray awkwardly, I return to the table where Chava and Benjamin sit. And I thought only waitresses carried trays! I am a little put off by the bare tables as I think of the crisp white tablecloths Marysia used to put on our dinner table in Łódź. The din in the dining room reverberates in my ears. Maybe it's my own discomfort that amplifies all the sounds around me. I hear the serving spoons clanking against the metal bowls, the used trays being stacked with a thud and the glasses being filled with soda water from a hissing machine.

What disturbs me most is the *tsiburit*. It's an innocent looking, medium-sized metal bowl into which those seated at the long table casually spit out and toss in bones, pits and morsels of food they find distasteful. How disgusting! The image of peasants comes to mind, but I try to push it away. I can't imagine how Mama will stand this when she comes for a visit. She is elegant and fastidious; this *cheder ochel* will surely turn her stomach.

Unable to participate in the conversation around me, I smile an idiotic grin at my cousins across the table. They seem even more tanned than yesterday. I crane my neck searching for Daniel, but now he is nowhere to be seen. Chava notices and says, "Dani's group must be finished eating already. Kibbutzniks don't linger over lunch. Work awaits!"

"But he isn't working yet, is he?"

"Not yet, but I believe today they are showing him the *lul*. He'll probably work there."

"What does *lul* mean?" I ask, unable to see my little brother working anywhere, no matter what it means.

"It's the chicken house," she says breezily as if all eleven-year-olds know how to feed chickens and collect eggs.

"How many chickens are in it?" I ask.

"I don't know the exact number. Hundreds," she says.

An image of Daniel surrounded by hundreds of clucking hens and pushy roosters comes to mind. He runs and screams. The feathers fly. I hope I am wrong.

"I have to get back to work," Chava says. She is a *metapelet*, a caregiver in one of the children's houses. Her charges are toddlers, not chickens. She cares for them while their mothers work. The children remain in the children's houses even at night, looked after by women on childcare duty. Chava puts away the lunch trays quickly. For a large woman she sure can move fast! "My babies will miss me if I'm gone too long." She speaks of them with as much tenderness as if they were her own.

"Do their mothers ever get to see them?" I ask.

She laughs showing her perfect white teeth. "Of course, they will come as soon as they finish working for the day and, again, first thing in the morning. They also come to nurse the babies that still need mother's milk."

"How do the mothers know the babies need to nurse when they aren't with them?"

"We have a system for that. A buzzer goes off in their apartment if their baby can't be soothed by a *metapelet*."

"You have a system for everything!" I can't get over how things work here.

Then Chava adds, "And the parents of the older ones come to read them bedtime stories and tuck them in."

"So both children and parents get a good night's sleep," I say, beginning to realize the advantage of these unusual arrangements.

"You are getting it, Anat. Everything here is organized for mutual benefit and fairness," she says.

I leave the dining hall trying to think if there are other societies that work like a kibbutz, but all that comes to mind are ant colonies I studied in school.

We approach cousin Rami's workplace. I imagine him sitting at his desk in an office, like my father's in Łódź, but I start smelling a strong unfamiliar smell. It is pungent, but not terribly unpleasant. A long cowshed stretches before my eyes. Rows of huge cows stand patiently with some sort of a mechanism attached to what I imagine must be udders, though I have never seen a cow up close, and certainly not its private parts. Chava smiles at my puzzled expression, "Those are our electric milking machines." Milk and electric—the two words don't fit together in my head, but why worry, not much here does.

Rami greets us warmly on the path. His *kova tembel* sits askew on his head. Brown sandals show his toes. He is wearing jeans. I recognize them from the Polish journal about America. They wear jeans here too?

"You have come just at milking time. I can't really spend any time with you now. I must attend to my cows," Rami says, sounding like a grown man. I stare silently. So Jews can really be farmers? The idea still seems incomprehensible, but I have the living proof before my very eyes. "*Shalom*, Anat," he says. This I understand. I whisper *shalom* under my breath and turn away quickly so he won't see me blush.

6

I have spent the last few days getting to know the workings of a kibbutz. Now I am sitting in Chava's apartment writing letters to my friends in Poland. My small red address book is at my side, but I know the addresses by heart. The trouble is Ala and Ania were leaving Poland too. I don't know when. Who knows if my letters will even reach them? For all I know, they may be en route to France or Australia. Slawka's family was going to Israel. Maybe our paths will cross.

Chava's puttering in the galley kitchen on the balcony distracts me. She is making an after-school dessert for her children. I write my opening sentence over and over tossing the crumpled sheets into the wastebasket. I don't know where to begin. There is so much to say. Finally, I get inspired, "I have landed on the moon..." I write. The smell of cinnamon is intense. The pots clatter making me think of Marysia. I will write to her too, but Chava says, "Anat, I'm done here. Let's get your things and go."

I'll never finish these letters. "Go where?" I ask, trying not to sound annoyed.

"Ruthi told me your bed is ready in the seventh-grade children's house."

"Am I moving *now*?" I ask.

"Yes, aren't you excited?"

The sudden announcement has caught me by surprise. I knew it would happen, but I didn't know *when*. Now I don't know *how*. My hands feel moist and my stomach is queasy. I don't know these girls and boys and I have to live with them side by side, like a mute?

I begin stuffing my things in my tan leather suitcase. It's brimming with dresses, some beauties made by Mama, some by her favorite seamstress. The multicolored sweaters knitted by Marysia with berets to match are not likely to be needed in this heat. I squeeze the bulging bag, trying to get it to close. Chava comes in and watches my struggle. She chuckles. I am embarrassed and the hated blush spreads on my cheeks. "Ania, you won't be needing any of this. I already sent your whole new wardrobe of shirts and shorts, even a pair of sandals, to your new room. If I know my Ruthi she has probably put them in your cubbies by now."

"So, so... what do I do with these?"

"Leave the bag here for now. We'll figure it out later."

"But... my dresses..."

"You haven't seen any girls wearing dresses here. Have you?"

I can see it now, I will have to stuff my plump butt into shorts and my fat, white legs will stick out. How embarrassing!

On the way to my new home, Chava reminds me that Ruthi will be with me, that I have nothing to worry about. That calms me a little. I like her, but she doesn't really know me. If only I could make myself understood.

As we get closer to our destination someone calls out in the distance, "Anat, Anat," but I don't respond; I just keep on walking. Chava taps my shoulder and chuckles, "It's Golda, the house mother for your group; she's the one I introduced you to yesterday. Remember? You don't seem to own your new name yet." I am mortified.

Golda approaches with a smile and says, "*Shalom.*" She pats my head as if to say, it's okay you'll learn your name soon enough. And though I know she's trying to be friendly I am irritated at being treated like a child.

"Anat is moving in today," Chava volunteers.

"I know, I know," Golda says approvingly. "I have already sent clean linens for her bed."

We arrive at a low cement building. It looks freshly painted, but unlike most houses here on the kibbutz, it is devoid of fragrant bushes and flowerbeds. It looks more like an army barrack. Its severe exterior makes me think of the Łódź building we lived in, not because they are similar, but because they both make me feel nervous, as if I belong elsewhere.

Chava must have read my mind because she explains, "This building, and the other ones in this section, were part of a British military base before we kicked them out."

"Yes," I say, thinking that I really know nothing about Israel's history.

Ruthi is already at the open front door. She stands there like a sentinel, stunning in her calmness. Her mouth with its shapely lips has a determined look about it, her shiny black hair falls into perfect shape as she tilts her head back and laughs. "*Shalom, shalom!*" she greets us. Just behind her, a bunch of girls has gathered to see the newcomer. They hang back but crane their necks over one another to get a better look. I bet they can't wait to evaluate me. The boys that live here are nowhere to be seen. "May we come in?" Chava asks.

"Yes, yes, we have been waiting for Anat," Ruthi sweeps her hand and points down a long corridor. We enter and follow her.

Wide-open doors of the rooms we pass look neat and are sparsely furnished. Seven rooms and no clutter anywhere. But all those open doors! Forget privacy here! I sigh and wonder if these girls ever find a way to be alone with their thoughts. Several girls, all about my age, are milling about. All of them wear short shorts and thin, sleeveless cotton tops. Some have pert little breasts sticking up too obviously under the thin fabric of their blouses. Another wave of anxiety washes over me. They will laugh when they see I'm wearing the training bra my mother made. They've probably never seen such a contraption. And just for a moment I am glad to be covered by my heavy dress.

"Here we are," Ruthi stops at one of the doors near the end of the corridor. "This is my... this is our room, Anat." Chava translates and we go inside. I walk in cautiously as if I were expecting a strange beast to jump out from behind a piece of furniture, except there is practically no furniture here. The sun streaming through the wide curtainless windows lights the room brightly, but it is very austere, not at all my idea of home. It looks more like a place nuns would live, at least that's what I imagine from stories Marysia told me. A couple of metal cots, a small desk, some shelves for clothing, a few hooks on the wall. No pictures, no knick-knacks, nothing to clue me into the personalities of the girls who live here.

Ruthi spins around the room pointing to objects and saying their names. She takes my hand and I feel like a blind person. She leads me toward the shelves where my new kibbutz clothing is stored. "*Hine*," she points. Here is your stuff. She says something else I don't understand and Chava translates, "She wants to show you the shower room now."

"Shower room?" I ask.

"Yes, you know... where you wash."

"Is there no tub?"

Chava laughs. "A dozen girls wouldn't fit into one tub!"

"What? They shower together?"

"Of course!"

I am mortified. I will have to get naked in front of these girls? Will the boys try to poke their heads in?

We enter the communal shower room. It is just a cement floor stall. There isn't even a shower curtain. I learn quickly that the long-handled squeegee in the corner is used to push the water into the center drain. How different this place is from the home I left two weeks ago—or was it two centuries ago? My bed, covered with a fluffy down quilt and pillows in white, hand-embroidered linen, our mahogany table and chairs, the ornate chifforobe, the porcelain tile stove reaching the ceiling—they seem now to belong to another time, to a different family. I stand there with my mouth open. No words come out.

Now that I've been inducted, several girls approach us in the hallway. A few boys, too, appear out of nowhere. We are introduced: Navah, Chana, Chemda, Ziporah, Shoshana, Yoram, Nachum. One by one I repeat their unfamiliar, unpronounceable names. So many harsh "ch's" and "sh's", so unlike the soft, undulating Polish I am accustomed to.

These will be my classmates in the fall. Two of them have made me curious—Ziporah, with her flaming red curls and Nachum, the boy with the blue eyes. I wonder if we'll become friends.

7

Several weeks have passed since I moved into the group home and it doesn't feel quite as strange as it did at first. By now I know all my housemates and they don't look at me as if I had horns. And things are going really well with Ruthi. I think she could become the sister I never had. The patience she shows each and every day in schooling me in the kibbutz customs is remarkable for anyone, but even more so, a girl my own age. She never snickers at my braids, or the way I grope for words. When I thought one of our classmates made an insulting remark about me the other day, I saw Ruthi's dark eyes darken a shade and a string of words shot out of her mouth like bullets. That girl was never unpleasant to me afterwards.

Ruthi is my confidante and protector, but she is not my only friend. I have already begun forming friendships with a couple of other girls in my class. Chemda, with a big black bun on top of her head, olive skin, long eyelashes and darkish fuzz on her upper lip, and Chana, whose perpetually squinty eyes make her seem older though she isn't. I know it is rude to stare at imperfections on people's faces, but sometimes I can't take my eyes off the brown growth on the side of her eyebrow as large as a pea. She told me she wants to become a nurse and I thought that would be a very fitting profession for someone so quiet and gentle and a bit homely. Embarrassed by such unworthy thoughts I keep them locked in a place where all my shameful thoughts are stored. Navah is the most interesting girl. Her eyes are deep dark lakes and her oval face always looks thoughtful, as if she were considering important decisions. But there is one other special pal—Nachum.

I count him among the people I can really talk to. What a surprise it was when he approached me in the dining hall a few days after I moved in, looked directly into my eyes and said, "I am glad you came." I don't think anyone had actually said that. I looked up into his face—he towers over me—and again saw those piercing blue eyes on a plain broad face. Somehow, I couldn't say why, I didn't think a big guy with a crew cut would have any interest in talking to someone like me. But it was exactly that crew cut that made him stand out. Other Gvat boys have untamed hair, long or curly. Nachum looks like a military recruit, though his persona is anything but! He is soft spoken and his dimples look so incongruous with his brawny physique. Hardly anyone would imagine just looking at him that he is shy, but he is not like that with me.

Yesterday he stopped me on my way to my room and called out, "Anat, do you have any time?'

"When?" I called back.

"Now," he yelled across the lawn.

I am free till dinner, I thought. "OK!" I called out and he came bounding over the grassy divide with a big smile on his face.

"Let's take a walk," he said. "I'll show you the back part of Gvat you might not have seen yet."

And we walked in awkward silence for a while until we came to a grassy expanse, way beyond the cowsheds. "Look over there," Nachum instructed and pointed toward the distant Galilee hills.

"What are you trying to show me in the mountains?" I asked.

"No, not that far. Look at the runways."

"What runways? Those grassy strips?"

"Yes. Watch and you'll see planes taking off," he said, as if he were divulging a secret.

"What planes?"

He laughed and just then I heard an airplane whizzing overhead. He told me it was a military airstrip.

"From the British times?" I asked.

"Exactly, but now it's ours," he said with obvious pride.

Other than the occasional fly-by we were alone except for the bees buzzing.

It was quite late in the afternoon and soon the mosquitoes began their dinner hour but we were too engrossed in our conversation to keep swatting them. We sat on two large boulders facing one another.

"Have you ever felt like a stranger in your own family, Anat?"

"Well, not in my family, but I did feel that way in the city where we lived in Poland," I confided.

"My father and brothers can't stand me," he said, his voice thick with emotion.

I had no idea how to respond.

"Maybe they don't hate you. Maybe something else is bugging them," I said, but immediately felt it wasn't helpful.

"No, I know it's me. They don't like how I look, how I comb my hair, how I like flowers."

"Flowers?"

"Yes, I planted a garden in front of my parents' apartment and my father just curled his lip like a snarling dog."

"What about your mom? Did she like it?"

"I think so, but she seems to be afraid of my dad."

We sat quietly for a while. I thought it was strange because from the outside it looked like everyone in the kibbutz got along with everyone else. Then Nachum looked at me intently and said, "My father thinks I'm not a real man like my older brothers."

I felt so bad for poor Nachum but didn't know what else to say, so I began telling him my story of the Greek sailor on the ship to get his mind off his problem. Anyway, I wanted to tell someone. I stopped speaking when several planes flew over us in quick succession, but Nachum said, "Don't stop the story now, I want to know what happened."

"You really find it interesting?" I asked.

He leaned forward and said, "Anat, you are like Scheherazade spinning the story of your voyage." I blushed because of what he said and because I thought he might kiss me. I stood up and began scratching the mosquito bites on my legs. He laughed, lighter now, and said, "You'll get used to them. See, they haven't bitten me."

Nachum is a good listener and I appreciate the way he waits while I grope for the right Hebrew word, and how he tries to figure out what I'm trying to say and helps me. I feel my secrets are safe with him and now that he told me these personal things, I can tell him almost anything, even the things I might not reveal to Ruthi.

When it began to turn dark I said, "We better head to the *cheder ochel*, or Ruthi and my group will send out a search party for me."

He stood up stretching and looking like a kind giant, then said, "From now on these rocks will be our private talking spot."

It was getting dark. I returned to my shared room, sat on my bed, and picked up Thomas Mann's *Magic Mountain*, the book in Polish I'd been trying to finish. The sanatorium reminded me of my time in Otwock, but its frail and nervous inhabitants were nothing like the wiry robust young men in Gvat. My eyes were closing. I put the book aside and wondered when I'd be fluent enough to read a Hebrew novel. It excited me to think that was a possibility.

———

Kibbutzniks are tough, at least on the exterior. This is why they are called sabras—all thorns on the outside with a sweet interior. I have already glimpsed their soft core, first with Nachum, and just last week when Chana and I were on our way to the laundry. She said, "Just give me a minute, Anat, I want to stop here for a moment."

"Why here? It's the old folks home."

"Do you know Shifra?"

"No," I said, but wondered if she was talking about the shriveled small woman whom I've noticed sitting on the bench in front of this building.

"Is she your grandmother?"

"No, but she has no children of her own. I'll just drop off this piece of apple strudel. It reminds her of her home in Hungary. I think she only smiles when I come to visit."

I waited for Chana in a spot overlooking the valley. Before me, an emerald panorama of lush plantings in variegated shades, occasionally alternating with gentle tans of wheat fields. In the distance a flock of sheep—cream-colored puffs that looked like clouds fallen to earth. With most workers enjoying their afternoon siesta the place had the soothing quietude of a library. If I were ever to leave Gvat, which I don't plan on doing, I think I'd miss it more than any other place on earth.

8

In Gvat school is out. June temperatures soar into the mid-thirties on the Celsius scale (nineties in F°), about fifteen to twenty degrees hotter than June in Poland. My body is struggling to adapt. On some mornings I can barely breathe; I sit on my cot mopping my brow. Then Ruthi suggests, "Let's take a cold shower." And we race down the hall to the shower room letting the cool water run across our bare backs, buttocks, and legs. We giggle and barely soap up. Then we come out with our hair dripping all over the hallway floor, refreshed and ready to face the day.

By now all the kids have been assigned jobs. Now that I'm a regular Gvat resident, I, too, get my work assignment from Golda, the tall business-like woman who is in charge of our house.

"Anat, your job will be picking grapes in our vineyards," she says, handing me a sheet with some instructions.

"Vineyards? Where are they?" I remember passing them with Benjamin on our first day, but by now I have no idea how you might get there.

"Oh, don't worry, your cousin will show you," she says.

At breakfast we run into Chava. "How is my favorite niece?"

she asks brightly. "Are you happy in the group house?"

"It's nice," I say, unsure exactly how to respond. "I have my work assignment." I hand Chava the sheet.

She looks at it and raises her eyebrows in surprise, "How did you manage to snag one of the most coveted jobs in Gvat?"

I shrug my shoulders and look toward a new group of young men, close to my age, who have just come in from the fields, *kova tembels* on, rolled up sleeves and bits of hay clinging to their trousers. As they pick up their breakfast trays I can't help but stare at their beefy biceps. They look ravenous and seem to be jesting with one another. I can't believe I'll be joining their ranks.

I don't relish waking up before dawn, but Ruthi and I dress quickly so that we won't miss the pickup truck that takes us to the work site. It takes no time to slip on the sleeveless top and shorts. I don't even bother to braid my hair. I just make a ponytail, buckle my sandals— what freedom my toes have now—and I'm ready to go.

We need to start work very early in the morning so that we can complete our job before the brutal mid-day heat. The sun is just coming up as we arrive in the vineyard. The sunrise mesmerizes me. I am witnessing it for the first time in my life. A blazing otherworldly pinkish light comes up from behind the hills illuminating wispy clouds. The coolness of night recedes quickly as golden rays, emanating as if from a crown, melt the darkness around us. I stand there silently for a moment absorbing the beauty of it. I have never seen such a stunning sight.

"Are you okay, Anat?" Ruthi asks.

"*Ken, ken, hakol b'seder,*" I tell her in my elementary Hebrew. Everything is fine, very fine.

The vines are taller than I imagined and covered with cool dew. We move in an orderly fashion down each row, along with others assigned to this job, cut luscious clusters of celadon colored grapes, and place them gently in enormous wicker baskets. We must be careful not to bruise them. They will be put up for sale in the markets of Haifa or Tel Aviv. I look around and notice other workers popping grapes into their mouths.

Ruthi looks at my face and must know what I am thinking because she says, "It's okay, you can taste some too."

"Really?"

"Sure, go ahead," she winks at me.

I feel like a goddess having her first taste of the sweet, fragrant nectar. I love how they pop open in my mouth, exploding with juice at the barest touch of my teeth, their oval shape similar to olives, but so wildly different in taste. Is that how grapes tasted to Cleopatra? I doubt I'll want breakfast when we take a break. This is all I ever want to eat.

Some vines are quite tall, so shorter workers, like me, must step up on a ladder to reach all the ripe grapes. By the end of our assigned vineyard section I am very tired, but in an unfamiliar, good way. My calf muscles twitch from the strain of repeatedly climbing the ladder; my arms are so tired I can hardly lift them. I must be developing new muscles.

At night I lie in my cot thinking of what my fate will be some months from now. School here on Gvat or in Tel Aviv? I listen to the sounds outside: frogs and a strange distant chattering laughter. For all I know, it might be a striped hyena. The sound doesn't scare me. I feel content and productive. I could sleep for three days straight if I were not to wake again before dawn. I don't mind working for my keep. Oh, those vineyards, I could work in them for the rest of my life!

I tell myself that I better fall asleep quickly, but the image of Cleopatra keeps me awake. The night is hot without the slightest breeze through the open window. I unbutton the top half of my nightgown and imagine her reclining on a silken couch while Marc Antony feeds her succulent grapes from a golden vase, his fingers gently brushing by her lips. I long to become her in my dream.

The kibbutz system is strange. Nothing like our isolated lives in Poland. But there is one similarity. Here you must do what you are told, except the rules are made by people you chose to live with, and in Poland it was the government of people you were forced to elect.

There are some kinds of committees that meet regularly to map out the work that needs to be done and decide who can do it best. Work assignments are posted in the dining hall. Most people are matched to jobs according to their skills, but for the big jobs where important decisions are made, people get elected and must rotate every year or two. Everyone, it seems, has a chance to be the boss here. I still don't know so much about this system. All I know is that I am off the vineyard detail! Now someone else will gorge on grapes and marvel at the sunset.

My new job is on a potato picking detail. The best thing I can say about it is that I don't have to get up before dawn. You need daylight to see the potatoes as they are brought to the surface by a piece of oversized farm machinery. Our group works in a long row, following closely behind the machine and stooping to pick the potatoes with our bare hands out of the moist brown soil. It's a dirty, backbreaking job even for our young bodies.

The worst part of it is the myriad bugs that crawl out of the freshly turned soil. They crawl up my bare legs and bite mercilessly, making me itch and scratch raw. Sweat runs down from my forehead and stings my eyes; I can taste the salt as it reaches my lips. Dirty rivulets of sweat and mud run down my calves and shins too. The sun beats down on my head. Had I not finally succumbed to the *kova tembel*, I might have collapsed with sunstroke.

In the evening, exhausted and itchy, I dash off an angry letter to my parents in Tel Aviv.

"How could you have left me here to be subjected to labor such

129

as the Egyptians had us do? If you could only see my poor sunburned and scratched up body, you'd immediately take me out of this hell."

Luckily, my ordeal in the potato fields doesn't last very long, though while it does, it seems that each day is made up of three Mondays stuck back to back. To my great joy, after two weeks of misery I am transferred back to the grape picking detail. Yay!

But Daniel, my poor brother, has been stuck all these weeks in the *lul*, the chicken house, just as Chava predicted. His first day there he was overwhelmed by the stink. "I thought I'd choke to death," Daniel told me on one of those the rare occasions we saw one another. The separation of the groups by age makes it difficult for us to find time together. The only way we can speak these days is whenever we stop by at Chava's in the evenings for snacks. But even there we don't want to chat in Polish too much as not to offend our cousins. We sit on the terrace and exchange the crucial events of the day.

"Ania, you would not believe the racket a million chickens can make."

"It's not a million."

"And they can peck you to death if you aren't careful."

"How do you know what to do?"

"Menucha, the fat gray-haired lady we met the first day, showed me how to collect the eggs and still come out alive by the end of the shift."

Chava is preparing a plate of cookies and I know she overhears us because a loud chuckle comes from the living room, then the door pops open and all four of our cousins pile onto the terrace.

Tonight we are doing something special with our entire class and some others from the area. Ruthi tells me this as we sit on our cots after work. She calls it GADNA and tries to explain, but it doesn't make too much sense because it seems to be connected with the military. The military?

It's some sort of a group game, at least that's what I gather from Ruthi's explanation. A torrent of words tumbles from her mouth and strains my limited vocabulary. I ask her questions trying to understand better and finally she says, "Never mind. You will see for yourself soon enough." Then she hands me a pair of ugly brown boots and a green knapsack. "Put these boots on and bring the knapsack when you come to the bus."

"But I haven't tried them on to see if they fit."

"They should be fine, I know your size," she says and runs out with a wave of her hand. "I have to get some other supplies," she yells as she's practically outside.

In the late afternoon, several of our kibbutz classes pile into the bus waiting for us at the main gate. Were I not made to wear these heavy army-like boots with thick socks and carry this heavy canvas knapsack, I might think this would be fun, but the shoes bother my toes already.

At dusk we arrive in an area that looks strangely like the desert, sand dunes everywhere I look, nothing else. The teachers divide us into two groups—two warring armies. The leader of our group gives instructions as dark falls. He is a tall, gray-haired man in a military uniform and his words come out harsh and loud. But he speaks rapidly and I don't understand most of what he says. Luckily, Ruthi ended up in my group so I decide to follow whatever she does. The sock bunched in my boot is really bothering me, but we move on and there's no time to adjust it.

First, we walk in silence, single file, for eternity. I am perspiring and wishing to fix my sock, but everyone is moving forward at a quick pace so I can't stop. I try to say something to Ruthi but she shushes me. Now a steep hill looms in front of us and we begin the climb. I feel huge blisters developing on both my feet and the knapsack is getting heavier with each step.

The air is cold now but my face and neck are covered in sweat.

My body is like a magnet for all the mosquitoes in the area. I itch wildly and try not to lose sight of Ruthi, but she moves ahead faster. I can barely keep up with her and am terrified I'll be lost in the inhospitable blackness that surrounds us. This is surely worse than working in the potato fields! I think this ordeal will never end until I hear gun battle sounds up ahead. God! I hope these are simulated, not real sounds.

What is going on? I have no idea. Soon we arrive back where we started, or at least that's what I guess because it is too dark to see. I'm so tired I don't even feel my feet. Ruthi helps me pitch our tent next to others and I crawl into the clammy sleeping bag without speaking with her.

"*Layla Tov*," she says and lets out a little chuckle. I don't have the energy to reply good night or even to ask where I can find band-aids for my throbbing blisters. My last thought as I close my eyes: if this is what the military is like, I am not going. Let them arrest me for all I care! Then we both fall into comatose sleep.

No matter how hot the week has been, or how hard the work, I look forward with excitement to Friday evenings. Daniel does too. Though my ability to communicate grows better each day, I am still hard pressed to understand all of the lyrics of the songs we sing each Friday night around the campfire, or *kumzits*, but it doesn't matter. Each Friday, Ruthi and I and our housemates rush to our rooms after supper to shower and primp. Getting ready for the *kumzits* is a sacred ritual here.

"Do you like the way I've done my hair?" Ruthi asks.

"Yes, it's nice," I tell her, wondering what I should do with mine.

"What about my top? Should I wear the embroidered one, or the striped?" I consult her. Ruthi points to the white-on-white embroidered one and nods approvingly. I put it on and strain to see my reflection in the window, but it's not like a mirror. I can't make out any details, but I do notice that my shape is becoming more streamlined and that there is less baby fat on my arms. "See you later," I say to Ruthi and run back to the shower room to fix my hair. I make a very straight part and comb it to the side, letting my long sun-bleached hair brush just past my forehead. Now, that's different! I'll try it out.

Young people, my classmates and those of all grades, stream toward the giant bonfire. We all wear our freshly laundered, starched shirts, crisp and looking nothing like our dusty, sweaty workaday selves. Just by looking at us, anyone can tell that Fridays at the kibbutz are special.

As dusk turns to darkness sparks rise from the bonfire like so many brilliant stars. We sit cross-legged on the ground close to our friends, smelling of nothing but soap, our hair still damp from the showers, our faces bathed in a pinkish glow. We encircle the fire and sway to melodies sung loud and clear, songs of new love, of sweet-smelling roses, of a lonely soldier in the hills of Dimona. Our voices rise into the velvet sky and fill the air around us with longing. The camaraderie is palpable. In this circle everyone belongs, everyone is welcome, even Daniel and me, creatures of Europe, unfamiliar with the warm cocoon of belonging.

Aside from the magical atmosphere, and the fragrant night air suffused with the spicy sweet scent of myrtle, I am now aware of girls and boys exchanging glances. Maybe it's the cover of darkness, or the languid mood, but it seems less embarrassing to cast your eyes at a boy whose attention you want. I, too, steal glances across the circle at Dani, a tall young man with curly brown hair and a fetching smile, but I don't think he's even noticed me. "Will he be in our class in the fall?" I ask Ruthi when we return to our room.

"No," she says. "He is two years above us."

Embarrassed to have revealed my interest, I feel my cheeks get hot.

During the week I look for him wherever I spot groups of kibbutz boys, hoping against hope to catch his eye.

Whenever I think of Dani my stomach flutters. It makes me feel odd and awkward in my own skin. I didn't pay much attention to the opposite sex in Łódź, with the exception of my math teacher, Mr. Artykiewicz. He was tall and blond and very handsome. But Dani is different. His rippling muscles, bronze skin and an air of assurance are not something I've observed before. Come to think of it I didn't know any Jewish boys in Poland. The few Jewish men I knew, my friends' fathers, were all short, pale-faced and carried the weight of the world on their shoulders.

Three and a half months have flown so quickly in a blur of new faces and new words. The end of summer is approaching and I am getting excited about the prospect of attending school in Gvat. By now I know all the girls that will be in my class and there is one special boy that will be there as well. The teacher will be a lovely woman, Miriam, whose bright eyes, and easy smile tell me I will like her. I have now been out of school almost sixteen weeks—it feels like forever! I realize that I have actually missed going to class and learning new things. I am definitely not one of those students who hate school.

Today I overheard something worrisome when we came over to Chava's apartment. She and Benjamin were whispering that my parents might be moving us to the city. I hope these are just speculations because Gvat is beginning to feel more comfortable.

Though I prayed to be rescued from here, especially while I worked on the potato fields, I'd be heartbroken if I really had to leave. As I think about my life in Gvat all these months, the city people-farm people dichotomy suddenly begins to lose its previously defined borders. I have come to love Gvat's endless farms with their rows upon rows of neatly turned over soil sheltering tiny green leaves, the vineyards with their promise of sweet nectar, the aromatic citrus groves and even the gentle, black eyes of the cows. I can almost see myself as a farmer one day. I can even see Tinek wearing that label, but Mama—never.

My Hebrew, now almost fluent, has enabled me to make many new friends. Ruthi with her bubbly laugh and warm acceptance of my odd European ways is slowly replacing my Łódź friends in my heart. I wake up with my classmates; we shower together, try out new hairstyles and talk about the boys down the hall. I have even learned how to walk around barefoot! The pebbles are nothing to my once delicate feet. Now my soles are hard and rough as shoe leather.

Each Thursday I begin thinking of the next day's *kumzits* and I no longer ignore calls for "Anat." And there's one more thing that makes me feel good. I am getting used to eating salad for breakfast, though I would still avoid the olives if it weren't for the teasing of my friends. "Go ahead, taste another one," they say as they laugh and dare me to be more like them. These olives do seem to get a bit less bitter each day. I taste one, or two, just to prove my potential for becoming a *sabra*. Not quite, but almost.

All my wishing to remain in Gvat was for naught. This afternoon Chava handed me a letter from my parents saying they will be coming next week to take us with them to the city. I can't believe it! Chava sees my distress and says, "Don't worry, it may not be final. You can come back anytime. We like having you with us." Then she offers me some cookies to make me feel better. But cookies will not cure me right now. I must find Ruthi and speak to her and the other girls in my house. After we scheme about how I can persuade my parents to leave me in Gvat, the word of my imminent departure spreads like wildfire.

9

Mama and Tinek have come to collect Daniel and me this morning. We are moving to Tel Aviv. I've missed my parents and am happy to see them but I do not want to leave Gvat. I belong here! We hug and kiss in Chava's apartment but I feel awkward with my cousins looking on. They never seem to kiss or hug. They keep their feelings deep inside. After we're done with the greetings I ask, "Tinek, have you found a job yet?"

"No, not yet, but don't worry. I have friends helping me. It will happen soon."

"Mama, what about you?"

"I am setting up my corset workshop."

Chava asks Mama, "Where did you find an apartment?"

"Oh, it's a nice sublet on Arba Aratzot Street."

"Fancy, very fancy!" Chava looks at my puzzled expression and explains, "It's a fashionable, new section of Tel Aviv."

"What's a sublet?"

"The apartment belongs to a professor who is moving to Europe for a while, and we can live there," Mama explains.

"With all his stuff?" I roll my eyes. I have never heard of such a thing.

"Yes, why not?" Tinek says.

"But for how long?" I am very alarmed.

"Two years," my parents say in unison.

"What then?"

"We'll see," Mama says. There's that answer again.

I'll be unsure of what will become of us for two whole years. Tears well in my eyes and I dive into the bathroom. I don't want Ruthi to see me like this. When I emerge from the bathroom Benjamin is explaining something about the name of our street. "*Arba Aratzot*, The Council of Four Lands," he says, "comes from the sixteenth century council of Polish Jews from four regions who met to govern Jewish affairs."

I want to say, who cares? I'm so upset I could scream. Then it occurs to me: Poland's history is determined to follow me wherever I go.

"Let's sit out on the balcony for a while," Benjamin suggests. "It's stuffy inside."

Chava brings out a tray of glasses with cold lemonade. The adults chat for a long while outside, savoring their visit. Daniel and I walk in and out, pacing nervously, waiting for our cousins to show up. I walk out to the balcony to see if Ruthi is on her way, because the Tel Aviv bus will be here soon. Tinek looks at his watch and says, "It's late," in Yiddish, his preferred language.

"Nachman, Yiddish is the language of the Diaspora, now you must speak Hebrew—the language of our nation," Chava says in a tone that sounds high and mighty. I've never heard her speak like that! She underscores *our*, with pride. Her comment is so at odds with her warm personality. What's got into her?

Something in me boils seeing my father's mother tongue dismissed like a bunch of gibberish. Tinek doesn't respond, but his expression tells me he feels exactly as I do.

"*Coiciu*, Auntie, what about our relatives who lived in Poland... until they were killed?"

"What about them? I don't know what you mean."

"They spoke Yiddish. To which nation did *they* belong?" I feel like saying they sang and said 'I love you,' in Yiddish too, but I don't want to sound more impertinent, so I keep silent and look down at my dusty toes.

"Ania, don't be rude," Mama jumps in.

"We can't afford to cling to the old ways," Chava responds after pausing for a long moment, as if she forgot something important, but can't remember it now. She looks guilty as she looks at my father, but I can't tell if that's just how it looks to me because I *want* her to feel guilty. It is very clear that if we *all* don't speak Hebrew we won't belong here either.

Benjamin is the first one to diffuse the tension. Good old Benjamin! "Look at that motley crew," he points to our cousins and friends on the path below the balcony. "It's your goodbye committee."

Mama and Chava go into the apartment and speak silently with one another. A short bit later we pick up our bags and the whole Gvat contingent, my cousins, the girls from my house, Nachum and two of Daniel's best friends, walk us to the bus stop near Gvat's main entrance. Across the road from the stop Gvat's orchards make me sadder than I've ever felt before. Ruthi says, "You will write to me, Anat."

"I will," I mumble.

She smiles, "Now, you have no excuses. You already know how to write in..."

The EGED bus pulls over and cuts her off in mid-sentence. I clamber on board without one iota of enthusiasm and plop into the seat as the bus pulls away. I see them all waving, but Nachum waves the longest until he is just a dot in the distance.

It will be a two-hour bus trip if all goes well; not enough time to swallow the bitter tears still at the back of my throat. It seems hardly possible that the strangers whose guttural utterances I thought I would never comprehend when I first arrived have become my dearest friends. Thinking of how much I will miss even Chana and Chemda underscores to me the depth of my grief over this sudden, unwelcome departure. At least I've packed my *kova tembel* in my tan suitcase. The thought makes me smile—my new favorite fashion item.

The crowded bus rolls toward Tel Aviv. Many young soldiers sit among the passengers, others stand in the aisles, bobbing and weaving as the bus hits potholes. They don't look so much older than I am. Their green uniforms are handsome, but the sight of rifles slung over their shoulders both scares and impresses me. I never knew Jews could be soldiers defending their own country. I knew my father had served in the military before the Second World War, but he was a rare exception: most Jews did everything possible to avoid the Polish military.

Daniel and I are seated in front of my parents. I ask Daniel in Hebrew, so our parents won't understand, "Do you think we'll have to move again in two years?"

"I don't care," he says. "I want to see Tel Aviv." He doesn't seem to be as heartbroken as I am to be leaving Gvat. "Do you know the Hebrew word for sublet?" he asks me.

"Stupid, how should I know?" I am too unhappy right now to be civil.

Tinek taps on my shoulder, leans forward toward my head, and says, "Ania, we have already enrolled you in *Ironi Aleph*—#1 City School in Tel Aviv."

I am not sure how to react. No one consulted me.

Then Mama adds, "It's a very good school, one of the best."

"Okay," I say. Since I like school, this is the first positive thing I've heard today.

Tinek taps my shoulder again and whispers loudly enough for me to hear, "Now, don't be surprised, but in addition to regular subjects, you will study the Torah and the Talmud."

I crane my neck back toward him and give him my wide-eyed, raised eyebrow 'what are you talking about' look and say, "I don't know what these subjects are."

"They are a part of religious studies."

"What? But we are not religious."

"Don't worry, I'll explain."

Mama elbows him and whispers, "Not now, Nachman."

"Why should I be taking these subjects?"

"Later," he whispers.

I sit there confused. I thought my parents had rejected religion. They don't seem as disturbed as I'd expect them to be that I'll be studying religious books. What's going on?

The bus lurches forward and back on the bumpy road. Every now and then I hear my parents' voices rise above the din of other conversations in the bus. I detect notes of tension that transfer to me through the sticky air and give me a nasty headache, like a metal clamp around my temples. I close my eyes and press my forehead to the cool windowpane of the bus. I try to shut off my brain, but every fragment of my parents' conversation brings on new questions. "Dora, do you still want me to design advertising flyers for your new shop?"

"You know I do. No one can draw better than you. But you must make it clear how to get to our apartment." Our apartment? What could she mean by that? She can't mean the apartment where we are supposed to *live*.

"Please, Dora, let's not take too long thinking. I must spend every minute on the job search."

Oh, so he *is* worried about finding a job! The two facts hit me in the face. Mama's corset shop will be right in our apartment! That must be it. There will be clients coming and going! What about our privacy? Will there be fabric, ribbon, whalebone ribs, snaps, hooks and other components of my mother's craft strewn about in the living room like in her shop? Where will her clients come from, anyway? No one is aware of her talent here, and she doesn't even know how to say, "bra" in Hebrew. And Tinek hasn't found a job the whole time we have been in Gvat. This explains why they seem so tense. Now I am anxious too.

I'm glad Daniel has fallen asleep. He shouldn't listen to all this. His head is bouncing like a ball and onto my shoulder, but I let it stay there.

Several hours on the bus with all this unwelcome information rattling around in my brain makes my temples pound. I feel exhausted. The temporary nature of the sublet apartment, the unfamiliar subjects I will be forced to study, the idea that strangers will be wandering in and out of our home, none of these things make me glad to be in Tel Aviv. The bus pulls into the central bus station. We are here.

"Wake up, Daniel." I shake him.

He rubs his eyes, "Where are we?"

10

We take a bus from the central bus station to our new neighborhood. Several stops and we get off. "It's only a short walk from here," Tinek says. We make our way along wide, modern boulevards and my mood brightens. This city is so different from the dinginess of Łódź!

I have never seen so many new buildings clustered together and beckoning to passersby: come in and see our interiors; surely you will be impressed. The light-colored buildings are fresh and bright like children's new toys. If they were people you would say they were happy. The streets are broad and elegant as if they were expecting a festive procession at any moment.

"So how do you like it?" Tinek asks.

"I don't know yet. I am tired," I say.

"What's the name of this neighborhood?" Daniel wants to know.

"This is *Tzafon*. It's a new section in the north of the city. Here people buy the apartments."

I have never heard of such a thing as buying an apartment.

"How can you own walls, doors and windows? You can't take them with you when you move."

Tinek laughs and assures me that the professor does own the place we are subletting.

There isn't much to settling in at our sublet on Arba Aratzot Street. Though our brains are packed with questions, our luggage is light. We have brought only some clothes and a few bundles of essentials. Our packing crates haven't arrived yet from Poland. As soon as we enter the apartment Daniel and I wander cautiously through the rooms. They are filled with other people's furniture, knick-knacks, and photos. It is an odd feeling. I feel like an uninvited guest.

"Don't touch anything here," Tinek warns me as I pick up a framed photo of a woman on the beach. I wonder who she is. I put it down, but Tinek continues his lecture. "It's best not to touch things here, not to break things, this is not our home, you know." Well, of course I know. He is so on edge. This is not like him. How far we have fallen from our comfortable life in Poland. Now we have to live in other people's homes.

"Hey, Ania," Daniel calls out from somewhere.

"Where are you?"

"Come out here, see this huge balcony!"

I join him outside and admire the space and the fragrant pine trees overhanging it.

"We can have dinner outside, there's room enough for a table," Daniel is excited about this place.

"Are you sad we had to leave Gvat?" I ask him now that we are alone.

"A little, but I won't miss the *lul*, that's for sure."

We chat a while then go back inside to get a closer look at the rooms: living room, one bedroom—again he and I'll be roommates— a long dark kitchen at the back and a huge bathroom. It has a tub! But now I'm used to a shower.

At our first dinner in Tel Aviv I broach the subject that weighs on my mind. I am afraid to ask, but I just blurt it out. "Tinek, why can't you find a job? You have been looking for four months."

"Tell me about it." He sounds discouraged.

"You were such a big boss in Łódź. You have a lot of experience. Don't you?"

"Oh, Ania, here my management experience is useless. I don't speak the language."

"So why can't you speak Yiddish?"

"Yiddish? You heard what Chava said."

"Why do they hate Yiddish so much?"

"I suppose it reminds them of the old country and the way people insulted them in Poland, Hungary and other places, whenever they heard Yiddish spoken."

Now Mama weighs in, "Look, it's a new country, there are Jews here from all over, unless they speak one language it will never be unified."

"Ah, Dora, you'll always defend Israel," Tinek says, waving his hand.

Mama gets up from the table aggravated. "You know darn well I don't like the disdain for Yiddish either, but I understand it."

She picks up the plates and goes into the kitchen, but Daniel makes an interesting observation. "Dad, didn't we hear Nechemiah and his kids speaking Yiddish?"

"Yes, you are right," Tinek says.

"So, why don't they speak Hebrew? They were born here."

"Ach..." He hesitates and looks as if it's not something he'd care to discuss. "They are Hassidim, super religious Jews. They consider Hebrew the holy language, not to be sullied by everyday use. For them, Hebrew is reserved for prayers. Yiddish is their everyday language."

"Hmm..." Daniel knits his brow. "Well... maybe you can make

friends with some of them. Then you can speak all the Yiddish you want."

"Daniel, you don't understand. I could never be friends with these people. They are religious fanatics."

Mama comes into the living room. "Were you talking about my brother?"

"No, I don't really know him enough. He did seem different when he met you at the port."

"We'll visit him soon. You will like him," she says. "He is not like the rest of them."

"You know what, Nachman? Let's take the kids for a walk on Dizengoff Street. Let them get a sense of this city."

"Good idea, I need a walk," he says.

"Can we get ice cream?" Daniel asks.

"Sure, why not?" Tinek shrugs and we are off.

It's getting dark as we approach Dizengoff. Mama and I walk arm in arm. Tinek and Daniel trail behind us in animated conversation. The city's main artery leaves me speechless. I have never seen people sitting at little tables on the street sipping coffee from elegant demitasse cups. Right on the street! Crowds fill the sidewalks and spill onto the roadway as we pass Café Kassit. This one seems more popular than the others, but all are full of patrons eating, smoking, reading newspapers. Shoppers carry swollen bags, noisy bars emit sounds of loud music, neon signs blink, people mill around, laugh, and yell. "You have never seen street life." Mama notices my wide-eyed look. "This is exactly how Warsaw's streets looked before the war, full of people, full of life..."

"Look at all these people, they all look so different," I say.

"Different from what?" she asks, as we cross Jabotinski Street.

"I don't know... different from us."

She laughs. "They are all Jews from different parts of the world."

"All of them?" I can't quite believe it.

"Well, certainly most of them."

"What about the Arabs, are they here too?"

She chuckles, "Yes, some, but you couldn't tell them apart, they look just like us."

Tinek and Daniel soon catch up to us. We sit on a bench in front of a tiny ice cream shop. Mama dips into her purse and counts out the change. She asks what flavors we want and goes in to buy us the cones. I sit and stare at the procession of people walking by.

Jews of all skin shades pass in front of us: old Moroccan Jews with skin like raisins, Ethiopian women whose chocolate skin is smooth and silky and Russian Jews with wild red hair and freckled faces. Beautiful North African girl soldiers strut in their green uniforms, vendors toss garlic-laden falafel balls in the air. A Babel of languages assaults my ears. The immigrants are still speaking their own languages; Hebrew has not yet stuck to their tongues. I notice hair colors ranging from the blondest blond to auburn, to jet-black, straight, kinky, curly, and still can't get over what Mama said. "Tinek, are all these people really Jewish?" And he explains.

The 1950 Law of Return allows anyone in the world who claims to be Jewish to come into Israel and become a citizen. Many waves of immigrants have created this incredible tapestry. I had no idea that Libya, Iraq, Yemen, Egypt, Tunisia and even India were home to Jews. Reverberating with sounds, smells and sights of the Middle East and Africa, Israel is so alive! Nothing at all like the gray industrial city we left only five months ago. I feel as if landed on a different planet.

"Your ice cream is dripping on your blouse," Mama says.

Shaken from my hypnotic state I ask Dad, "Who was Jabotinski?"

"Who?" He looks at me blankly.

"Remember that street we passed on our way here?"

"Oh, that! Yes, he was a Jew from Odessa who fought for the establishment of Israel."

On our way back we pass many streets whose names catch my attention and Tinek uses them to give us a lesson on Israel's history from the ancient Jewish King Solomon to King George, the British monarch. I had no idea Tinek knew so much about Israel. Through the entire walk I watch the people, crane my head this way and that as if I were on another planet. I can't believe there are so many of them on the streets, even women pushing strollers at ten-thirty in the evening!

11

In less than a week Tinek has finished designing a small advertising poster for Mama's new business, "Deborah." It promises the finest undergarments in Tel Aviv, garments with a European flair. Together they plan to outfit a rented glass display case near our street corner. It will advertise the business and point customers to our apartment nearby.

"Let's put this porcelain figurine in the street display case," my father suggests. The figurine is one of my mother's treasures from Poland. It's a delicate naked woman, reclining languidly and showing off her perfect figure.

"Nachman, that is a brilliant idea! I will even sew a miniature brassiere for her little round breasts."

He laughs. "We'll depend on this porcelain lady to entice customers."

Their laughter and the elevated mood make me hopeful, but I still worry when night comes. What if clients can't find their way to our apartment? Will Mama earn enough money for us to live on until Tinek finds work? Will we have to go back to Poland in disgrace? I shift around my pillow, turn it over, but sleep doesn't come.

Suddenly I sit up startled: might Mama get the idea of teaching me how to sew bras and corsets the way she learned how from her mother who used to say, "You never know what will happen in life. Women need skills to survive. You can't always depend on a man." I don't like sewing, or any of the "domestic arts"; I'd rather work in the potato fields. I get out of bed and tiptoe to the window to pull down the shade. The bedside clock says it's two in the morning.

By a stroke of luck, Mother's first client is Moshe Dayan's wife. He is the most revered general in Israel having presided over the victory in the 1956 Sinai campaign against Egypt. Mrs. Dayan is a great customer who found her way to Mama's workshop because the figurine with a tiny lace bra worked its magic. Mrs. Dayan is the best advertisement Mama could ever have wished for. She heartily recommends my mother's corsets—works of art she calls them—to all her friends. Now Mama is in better spirits than she has ever been. Her business is beginning to take off. New clients arrive daily.

It is not just her business that makes Mama in good spirits, people who care about her surround her in a protective circle. Esther, Mama's older sister who arrived in Palestine in the 1920s, lives in Tel Aviv and they see each other often, talking over one another in excited loud voices and laughing so hard, tears come to their eyes. Mama's laughter is an unfamiliar sound and I relish it as if it were music.

There are also the brothers: older half-brother, Maxim, and Mama's youngest brother, Nechemia, the one with reddish beard who was the first to meet us in Haifa. There are several cousins and friends from Warsaw too, people who knew her when she was younger and carefree. Mama basks in the glow of family and friends. But the happier I am for Mama, the worse I feel for Tinek.

He has no family or friends here and the fruitless job search has made him irritable. "Not now," he says whenever I ask him questions. When Daniel makes a mistake practicing on his accordion, Tinek gets annoyed. He was never like this before. We always knew him as the family's eternal optimist, the one who could make us smile no matter what, who always had a whistle on his lips. Nothing ever seemed to upset him. Until we came to Israel very little could disrupt his calm. Sometimes Mama would become annoyed at his perennial easy-going demeanor and he laughed whenever she made dire predictions about the future.

God knows, Tinek is not averse to accepting even the most the menial jobs that require no language skill: stacking lumber, or groceries, or making deliveries, but time and again he is told he's too old. Israel is a young country that has no use for people over forty and Tinek is already forty-eight! Our family seems oddly unbalanced now: Mama, Daniel and I are adjusting to our lives in Israel, but Tinek is not.

This evening after dinner, I plan to ask him about what he said on the bus, about the religion classes. Maybe he'll be calmer at the end of the day, after Mama's tasty meal.

"Daniel, it's your turn to wash the dinner dishes," I say.

"You must be kidding," he says, full of bluster. "I did them just the other day."

I challenge him. He doesn't stand a chance. "What day?"

"Uh... yesterday," he says haltingly.

"No, yesterday we had dinner with Aunt Esther in her house." I'm triumphant, but he looks so crestfallen that I stack the plates, pick them up and carry them to the kitchen. "Here, I've helped you, the rest is a snap." Daniel walks out giving me dirty looks.

Now I can ask Tinek my questions. "So what did you mean about religion classes? School starts next week. I have to know."

"It's something normal here in Israel. All the schools teach the Torah basics," he says.

I am very unsettled. "But why? Are people required to be religious here?"

"Well... I have some problems with this myself, but—"

I interrupt him. "But what? What?"

"First of all," he says, "they are required and, second, there is a huge body of Jewish thought contained in these books. It is not such a bad idea for you to become familiar with them."

"Hmm..." This is something I'll have to think about, but I'm not satisfied. "So why do you have problem with the idea, Tinek? Why?"

"Religion should be an individual choice. It should not be required," he says.

"But will they force us to go to a... synagogue too?" I am alarmed. I've never even seen one.

He laughs, "Not yet! Don't worry, just read those books and follow your teachers' instructions."

"I always do that!"

"OK then. It's settled," he says and leaves the room. My mind is churning though. I think I'll have lots of questions after I start those classes.

Just after my fourteenth birthday classes begin at my new school. The building is large and modern and nothing like Gvat's small low-slung building that would have been my classroom. The atmosphere here is overwhelming. The hallways are abuzz with students rushing in all directions. I am used to a school as silent as a library.

It has been almost five months since I attended classes and I feel a little excited about cracking open books. I love their new smell, stiff spines, and clean unmarked pages. Tinek taught me how to make book covers out of newspapers so I can keep them nice and fresh. I am squeamish though about the religious subjects: Torah, the Jewish Bible and Mishnah, centuries old rabbinical interpretations of Jewish law.

"Tinek, I've got my class assignments," I run into the house the first day of school. "Look," I pull out my schedule and wave it. "Here is a Mishnah class!"

"Don't sound so panicked, Ania, I think you'll actually like it," he says calmly.

"What makes you think so, Dad?"

"The Mishnah is part of the Talmud. It's a compilation of laws passed on orally by many generations of Jews. It's interesting," he says.

"How do *you* know that?" Now he has piqued my curiosity.

"I wasn't born yesterday. I am Jew, after all." Seeing my confused stare, he says, "Think of it as an intellectual challenge, not religion."

So he doesn't mind me learning the Mishnah? There are so many things about my parents that puzzle me. I think I only know their exterior layers, the ones that are shed periodically, like snakeskins, but the inner core where mysteries reside is so much more unknowable.

"Tell Mama to take you shopping for your school supplies," he says. "I want to hear about Daniel's first school day and then listen to him practice the new music pieces," Tinek says.

I walk into Mama's workshop. She hasn't yet heard about my new classes. The buzz of her sewing machine in the small room off the entry hallway keeps her separate from what goes on in the rest of the house. She's buried in half-finished bras and corsets.

A few weeks of Mishnah study and I am hooked! I find it more absorbing than any of my other subjects. Contradictory legal opinions are quoted on each page and their authors, rabbis like Akiva, Gamaliel and others are really fascinating. It isn't that I always like, or agree with their statements, but it is a real wonder to me that centuries ago they debated issues that are still relevant. The very first day of Mishnah class we debated this question: when a man walks in a field and finds a purse with coins, does the purse belong to him, or to the owner of the field? At first it seemed a simple question, but it sure wasn't! I couldn't wait to tell my parents about it.

I ran into Mama's workshop after school all out of breath, "You'll never guess what we studied today."

Mama put aside the unfinished corset in her hand and pushed her chair away from the sewing machine. "I don't think I have ever seen you so excited, except maybe after you did your first science experiment."

"Mama, can you believe the rabbis discussed whether women were persons, or possessions?"

The smile disappeared from her face. "Some husbands still treat their wives as if they didn't know the answer," she said, all bristly.

"Ugh... that's awful," I said. "I'll never marry someone like that."

When she calmed down, we spoke about another of the Mishnah rabbi discussions: "How do you define wisdom?"

"That's a tough question," she said. "Different people would define it differently, I think."

"What about you, Mama? How would you define it?"

She bit her lip and looked at me very seriously. "I suppose it's an ability to form your own opinion after thinking about all the facts... and staying open to new ideas."

Of all the women I know, Mama is the wisest. She always says something that surprises me and gives me a new way of looking at the world.

Unlike Tinek who is very straightforward, Mama is a

complicated puzzle. I long to decipher her, to assemble the odd contoured pieces. Just the other day everyone in Israel celebrated *Rosh Hashanah*, the Jewish New Year. In Poland the only holiday we observed was the New Year, which always came on January first. Now I've discovered that Jews celebrate the New Year in September and that it begins with the blowing of the *shofar*, a ram's horn! And this is where the puzzle about Mama grew more complicated.

First, she got all excited that the holiday was coming and cooked special sweet foods like carrots with raisins and cinnamon and meat with prunes. That was good, but not so surprising because she has always been a great cook. But when the evening came and the resonant sound of the *shofar* announced the start of the holiday, she closed her eyes and seemed to be transported elsewhere. I tried to say something, but she shushed me and said reverently, "Listen!"

I did listen and thought the sound was otherworldly and ancient. It didn't sound like any instrument I'd ever heard. It was like a cry in the desert, made by a wounded animal.

When it was over, I looked at Mama. Her eyes were still closed and she had a kind of a melted smile on her face. "Mama, do you believe in God?" I couldn't wait any longer.

"You know I don't, why are you asking?" She wasn't in the mood to discuss it and called us to the table. But I really wanted to know why she was so moved by the sound of the *shofar*.

Pig-headedly I persisted. "Mama, are you a little bit religious?" If I can unearth even a single kernel of truth behind her serene exterior, I may figure her out.

"Nonsense. I am not."

"But why did you close your eyes and smile when you heard the *shofar*?"

"Religion is one thing, tradition, something else—it's remembering your roots, where you came from," she said.

We sat to our special holiday dinner, but my gears were still going. In Poland, Mama used to instruct Marysia, on how to make our Friday night meals and it wasn't until recently that I figured out these were Shabbat dinners. I doubt Mama would admit, even to herself, that some of the Jewish customs of her Orthodox home are so deeply ingrained in her, she can't shed them. They are in her blood. These traditions must help her remember the family she lost during the war. I never ask. I think any question on this topic is like picking at a scab.

12

I hate when my parents argue. They don't do it very often, but it always makes me feel awful. Only a couple of weeks after we discussed the Mishnah, religion caused a problem in our home. Last night Mama said, "Let's plan to visit Nechemiah in Bnei Berak on Friday."

"What's the matter with you?" Tinek snapped. "Don't you know that everything in this country comes to a dead stop on Friday afternoons? The religious want all of us to live by their rules. There won't be a bus for us to return home."

"But I would like the children to see how the Orthodox celebrate the Sabbath," she said.

"What for? Who needs this religious nonsense?"

I didn't like being grouped under *children* with Daniel, but I said, "Tinek, I think we should see it. You know, just so I can make more sense out of my Talmud classes."

He frowned and looked at me surprised, as if I were a traitor—I usually side with him—but then he brightened and said, "Okay, maybe I can find one of my old gulag acquaintances to drive us back, but just this one time. You know how I hate asking for favors.

We'll have to take an early bus to get there." Then everything calmed down. I could tell by the upturned corners of his mouth that Tinek liked that I helped shorten the argument. None of us like to make Mama angry. It doesn't happen often, but once she gets truly angry she can stay silent for days.

Over breakfast this morning, Tinek calls me, *Ania Sprawiedliwa*, Ania the Just.

"Why did you say that, Tinek?"

"You like learning about laws and I like how you help settle disputes around here. It's a special nickname. It fits you." His eyes sparkle and for the moment he is the old Tinek from Łódź.

"Do you really think so, Tinek?" I ask because Daniel is snickering.

"You might be a lawyer, or a judge one day, Ania," Tinek says. "You never know."

"I have always seen myself as a doctor, but the law intrigues me too," I say smugly and stick my tongue out at Daniel, who is making faces. Mama smiles, gets up from the table and asks Tinek to clean up the breakfast dishes. "Make sure the kids get out to school on time. I have to get ready for two fittings this morning," she says and walks out.

"Dad, is Bnei Berak more like Tel Aviv or Gvat?" Daniel asks.

"Well, I haven't been there, but I doubt that it's like either. For all I know, it might look like a Polish *shtetl* before the war," Tinek says shrugging his shoulders.

"But why, Tinek?" Daniel looks puzzled.

"Hassidim live their lives isolated from modernity as if it were still the eighteenth century."

Mama walks back into the room. "Are you on the subject of Hassidim again?" She is peeved.

"Why not? I want them to be prepared," Tinek says.

"I was raised in a Hassidic home, so I'm the expert here," she smiles. "Kids," she says, "your Uncle Nechemia *is* modern: he is a mailman."

What an odd job for a Hassid, I think. After our meeting at the port I imagined him home in a dimly lit room stooped over the Torah, bobbing up and down as he murmured the holy texts. The image of him with ear locks and beard, in a gray mailman's uniform and a bulging brown mailbag seems so incongruous. I've got to see it to believe it.

I feel as if as if we are going on an anthropological expedition to observe a mysterious tribe that has escaped notice by modern society.

Bnei Berak is as different from Gvat or Tel Aviv as... I can't even find the word to describe the enormous difference. I see it as soon as we step off the bus. Unlike Tel Aviv, with its wide boulevards, fashionable streets, new apartment blocks, traffic, and elegantly attired couples strolling its main avenues, Bnei Berak is a picture from a dusty history book. Tinek was right!

Many of the streets we pass as we walk from the bus station toward Nechemia's house are named after rabbis. Oh, here is one I recognize, Rabbi Akiva from the Mishnah! There's also a Jabotinski Street, just like the one in Tel Aviv. But that's where the similarity ends.

The city is small, but densely populated by people dressed as if they were on a movie set in a film about eighteenth century Poland. A kaleidoscope of balconies draped with multicolored laundry gives the buildings a shabbily festive appearance. In stark contrast, the men wear black satin coats and black felt hats with broad brims. The women dress very modestly: long skirts, long sleeves, thick stockings, headscarves, wigs, or hats on their head. I point it out to Mama and she says, "Exposing a small patch of skin here is practically a crime for a woman."

"Why?"

"I will tell you after we get back home."

All these people make me wonder if my grandparents, great-aunts, and uncles looked like them. The war swallowed them up and their photos as well, erasing them, so that now only my parents' descriptions of them remain. They are nothing but words, ephemeral as air. I will have to be satisfied meeting those few that survived.

Even young boys are part of this movie set; they wear skullcaps and ear locks that are supposed to be tucked neatly behind their ears, though they fly sideways, or dangle carefree over their ears. I try to picture Daniel with ear locks and the idea makes me laugh. Most boys here have *tzitzes*, showing from beneath their black outer garments. These fringed vests remind them of the *mitzvot*, the good deeds commanded in the Torah they need to perform daily. The strange thing is that despite their unusual appearance the boys behave as boys do everywhere. They run and shout, throw balls and chase each other into their courtyards with laughter.

As we near Uncle Nechemiah's block, Mama and Tinek get into another argument. "Nachman," Mama says, as she opens her bag and pulls out a hat, "Please put this on."

"What's this? I don't wear hats."

Ugh, not again, is all I can think of. It seems any talk about religion sets Tinek's teeth on edge.

"Nachman, I don't want to ask you again, please..." It's hard to tell if she's insisting or pleading.

"No, I won't," he says, shaking his head.

The argument continues until we reach the small lobby of Nechemiah's building.

The aroma of cooking smells permeates the lobby air and mixes with the tension we brought in, like an extra unwelcome guest. Mama asks again for Tinek to cover his head, the custom among religious Jews. "After all," she says, "we are in the seat of Hassidism, no less Orthodox than Jerusalem itself. Let's show some respect."

"I am always respectful to people. Have you ever seen me otherwise?"

"Nachman, be reasonable. I don't want you to offend Nechemiah," Mama is pleading now and pushing the hat toward him, but he keeps shaking his head and looks baffled.

"Haven't you ever seen a hat?" Mama's face gets red. She is thoroughly frustrated.

"Is the hat an admission ticket to my brother-in-law's house?"

I knew he'd refuse to put on any sort of head cover. Why didn't Mama know it?

"What's happening with you?" he asks. "This is so unlike you."

Now the conversation is getting too loud. I'm mortified. Daniel is peering out the entryway at the boys chasing one another and pays no attention to our little drama.

Unbeknown to us, Uncle Nechemiah awaits us at the open door of his first-floor apartment and overhears the whole argument. He comes down the stairs with a broad grin, puts his arm around my father's shoulder and says: "Come in, Nachman, come in. In my home you should be yourself, no need to pretend to be something you are not."

"*Vos macht a Yid?*" Tinek greets him in Yiddish and up they go together.

Mama smiles, and motions for Daniel and me to follow.

———————

Skinny, pale-faced Chayka, Nechemiah's wife, hugs Mama as we enter and she speaks to us in Yiddish that I don't understand very well. Our cousins stand behind her eyeing us. We must look like aliens. There isn't much small talk. A few minutes after our arrival Nechemiah invites us to sit down to dinner with a broad smile. By this hour, his mailman's uniform is already off and he's in his black coat, like the other men on the streets of Bnei Berak. He doesn't look modern, but it doesn't matter. I like his lively eyes that crinkle at the corners, just like Chava's. Now I see the family resemblance that is hard to notice on a bearded man's face.

I like him even though he never addresses me directly. I am a girl and therefore I must remain invisible to him. But Mama's affection for him rubs off on me and I cast furtive glances in his direction.

Chayka lights the candles and blesses them. Nechemiah chants prayers and the meal begins. Tinek looks as awkward in this setting as if he were about to be cooked by cannibals, but Mama is perfectly comfortable. She doesn't pray, of course, but she looks lovingly at her brother, admiring the only survivor of Auschwitz from her large family, the man who keeps the flames of tradition alive. Daniel and I are fidgeting at first, waiting for the prayers to pass, but then I get caught up in their sound.

As I listen to Nechemiah intoning the prayers so fervently, something unexpected happens to me. Tears come to my eyes and some deep cord within me is touched. I don't know why; I don't understand their meaning. What is going on? I feel stupid and slink off to the bathroom to dry my eyes and blow my nose. When I return, the meal has begun, but I am still thinking: how is it possible to have a fondness for the sound of prayers not knowing their content?

The meal is as modest as the sparsely furnished apartment. First Chayka serves the chicken soup. It is flavorful and the matzo balls light as air. The sweet smell of the freshly baked *challah* makes up for the meager portions. Next, Chayka carves the chicken carefully. There are nine of us and I wonder how she will manage. First, she puts the drumsticks on Tinek's and Nechemiah's plates. Then she cuts the breast into four pieces and gives them to the four females: Mama, me, cousin Atara, and herself. Daniel gets a thigh and her two boys get a wing each. "There, we still have a few pieces left if anyone is hungry," she says shyly, spreading the remaining pieces on the platter. There are plenty of assorted vegetables, a bowl of sour pickles and apple cake for dessert. The cousins cast amused glances in our direction as we eat. They have probably never seen males with bare heads like my father's, or Daniel's, or girls in short-sleeved blouses like mine. After the initial awkward moments, the younger of the two boys pipes up in Yiddish, "Why are we having such a fancy meal tonight? We don't eat like this on all nights." Chayka's cheeks turn red and she says, "Don't talk so much, finish up and go play."

After dinner Nechemiah prays again. Later, my parents talk with him over endless glasses of tea while Chayka disappears into the kitchen. If it weren't for the racket Nechemiah's children are making as they run around the apartment bumping into the rickety furniture and laughing with abandon, I would listen in on the adult conversation. As it is, in between the shouts, I overhear fragments of sentences about Auschwitz. They are speaking in Yiddish in low voices.

The evening ends early. We must rush to meet Edek who is picking us up on the edge of town. "I hope he doesn't get stoned for driving around here," Tinek says as we descend the stairs.

"Don't be ridiculous," Mama says. "He'll be fine."

"You know they do this kind of thing here," he says.

"Yes, yes, just like in some parts of Jerusalem," Mama concedes. "I know what you are thinking."

"Actually you don't. I was just thinking I like your brother. He is a decent man. I doubt there are many as broadminded as he in this community."

Mama doesn't answer. I think she's still sore he refused to wear the hat.

"Dad, I thought you had a problem with Hassidim," I say in the car on our way back.

"Well, I do, with some of them. Nechemiah is employed—not *schnorring*, living off handouts, under the pretext of studying the Torah, like most others."

Edek looks at us in his rearview mirror and joins the conversation. "These people know nothing of the arts and sciences.

162

They fear the world, they even fear pushing an elevator button on the Sabbath."

"And from what I heard," Tinek continues with a bitter edge in his voice, "they hide in the Torah to avoid military service. Most of them don't really care if the State of Israel exists or not, so long as it provides subsidies so they can pray all day and dream of a better world in the afterlife."

Mama chimes in, "Nachman, don't be such an antisemite."

"Don't be silly. I am every inch a Jew, but I can't stand people that don't pull their weight in society and who impose their beliefs on others."

If my parents can't agree, it's no wonder the secular and Orthodox Jews here are so much at odds! And what does that say about the conflicts between Ashkenazi Jews and those from the East?

The tall modern buildings on northern Tel Aviv begin to come into view. Thank goodness, we are almost home.

13

These days I spend almost every waking moment improving my Hebrew, reading, reviewing vocabulary and grammar rules. I want to do well on my midterms because my school is very competitive. And I need to go beyond just everyday vocabulary if I am to understand the nuances of the Mishnah.

With the Bnei Berak visit behind us, I am looking at my Mishnah study with even more enthusiasm, hoping that Jewish wisdom with its mystical power will seep into my pores and link me to my ancestors as I was never linked in Poland. I realize now that this connection had been missing during our lives in Łódź even though I was hardly aware of its absence.

The Hebrew language, so impossible when we first arrived, is now such a part of me that I wake up knowing I had dreamed in Hebrew. That must mean something! I'd never want to leave here, but trouble is brewing.

Last night I overheard Tinek saying, "Dora, if nothing happens with my job applications, I will have to take another tack."

"I will ask Maxim if there's anything he can do," she tries to cheer Father up.

"I don't even think God can help me," he laughs, but it's not like his usual laugh. It sounds strained. "It is taking much too long."

"I am expecting two new clients next week," Mama says. "I hear they intend to make sizable orders. It should cover the rent."

"But they are not my clients," he says. His voice sounds tired. Tinek has hinted before that if no job materializes soon, he might consider looking for work in America. I know the idea terrifies Mama. Me too. She obsesses about it as if it were a reality already. She has just rediscovered her sisters and brothers and can't bear the thought of leaving them. In Israel, Mama is free of harassment by tax inspectors. She is a mistress of her own fate. How ironic it would be if we had to move again to a new country. No, not ironic. It would be a disaster!

I wake up early to study when no one is around to disturb me, but Mama and Tinek are already in the kitchen in a heated discussion. They are talking about the subject that is forever on their lips: his employment, or the lack of it. I stand quietly in the hallway listening with my ears pricked up like a rabbit and can only see Mama's face in profile.

Suddenly Tinek drops a bomb. "Dora, would you be willing to move to the kibbutz? I know they don't accept everyone, but I'm sure Chava could help us get in as members."

I freeze and feel a rush of blood to my temples. The kibbutz! We may move back there? Dare I hope?

"What? Are you suggesting that I give up my shop and go into the fields to gather potatoes, or cotton? You can't be serious..." Mama's voice rises with each word.

"Well, I just think—"

She cuts him off. "Nachman, stop thinking such nonsense." Her voice gets louder and her words come out sharp like shards of glass. She looks at him as if he were mad.

"Chava is happy there," he says.

"I am not Chava!" she yells. "I couldn't live in such a small, closed society where everyone knows everyone else's business, where you break bread over a *tsiburit*. You may be cut out for it, Nachman, but I am not."

"Calm down," he says. "Your ulcer's going to act up."

Still fuming, Mama says, "Just remember, I am *never* moving to Gvat, or any other kibbutz."

I skulk into the kitchen. They look at me. Mama looks drained, and Tinek asks, "Did you hear us?"

Now Daniel shuffles in. Sleep still adheres to his face. His hair sticks up in all directions. He rubs his eyes and says, "What's going on?"

"Why not? Let them hear. This is not a secret," Mama says, her voice an octave lower. "I have an appointment with a customer soon, have to get her bra ready for a fitting." And she walks out leaving us to finish breakfast in silence.

For the rest of the day all I can think of is that argument. Every time I open my book it obscures what I'm supposed to be studying. In the bath, as I dress, on my way to school, over lunch, between my classes and on the way back I keep thinking about it. Now the threat of America is hanging over us and I can't get it out of my head.

Actually, Mama's response to the idea of settling on a kibbutz doesn't surprise me at all. I have always known my mother to be a fiercely independent and private person. Sometimes when they argue Mama insults Tinek in Yiddish, *"Bist a poe,"* you are a peasant. I am glad she didn't say it today. His standard reply is, *"Und di? Di bist the Engelishe koenigen?"* And you? Are you the English queen? Now he knows, the English queen will never live on a farm.

Tinek—well, he is at the opposite end of the spectrum. Raised as a socialist, he likes the collectivist policies of the kibbutz: one for all and all for one. No one earns a salary, everyone is equal and basic needs are equally provided for all. Every member is the boss *and* a worker. That sounds like a good life to my father, except for

America, of course. America—the capitalist opposite of the kibbutz —is his unattainable dream.

Daniel is practicing on his accordion on the balcony after school. I go outside to ask him what he thinks. "Would you have liked to live in Gvat permanently?"

"What? You just messed me up. Why are you interrupting me?"

"Pardon me! I was just curious what you thought. Never mind." I start walking out.

He calls, "Wait! Why do you want to know?"

"Because..."

"Are you nuts? I hate the *lul*. I love the city," he says, then punctuates his reply with a pull on the accordion bellows, letting out a long groan.

I am on my father's side. I have come to love the kibbutz after just a short time though I don't fully understand its workings: who gets the hardest work assignments, how vacations are calculated, who decides what. I am impressed by the freedom teenagers enjoy.

I try to look at our situation through my parents' eyes. But I always end up feeling I am betraying my mother. I can't shake off this split in my loyalties. Where to live? In the city, where Mama is an independent woman, but Tinek an unemployed assistant in her corset shop? Or, on the kibbutz where we all become farmers? This is not the kind of conflict I can adjudicate, even in my role as "Ania the Just."

I pick up my book bag and look for my worn copy of the Mishnah.

Gentle strains of Clementi's *Sonatina* waft in from Daniel's accordion and I listen with my eyes closed, the Mishnah unopened on my lap.

14

I have found an unlikely champion—Edek, the very same friend of my father's who picked us up in Bnei Berak. When they were imprisoned together in the Soviet gulag, my father did everything in his power to help fellow inmates. He was appointed by the Russians to be the squadron "supervisor", and in that role was able to save Edek's life. Now Edek wants to help any way he can.

Every time Edek asks my father if he can do anything for him, Tinek says, "I did what any decent human being would do. No one needs to thank me." But Edek knows Tinek isn't working, so unbeknownst to either me or my father, Edek has secretly arranged and paid for a private tutor for me. Not that I need or want one. I am doing quite well in my classes, but Edek is so amazed by my progress he thinks that with some extra help I can skip a grade.

To my great embarrassment it turns out he has hired the school's assistant principal to be my tutor. I am to come to his apartment every Thursday for lessons. The assistant principal, Mr. Amnon Shalit, is an impressive figure. He is tall and broad shouldered; his handsome, deeply tanned face covered by a hint of a five o'clock shadow. The girls at my school whisper that he is a decorated pilot from the recent Sinai war. His lean muscular physique and short haircut are the only hints of his recent military service, but one unruly curl already escapes down his forehead, giving a hint of his new civilian status.

As he walks through the hallways, girls cast knowing glances to one another and smile shyly. They all have a crush on him, but I don't even look in his direction. My experiences in Poland have left me wary of those in authority and he'll be my tutor! I am too nervous to contemplate the tutoring sessions that are to begin next week. My stomach is in knots. I bet he will now discover how I struggle with math. I wish Edek had stayed out of my business.

At last, the dreaded Thursday arrives. Mr. Shalit approaches me right after school. I want to sink into the earth, or to run, but his black eyes are smiling. He radiates a kind of movie star cool and charisma: Robert Mitchum chin, Omar Sharif eyes and complexion.

"Are you ready for your first lesson?" he asks in a friendly way that causes my knees to buckle. We step outside the school building where groups of students congregate and chat before heading home. Mr. Shalit points to the sidecar of his motorcycle. "Get in, Anat," he says.

Get in? I am totally flummoxed. Is he going to drive me to his house? My cheeks are flaming red by now. I climb into the motorcycle in a trance. I can't think or speak.

Some girls I know are staring in disbelief. Out of the corner of my eye I see them whispering and pointing. I have never sat on a motorcycle, or even imagined riding on one, much less in a sidecar. I am not sure what to do with my feet stuck in the pointy end, where to put my book bag and where to hold on. The motorcycle takes off after a few loud noises as Mr. Shalit guns the engine. He doesn't say anything, just smiles that broad grin of his and flashes pearly white teeth. That's just as well, I couldn't hear much over the roar of the machine and couldn't find words to respond anyway.

The wind musses my hair as the motorcycle gains speed. A ribbon, holding one of the braids together, slips off. It flies off like a crazed dragonfly. I pull the other one off, just to be even. Then my braids come completely undone and my long hair blows behind me, flapping furiously, like a flag in the wind.

Time seems to be just like putty. It can stretch and stretch, or you can squeeze it into a small ball. Unlike in Poland, for me, time here in Israel is compressed. Six months in this miraculous country have flown as if in a dream. If I just think about it too hard, I might wake up back in the bleakness of the Łódź winter. Here, I feel a part of something, though I couldn't yet say exactly what that is. The sessions with Amnon are helping me, and not only in school. I feel better about myself, more grown up. Despite the rapid flow of time, the days between our tutoring sessions seem exceptionally long.

Another Thursday has arrived and with it my lesson with Amnon. By now I have become more accustomed to the stares of my classmates as I board his motorcycle though not to the whispers that I hear in the hallways during recess. I overheard one girl saying to another, "Something strange is going on between the new girl with the braids, and Mr. Shalit. Maybe that's why her grades are so high."

The other one replied, "That can't be true, he is married and at least twenty years older."

They don't know the truth and they are wrong whatever they are thinking. It would be useless to explain it to them; I hardly understand it myself. In a strange way I take guilty pleasure in their jealousy. What else could it be? Amnon is a real man, nothing like their scrawny boyfriends. His gruff military exterior camouflages the patient and gentle teacher in Amnon.

I am now more comfortable asking him questions about study passages I don't fully understand, but his wife's furtive glances as she moves in and out of their kitchen to the living room, where we study, make me nervous. She is a slim, ravishing Yemenite with cascades of black curls. The elaborate long silver earrings that dangle from her ears accentuate her elegant neck; their tinkle announces her presence. "Would you like some lemonade?" she asks.

"Thank you," I reply.

What is she thinking, I wonder as she sets two frosty glasses on the table in front of my book pile. Does she have any inkling of how much I like the attention Amnon gives me, the flutter in the pit of my stomach when I climb into the sidecar of his motorcycle?

Today, as we leave the school building I realize that I have forgotten a book I need for the study session. I am very embarrassed by my sloppiness, but Amnon says, "Don't worry, Anat, your home is on the way. I don't mind stopping so you can pick it up."

His motorcycle pulls out of the schoolyard leaving a big cloud of dust in its wake. Amnon zigzags with panache through the crowded streets. All of a sudden, he stops and asks me to wait a moment. I see him enter a florist's shop. He comes out with a bouquet of flowers in his hand. I am puzzled. Why the flowers? Then an unpleasant thought, 'He must really care for his wife,' flits by my brain, but is instantly dissolved by his radiant smile.

As we approach my building on Arba Aratzot Street, Amnon says he'd like to come in to meet my mother. I nod in agreement, but the bewilderment on my face must be obvious. Amnon says, "I must meet the mother of my best student." I blush from head to toe and lead him to our door.

Mama is clearly surprised at the unexpected visit, but gets up from her sewing machine, smoothes out her apron and welcomes Amnon. He hands her the bouquet. "It's for your Friday night dinner table," he says, charming her like a magician. She looks pleased. I am dumbfounded. Why? But something deep inside is leaping somersaults in the air.

When Tinek comes home from another day trying to find a job I can see the discouragement in his eyes. Mother tells him about the flowers, but I can see that right now he has no patience for such trivial news. He only asks, "Ania, are you making any progress with your tutor?"

"Yes, I am," I say, unable to suppress a big grin.

15

Over dinner, Mama smiles and says, "Nachman, I have an encouraging piece of news."

He looks up, eyebrows raised, eager to hear.

"I heard from my new client, Mrs. Peres, she's Ruth Dayan's friend, about the possibility of a job in a lumberyard. Shimon Peres's father owns it."

"*The* Shimon Peres, Director General at the Israeli Defense Ministry?"

"Yes, she will make the introduction for you."

"Great!" he claps his hands and rubs them together. "When?" His attitude improves instantly. There is energy in his voice. "So, tell me about it," he says, though I know work in a lumberyard is not exactly his dream job.

The next morning, Tinek heads out optimistically to the Peres lumberyard, but learns soon enough that the job is temporary. Very temporary. It is open for only a month, six weeks, at best. The manager for whom he will substitute has gone to Bulgaria on an extended lumber-purchasing trip. It's not easy to find experienced administrators such as my father, willing to work for just several weeks, but Tinek takes the job. Even Mrs. Peres' recommendation can't get him steady work. So much for Mama's high-level connections.

Sadly, this isn't my father's last disappointment. Other job referrals turn out to be as elusive. It has now been almost a full year of daily searches and nothing of substance has come of it, only a temporary stint here and there. The situation grows more acute each day. The land of milk and honey is not providing him any comfort. Yet this is the one country he thought would be the answer after the brutality of the war and after the communist regime's stranglehold on Poland.

It breaks my heart to see him walking around the apartment among my mother's piles of half-sewn brassieres. He looks lost. On some days she enlists his help in using a small hand-held device that inserts eyelets into the corsets she is getting ready. "Nachman, do you have a minute?" she calls out from behind her sewing machine, brushing the hair off her sweaty forehead. Of course he has time. Time is all he has.

"Yes, what do you need?"

"Can you help me with the eyelets again?"

"Why not? What else do I have to do?" he says with a sigh. This is not the kind of work he needs. He is humiliated to ask relatives for help with the job search; he has always been the one to help others, totally self-sufficient.

Mother's brother Maxim, and brother-in-law, Benjamin, have called on everyone they know trying to help with the job, but to no avail. And suddenly our fate is sealed: Tinek announces the worst news ever in a flat voice, "I am going to the American Consulate to apply for a visa."

Mama sits at the table with her head in her hands as if she'd been handed a death sentence. "Go, go, see if the grass is greener on the other side," she says resigned.

I run into the bedroom and throw myself on the bed trying to stifle a scream.

Daniel is sitting at the desk doodling. "What's wrong?" he asks.

"America! That's what."

His face erupts into a smile. "Wonderful!"

It isn't until the following day that I discover that Tinek can only apply for a *single* visa. In the unlikely event he gets it, the three of us will be left behind. What will become of us? I try to cheer up by telling myself that America has always been Tinek's impossible dream. He is so miserable here. Maybe he should go. He reads the worry on my face and says, "Don't worry, Ania, it may not happen for years, if ever."

"Why does it take so long?" I ask, glad that he has given me a shred of hope.

"Many people around the world want to live in America. They can't let them all in. Only a very few lucky ones get visas."

"I wonder if you will get lucky," Daniel pipes up.

I didn't even notice him lurking at the edge of the room.

"I hope my sister Rosa in America will help improve my chances," Tinek tells him.

I sigh and Tinek says, "You would be very happy in America. Both of you."

We don't speak much about the visa in the weeks that come. No use aggravating anyone.

16

In the meantime, two of Tinek's cousins, Gina and Ala, are coming to visit us all the way from Rio de Janeiro, Brazil, a land so distant and exotic all I can picture are the Yanomami tribal people of the rainforest, not my blood relations. Tinek is excited about this visit. It will be a good distraction for him; a welcome break from the discouraging, never-ending job search and wait for the visa.

Gina and Ala emigrated from Poland to Brazil in the early 1930s when some Jews already understood that the Nazi propaganda would only lead to more persecution and restrictions. Everyone in the family thought they were crazy. "What will young Jewish girls do in the middle of a jungle?" they asked. Tinek hasn't seen them in twenty-five years. In that time his adventurous cousins did quite well in Brazil, Gina especially, by marrying a wealthy jeweler.

The cousins' arrival breaks the tension in our household. Tinek squires them around Tel Aviv like a tour guide, temporarily forgetting his unemployed status. Gina is not only wealthy, she is generous. She takes me to the best store on Allenby Street to shop. I could never dream of shopping here, but she buys me a beautiful embroidered white blouse and a spectacular navy blue skirt that twirls when I spin around in front of the tall mirror in the store. At last, I think I'll look more Israeli. I can't wait to wear my new outfit to some festive occasion. I'd wear it for school so Amnon could see me in it, but I would be overdressed. Gina also bought some record albums for Daniel and a pair of new shoes.

When we sit down to a meal I have a chance to look at Gina more closely and marvel at the many rings on her fingers. The colorful stones sparkle and her gold bracelets jangle. I have never seen anyone as rich before. She laughs a hoarse laugh as she puffs on one cigarette after another, then coughs and takes another drag. There is a puffiness around her eyes and bags below them.

"Smoking isn't good for you," my father admonishes.

"Ach, *bubbe mayses*, old wives' tales," she says. "Look at me, no one will say I died young." Then she flicks the ashes into the crystal ashtray that no one else uses in our home.

And I can see her point. She is wrinkled like a prune, but oh, so cheerful. She is a great storyteller and tells us about the Carnival, the Ipanema and Copacabana beaches and the huge statue of Jesus that stands on a mountaintop. "We have Christ greeting our visitors, New York only has the Statue of Liberty," she laughs and starts coughing.

Her sister Ala is different, short and so thin you'd think she could break in half. Fragile, is the first word that came to mind when I saw her. She speaks more deliberately and her eyes have a hangdog look in them. Ala never married and has been living with Gina since her husband died.

There is one thing Gina never mentions and my father never asks about: her only son Jorge. He died a couple of years ago when he was about my age. There is a handsome photo of him in our album. It frightens me to look at it and I always flip the page quickly.

Despite everything, Gina is fun to be around. When Mama headed out to the market to get dinner provisions— vegetables being the mainstay of the Israeli diet— she asked Gina, "What's your favorite vegetable?"

Gina replied, "Chopped liver."

We all laughed so hard. I think I'll always remember that.

The weeklong visit evaporates as fast as a puddle on a Tel Aviv day. As our Brazilian cousins prepare to leave, I overhear a conversation between Gina and my father. They are chatting in the living room, waiting for Ala who is finishing a final fitting with Mama.

"Take this money," Gina says.

"I don't want to take it."

"But I know you really need it, Nachman."

After a long pause he says, "All right, but only if it is a loan, not a gift."

"You can repay me after you start earning some money in America. Don't worry about it. I have so much more than you," Gina assures him. I can't see Tinek from my spot at the kitchen table, but I can just imagine his mixture of embarrassment and relief. This gift of five-hundred dollars will really help my parents pay the mounting bills. They whisper about the bills every night after Daniel and I go to bed.

After the cousins leave for Brazil our home feels too quiet. All of us miss their lively stories about their lives on Rio's posh street, Visconde de Piraja, in Ipanema. For me, its very name evokes images of exotic bronze women with golden charm bracelets strolling the wide avenue. We visit relatives and friends more frequently now. Anything to muffle the anxiety.

My lessons with Amnon are always a welcome break from the routine and so is Daniel's music practice. On some days his music sounds like a private concert and Tinek's satisfaction is written in his wide grin and the way he keeps tabs on the tempo by tapping his feet. Mama loves to listen too, but often she says, "I have got to get back to the sewing machine. The client will be here in the morning."

This Saturday night we have been invited to visit Mama's older sister, Esther. She is so different from either of her surviving sisters —my mother, and Chava. Though they all share a short, stout stature and large bosoms, Esther is quite different politically. She is not as likely as her sisters to talk about social justice, politics or matters that pertain to others. She is very self-involved and moody. Everyone in the family talks about what a great beauty Esther had been in her youth and how bitter she has become since her husband died. I can see that she still revels in the attention of others to which she feels entitled in her widowhood.

Like the loyal sister she is, Mama defends Esther's every fault and won't allow anyone to criticize her. Mother's presence seems to cheer Esther up and when they get together they laugh, tell jokes, and turn into girls. This is so rare for both of them.

Tonight, Esther seems once again like the much-admired woman she once was, presiding over dinner in her modest studio. The chatting and laughter keep the sisters connected and energized; it sustains them. Their easy banter makes me a little jealous that I don't have a sister who can make me laugh until tears come to my eyes. Daniel is smart and funny when he's not annoying, but he's no sister.

We return to our apartment late. As we approach the front door it's obvious something is amiss. The front door is ajar. "Wait! There has been a break-in," Tinek calls out. "The lock has been tampered with. Stand back." He pushes the door open. My parents advance cautiously into the apartment. Daniel and I follow anxiously behind.

A scene of unimaginable ruin unfolds before us. All of Mama's works in progress lie strewn about on the floor and not just in her workshop. Chest drawers are on the floor, their contents spilling ribbon and hooks and thousands of pins, eyelets, and corset ribs all over. Loose bobbins with tangled thread roll under the furniture as my parents make their way into the bedroom. As she rummages through an open bureau drawer, Mama calls out, "The money from Gina, it's gone, all gone!" Her face is ashen, her hands tremble.

Tinek mumbles in disbelief, "I can't believe it. Our own people have violated us. Who would have thought there are thieves in Israel? No. It can't be. It's impossible. It's impossible." He seems more upset that the thieves were Jewish than the fact the money is gone.

My parents make a call from a neighbor's apartment to the police station and are told that break-ins are fairly common. "Come in the morning to make an official police report," a disinterested clerk says.

A peculiar quiet settles over the apartment after the initial shock. Mama and Tinek are cleaning up in complete silence. Daniel and I offer to help, but Mama says, "It's late, go to bed now." I can see she wants us to erase the whole sorry scene out of our brains.

I am only too glad to pull the covers over my head and not think, but thoughts keep me awake. I can't stop churning over this ugly incident in my head. Thieves? Tinek's question reverberates in my head: who would have thought there are thieves in Israel?

Daniel whispers, "Can you believe it?"

"No, I can't, but I don't want to talk about it now. *Layla Tov.*" I say good night because anger chokes me.

Jews robbing Jews! True, it seems more shocking than the robbery itself. I wouldn't have dared to think it. Jews are supposed to be scholars, inventors, scientists, and mathematicians—people of the book. I have always been told that Jews are intelligent, decent people who care about *Tikkun Olam*—repairing the world, not thieves. My people can't be thieves! It's such a revolting idea. I console myself with the thought that my parents have dealt with worse. They'll manage somehow, I conclude.

As I drift off to sleep I remember the silly game Daniel and I played when we first arrived in Tel Aviv. Walking down the streets we would call out a multitude of professions we had never, not even in our remotest imagination, associated with Jews in Poland. "Look, see the policeman on the corner," I would exclaim. "He is Jewish!" "Look across the street. See that beggar over there, he's Jewish too," my brother would reply. And we would continue this way naming Jewish repairmen, movers, barbers, gardeners, butchers, and nannies, even the mayor. It was as if we suddenly found ourselves in an alternate universe where we were no longer unique, or different, but enjoyed a camaraderie with unknown throngs, different in some ways, but more like us than any group of humans we knew in Poland. We felt we had won admission to a large, inclusive club—*we* were in! But we never could have imagined thieves would be lurking in our pantheon of Jewishness. All my assumptions about Israel have been shaken to the core and I feel ashamed for my people.

In the morning, Tinek comes into the kitchen and tells Mama that he has an idea for recovery of the stolen money. There is a hint of a smile on his face that makes me wonder how he recovered from last night's shock.

"Remember Weinstein, the fellow inmate from the gulag I told you about?"

Mama looks at him strangely, "Why are you telling me about him now?"

"A few weeks ago, Edek told me that he is living somewhere in Tel Aviv."

"What are you getting at?" Mama looks at him knitting her eyebrows.

"Well, do you remember what I told you about him?"

She gasps. "He's the thief from Warsaw! Do you think he robbed us?"

Tinek laughs, "No, no, he'd do anything for me. Remember, I saved his life? I bet he knows the thieves here and he'll find the louse that stole our money. I know he will."

Mama is horrified. "Nachman, what are you talking about? Just think about it!"

"Well, for all I know, he might be a decent guy now. He was a thief *before* the war," Tinek defends Weinstein, or himself. I'm not sure whom.

"Dad, you knew a *real* thief?" Daniel is wide eyed.

"Well, we were thrown together by circumstances. I don't think I'd have ever met him if not for the gulag. Anyway, it's strange, but he was honorable in some ways."

"Nachman! You will do no such thing!" She throws the dish towel with a snap at the table. Her cheeks are getting redder by the moment. "I do not want you to initiate any contact with such low scum," Mama says with disgust and falls silent. After a long pause she adds quietly, "We'll pay Gina back somehow. I promise."

That's how it is with my parents. Mama is not too fond of Tinek's acquaintances. Anyway, he has hardly any in Israel. Most of them are in America. In the end, Mama wins. The idea of locating Weinstein is never mentioned again.

The robbery has not only taken our money. It has taken a bite out of my comfort in my new country and the unquestioned faith that each of its citizens was a decent person. The joy I felt seeing Jews in all their wondrous diversity is tainted. I want to shake each of them and ask: are you a good Jew? Do you abide by the precepts of the Torah? I want something to happen that will erase this unsettled emotion churning inside me. I wish fervently to experience something that will bind me to my people.

The atmosphere in my home is too heavy this morning. I gather my books and am happy to be going to school. On the way I wish it was Thursday, time for my weekly lesson with Amnon.

17

The gloomy spell in our household has been swept out with the spring breezes.

Two special holidays will be here very soon: Passover, and Israel's tenth birthday celebration. I am getting very excited about both. I have never seen a Passover celebration and people say that the birthday celebration for our country will be big, really big, unlike anything they have seen before. Something tells me these festivals might change me, though I'm not sure why. I just know it in my bones.

The rains of March have given way to the azure sky of early April. In Poland at this time we would still be stumbling over piles of gray snow and feel it soaking into our felt boots. But it's not the weather that is so remarkable. There is electricity in the air. It seems as if all our neighbors are suddenly in a cleaning fit that is evident even outside their homes.

Women beat and shake rugs out on the balconies. They emerge with baskets full of laundry and pin it to lines running from window to balcony. Colorful clothes, like holiday decorations, flap on the lines of most buildings. Men hose sidewalks and whitewash walls with an extra dose of energy, as if these tasks were not mere jobs, but essential rituals. Potted plants magically appear in windows, in courtyards and on balconies creating small Edens. Girls speak with excitement about the fancy outfits they are expecting to get for the holiday.

From the frenzied activity and scraps of conversation I realize this is more than spring fever and so I ask Mama about it. She tells me that the buzz is all about Passover. "Why didn't we celebrate it in Poland?" I ask.

"Well," she starts slowly, as if my question is difficult, "it wasn't easy for us to be so overtly Jewish and we didn't want you to hear nasty stuff from the neighbors."

"Like what?" I ask defiantly, surprised that anything would have been withheld from me.

"Like the lie that Jews were using Christian children's blood to make matzo."

"Eew, blood?" I say lamely, knowing somehow that I should not press her with more questions, but it is obvious to me that this must have been one of those myths popular among the gossips in our Łódź courtyard. I heard something about it from the kids in the yard, but Mama doesn't know that I know. If I tell her, she will know I sometimes hung around the courtyard when I was specifically forbidden to do it. Now I know why we never celebrated any of the Jewish holidays Poland. It was too dangerous.

The energy pulsating in conversations on the streets and in the markets finally affects our family too. Soon we are swept up in the frenzy preparing for the holiday like everyone else. Mama takes me to the Shuk Ha Carmel market in the southern part of Tel Aviv near Allenby Street. She wants to order boxes of matzo. When we get to the vendor's stall I immediately recognize the picture on the box as the same flat squares she used to soak in milk and eggs in Poland, then fried and sprinkled them with sugar and cinnamon. This delicacy appeared on our breakfast table in the spring of each year. She called it a strange name, "matzo brei," but never explained, until now, that this was a kind of treat her own mother used to make at Passover.

The market is so crowded with shoppers we have to push our way through. Stalls overflow with fruit I can't even name. The array of shapes, colors and textures is dazzling. We never saw such abundance of anything in Poland.

As Mama picks up spices, vegetables, and fruits for the holiday from different stalls I am still wondering about the matzo. "Mama, how were you able to find matzos in Łódź?"

"One needed to know where to look. There was a tiny group of religious Jews in Łódź that survived the war. They baked matzo and made it available to those who knew how to keep quiet about it."

"I guess there were things you couldn't tell us in Poland."

She nods. "For your own safety."

I wonder what else they haven't told me. But I am beginning to understand only now why in Poland we were Jews, more or less, inside our home, but nothing in particular outside, why my parents always lowered their voices when they spoke to one another in Yiddish.

A week before Passover, after I wash the dishes, we sit at the kitchen table. A tray with tea glasses and sugar cubes still sits on the plastic checkered tablecloth. Tinek says, "I want tell you about something that happened on the first night of Passover fifteen years ago. Call Daniel, I want him to hear this too."

"You remember the date so precisely. Why?"

"I'll tell you when Daniel gets here."

I go out on the balcony where Daniel is reading the newspaper. He loves reading the news. I always find that funny for a young kid like him.

"Tinek wants you. He is about to tell us something important."

Daniel folds up the paper and gets up reluctantly. We go into the kitchen.

"This is something no Jew should ever forget," Tinek says. Then he starts telling us about the Jewish uprising in the Warsaw ghetto.

I make a quick mental computation. "Dad, fifteen years ago? Then it was 1943, the year I was born."

"You were born because Mama and I escaped to the Soviet Union. If I hadn't, you wouldn't exist."

My mind wanders for a moment, not able to comprehend *not* being born, a state of nothingness forever.

Tinek doesn't notice my puzzlement. He is continuing single-mindedly. "I don't ever want you to think that our people went to slaughter like sheep. They were brave even though they were so starved they could barely walk."

"So how did they fight?" Daniel asks.

"With primitive grenades and bare hands," Tinek says in a voice brimming with emotion, but his face looks calm. I can see the vein pulsating on his left temple and the clenched hands resting incongruously on his lap.

"You know my older brother, Natan, was among the leaders of that uprising. Don't ever forget that."

"He was the brother closest to your age. The one that died, right?" I ask.

"Yes, and he didn't just die. He was murdered. He and his wife lost their lives in the uprising. You should know that. Don't you remember the medal?"

"Do you mean the one in the navy box with the grainy blue-and-black ribbon and the raised insignia?" I ask, remembering that it always sat on my parents' bureau in Łódź.

"Yes. The Polish government awarded it to him posthumously. It's the *Virtuti Militari*, the highest medal for valor."

"But I thought that the Poles didn't..."

"I know what you are getting at, Ania, but after the war it was the communist government's policy to officially reject antisemitism. Unfortunately, that meant nothing to the population at large."

Now I remember how Tinek said he would carry the medal in his pocket and didn't want it packed with other things when we left Poland. It is his most prized possession. He has no other keepsakes to remind him of other members of his family that disappeared.

Since we are treading on a minefield, I decide to ask something that I really have to know. This is the right moment. If I wait, I might not get another chance. "Dad, did you *ever* believe in God?"

"I don't know, maybe, when I was a little boy, attending the *cheder*. But I have told you that my oldest brother, Yankl, took me out of there and enrolled me in a secular Jewish school."

"Tinek, does anyone believe in God after the Holocaust?"

"Yes, some people still do, but I can't understand them," he says. "Just think, Ania, would the Holocaust have happened if there were a God?"

That night I lie in bed thinking about what Tinek had said. I see why he can't believe in God. He lost twenty-two members of his immediate family. But he also said that the Nazis wouldn't have been as successful without the cooperation of some Poles. So how, I keep wondering, could he have been so friendly with the Poles? I can't come up with an explanation that makes sense to me.

I hear Daniel moving around in his bed. Maybe he's still awake. "Daniel, do you believe in God?" I ask, but all I hear is his snoring.

I strain to organize the shadows dancing on the ceiling into a coherent image, but nothing comes to mind. Instead, I try to imagine my father sitting down to dinner with all those relatives he lost and think what a noisy gathering it would have been.

18

A letter from Chava arrived inviting us to celebrate the Passover Seder at kibbutz Gvat. Goose bumps erupted on my forearms. "Oh, Mama, can we go, can we go?"

"Nachman, do you want to go? It would be nice, but the bus fare will set us back."

I thought he'd say no.

"Sure, let's go," Tinek said without a moment's hesitation.

Today we are actually going. I am thrilled at the prospect of seeing Ruthi and my friends. We are staying in Gvat only for two nights, because Chava can't put us up longer.

How different this bus ride is from the one we took eight months ago on the way to Tel Aviv. I feel so much more at home in this country. But I am nervous about telling Ruthi the big things in my life: my father's visa application and tutoring lessons with Amnon. I don't know why, but I worry about her reaction. Still, I can't wait to tell her.

After almost three hours on the bus, we get off near Gvat's familiar main gate. Yellow and white wild flowers sprout randomly by the side of the gravel road. Across the road I see Gvat's cotton fields and a pang squeezes my heart: I no longer live here.

It's quiet and clear that we have left the frenetic atmosphere of Tel Aviv. We walk up the path to Chava and Benjamin's apartment building.

Except for the buzzing of the bees, it's peaceful here in the afternoons; most people catch naps in the heat of the day. Even the air is still. We pass through Chava's fragrant rose garden and look up to the first floor. She is already on the balcony of the low stucco building and motions us to come upstairs. A broad radiant smile erupts on her dear face. "Come up! I've been expecting you." We climb one flight up to the modest one room apartment. Chava stands at the door, her arms poised for hugs.

A white baker's apron, clearly not designed for her squat frame, almost reaches her ankles. Matzo meal still clings to her hands as she embraces us. "I'm baking for tomorrow's Passover feast," she says grinning.

"Chava, you were always the best baker in the family," Mama compliments her efforts.

"Believe me, Dora, it's not as easy to bake with matzo meal as with flour."

"You can actually bake on this thing?" Mama, astounded, points to the *P'tilia*, a cooking device, like a camping stove. It sits somewhat precariously on a wooden stool, hugging the wall of the porch. They have no kitchen. I smell the kerosene she uses for fuel.

"Sure, it's no problem," Chava laughs making her bountiful bosom shake.

Her resourcefulness and can-do attitude must be why I admire her so much, except for her attitude toward Yiddish. But I won't think of it now. This is supposed to be a special visit.

***

It's early evening of the Seder night. There are just a few wisps of color left on the darkening blueberry sky. Passover has arrived. A veritable river of Gvat families streams toward the *cheder ochel*. Our family and Chava's are part of this festive procession. A gentle breeze churns the fragrant air and spreads the festive atmosphere into everyone's nostrils. We enter.

I am at once stunned by the extravagant transformation. The bare, industrial-looking space is totally different from the dining room I left months ago. The long tables are decorated with snow-white tablecloths set with sparkling wine glasses. Each table is decorated by a vase of colorful wildflowers. I cannot take my eyes off their delicate shapes and colors: dark blue serrated petals of cornflower thistles with improbable pink centers; tall lupines, velvety blue with just a touch of white highlights; wild sage with tiny pale blue flowers—a floral sea in all its magnificent moods.

Flowers festoon a stage made just for this occasion; red gladiolas stand tall in large buckets on either side of it. The windows are draped in more flowers. It's as though spring has chosen to make its worldwide debut specifically in this room.

Each large family is seated at its own long table. Smaller families share tables with friends and neighbors. There is a kind of uncharacteristic expectant hush. This is not the place where workers gather to get their daily sustenance. This is more like the stage set of a theater.

I crane my neck looking for familiar faces. And then I spot Nachum and Navah sitting with their families. Daniel waves to his friends. All the men and boys wear starched white shirts; the women and girls look luminous in beautiful white blouses and colorful ribbons in their hair. For once I don't look out of place in the beautiful outfit from Gina.

A master of ceremonies emerges on stage and welcomes the two-hundred families gathered here. About sixty people follow the master of ceremonies and line up in rows on the stage. There are adults and children from the second grade and up. Benjamin, seated on my left, whispers, "It's our kibbutz chorus."

They break into song. Their voices, like a thousand clear bells, ring out with a force that brings tears to my eyes. They sing of freedom and rebirth and suddenly I have an indescribable desire to join them on stage, though I know this is ridiculous given my lousy voice. I don't even sing in the shower! The voices rise and fill the entire space; they could shatter the windows or wine glasses on the tables. The music reverberates through the room. I am bathed in it until it gets into my chest and makes me lightheaded. Mama, sitting next to her sister pats her hand every now and then. They look happy. I see Daniel tapping his fingers on the table as if he were playing the piece on his accordion.

During a break in the singing, I ask Ruthi, who is seated on my right, "What is this ethereal music?"

"It's an oratorio composed especially for this celebration. It tells the story from the perspective of the Jewish slaves making the exodus from Egypt."

I lean and whisper into her ear, "But I thought people on this kibbutz were not religious."

She moves toward me, and whispers, "It's not told from God's perspective like the traditional *Haggadahs*."

Now delicious smells of food waft in from the kitchen. The metal self-service racks have been removed. Young men and women have the honor of serving the meal on shiny dishes without the usual nicks and scratches. "So, Anat, how do you like our Passover Seder, so far," Benjamin asks as we are waiting for the huge platters being placed on the tables.

Like? I am mesmerized. Can't he just see it on my face? "Yes, I really like it," I reply quickly because I have to hold back the lump in my throat. I don't want to burst out crying. Mama has a big grin on her face and her eyes shine. Tinek says from across the table, "What's not to like? Sure, we all like it, especially the music."

With each new segment of the Passover night, I feel excited for what comes next. There are beautiful poetry readings, songs, and dances from the *Song of Songs*. This is spring so we celebrate the rebirth of nature and life as well. The exodus and the renewal are so intertwined I begin to think of them as one extraordinary event. I have never felt such joy! Never felt so much part of one huge, loving family. I feel tonight I have been formally inducted into the Jewish nation, converted from a Polish Jew to a *sabra*, prickles and all.

After the Seder, Nachum practically leaps tables to reach ours. He says, "Anat, let's take a walk."

Tinek sees my glance at him and says, "Sure, go ahead, we won't get to bed early anyway."

Nachum's offer, the familiar look, and that sad smile means he needs to tell me something. How I've missed him!

We walk out into the balmy night air. I stop momentarily and look up at the sky thinking that on a night like this even the stars are dancing. Nachum tugs gently at my hand and we walk in silence past the cowsheds and the kibbutz small private zoo. We settle on our two boulders and Nachum says, "Anat, I want you to know something I haven't told anyone."

"Go on," I nod.

"Well, I have a secret dream," he hesitates.

"So say it. You can trust me."

He blurts it out, "I want to move to America."

"America?" I am completely flabbergasted. All I can think is if kibbutz members ever hear such talk he will be ostracized even more than he is now. Loyalty is expected here. It's what makes the kibbutz work.

"But... but why, Nachum?"

"To get away from my family! And because. Because, in New York people can be what they want to be." And he goes on speaking of New York with such longing that I begin to imagine it. He sounds like my father. Everything he says is so different from what the Polish papers and magazines said about America, starving people and bosses who exploit working people. "Nachum, can I tell you something?" I say afterwards.

"Yes, remember, Anat? We are at our talking stones."

"But promise you won't get mad at me."

He knits his eyebrows and says, "I promise."

"I couldn't imagine ever leaving Gvat if I lived here," I say quietly, not wanting to upset him.

"Not even to travel?"

"No, I am staying right here in Israel. Forever. Especially after tonight."

He screws up his face and puts his hand on my shoulder. "I wish I was more like you," he says. And I wish he could be more than a friend, but I know that as much as he likes me, it isn't because I am a girl. Tonight I don't want to linger here with him. I want to get back and find Ruthi. There's so much we have to talk about.

Ruthi pouts when I meet her at Chava's house. "I have been waiting for you forever. Where have you been?"

"I'm sorry. I had to be there for Nachum. Let's go out on the balcony so we can talk," I say, and in no time, we are deeply into my sessions with Amnon.

With her eyes as large as saucers she asks, "Don't you feel weird spending time in a strange man's apartment?" In the dim balcony light I can see she has a slight smirk on her face and I can't tell if she's surprised, jealous, or incredulous to hear this story from someone like me—the innocent girl with braids.

"He isn't a stranger," I tell her. "Anyway, where else should we have the lessons?"

"I don't know." She shrugs her shoulders.

"Look, he's an honorable war hero," I explain and she giggles, so I have to shush her.

Before we say good night, I say, "I'll tell you something I wouldn't tell anyone else."

She leans closer so I can whisper it, "I kind of like having him all to myself when his wife isn't around."

"I guessed that," she says.

I feel a blush from head to toe and am glad it's too dark for her to see it. "Oh, Ruthi. It's two in the morning let's go to sleep now."

I welcome the bus ride back to Tel Aviv because I am exhausted. The bus lulls me to sleep almost as soon as we board. When we hit potholes and the bus lists I open my eyes realizing I've been dozing, dreaming of the Seder mixed with scenes from our former lives in Łódź. Just like any dream the images are jumbled: us marching down Piotrkowska Street in Łódź on long gone May Day parades; Daniel at the head of the contingent from *Centrala Textylna*, Father's employer. Daniel on his bicycle festooned with Polish and Soviet flags. Behind him a huge banner proclaiming, "Long live Poland and the Polish workers!" The marching music blares. Tinek and I trail behind, but I see no sign of joy, or festive spirit in his eyes. Without being told, I know he must be seen marching.

Someone's child begins to cry and I wake up, but bits of the dream still cling to the edge of my consciousness. Tinek was different at the Seder in Gvat than in the May Day march in my dream. Did I imagine it, or did I see tears well up in his eyes when the choir's voices filled the room? His eyes shone with a special light and looked bluer than usual. When he joined in with the chorus I was surprised that he knew the words, and it was his voice that stood out from the others. I am beginning to understand better why we made such a hasty retreat from Poland when the gates opened.

I see my image reflected in the bus window. What a mess I am, sleeping on a bus like a baby. I pull out my comb and mirror from my purse to fix my hair.

19

Today, like every Thursday, Amnon drives me to his apartment for the tutoring lesson. The finals are coming soon and I'll be taking advanced science tests.

We sit side by side at Amnon's dining room table strewn with my notebooks. My eyes wander for a moment. The apartment is modern, stark white and quiet. The only splash of color a vase of red carnations standing precariously near the table's edge, pushed aside to make space for my textbooks. Today Amnon's wife is not here and I wonder if he bought the flowers for her.

"Anat, let's first review the Hebrew vocabulary from your astronomy text." He is right, of course, I am quite comfortable with everyday Hebrew, but science words are another story.

"You mean the ones from the lesson on planets and stars?" I ask, but I'm really thinking of those carnations.

"Yes, that's the one," he says. The carnations recede. I'm melted by his winsome smile and begin shuffling through my book bag, but he says, "You know, it will help you memorize the constellation names if you actually see them. Right?"

"Um... where?"

"Up there," he points at the ceiling.

I must look very bewildered because he laughs, "Anat, we can see them on the roof."

"Oh, the roof," I repeat like a parrot. I had no idea you could go out on the roof. Is that even safe?

We walk single file up a narrow staircase. He is ahead of me taking two steps at a time. He pushes the metal door open and we step out onto the roof. It's pitch black by now and the stars glow so brightly as if they were electric lights. We walk toward the center of the roof with our heads up. The velvet sky seems so close. If I reach up, I can grasp a star.

"It's so beautiful," he says and looks as spellbound as I am. I feel dizzy, almost drunk with some kind of anticipation.

"So here, look, Anat, this is the Capricorn and this one—he stands behind me and moves my shoulders to point me in the right direction—this is Sagittarius."

He points this way and that and I can hardly think. Standing under this fairytale sky, feeling his commanding presence so near to me, smelling his spicy cologne I feel something changing inside me. The evening is chilly and I begin to shiver slightly. Goose bumps erupt on my bare arms.

"Anat, you are cold."

"Just a little."

He takes off his jacket and places it over my shoulders ever so gently. "Here, that's better," he says.

My teeth still chattering, I stammer, "Thank you."

I am embarrassed, but delirious and feel as if I were floating. Amnon smiles his radiant smile and puts his big bear arm on my shoulders, pulling me close to him. "Look, there's the Big Dipper," he points skyward. At this moment I can't remember a single Hebrew word for the constellations he's shown me. How could I have imagined that my science class would lead to this intimate encounter between Amnon, the stars and me?

Downstairs, back in the apartment, I feel strangely aroused and flustered and hope his wife won't come home for a while. "Let's get back to the books," he says sounding like a teacher. And we start talking about the upcoming Independence Day celebration— Israel's tenth birthday. It occurs to me this would be the perfect moment to ask him about his military service and his role in the 1956 Sinai campaign. Maybe I'll find out why the girls in school say he is a decorated war hero. "Can you tell me something about the Sinai campaign?" I ask. "We are supposed to have a class discussion about it."

"Anat, you need to go to the library and do some research. It'll help your Hebrew." The dimples in his cheeks make him look playful and mischievous, more an imp than a warrior, but I am disappointed because he treats me like just another student.

I go home confused, but I study late into the night until Mama comes to the kitchen in her nightgown and says, "Go to sleep. You won't be able to get up in the morning." These days I've thrown myself even more earnestly into my books because Mr. Shalit, though I suppose by now I can just call him Amnon, will know about my performance in every subject. I would be mortified to disappoint him with less than perfect grades. And disappointing my parents is even worse. They expect Daniel and me to have the best grades of any of our classmates. They won't be satisfied with ninety percent on an exam. "So what happened to the other ten percent?" They'd ask. They don't yell, or get angry, but they make me feel like I have shamed them, so I always try to do better.

Last week must have been Mama's best. I could tell from the shine in her eyes that something wonderful had happened. She'd just come home from a parent-teacher conference in Daniel's school. She sashayed into the living room as if she were about to perform a dance. "So how did it go?' Tinek looked up from the want ads. "How is Daniel's schoolwork?"

"You wouldn't believe it, Nachman, when I walked into Daniel's classroom, the women already gathered there looked up at me and a murmur went through the room."

"Why? What was wrong?" Tinek looked alarmed.

She laughed, "Nothing. It was all good. Very good."

"Stop it with the riddles, Dora."

"They whispered, '*Ze ima shel hagaon*,'" that's the mother of the genius. She pointed at her chest. "And the teacher confirmed it."

"Don't tell Daniel. His head will swell," Tinek said smiling and put his nose back in the paper.

I looked around. Daniel was nowhere to be seen. Maybe he was still playing soccer in the backyard with the neighborhood boys. The smart alec didn't need a tutor. Now he'll be able to get away with murder!

I glance at the clock above the kitchen sink. If I don't get to bed right now, I'll surely fail my math test tomorrow. Numbers and equations bounce in my head giving me a dreadful headache. I pack my book bag and tiptoe to the bathroom. Brushing my teeth, trying not to splatter, I stare into the mirror. Could I graduate at the top of my class? I must get an A on this test. I must impress Amnon.

In the twelve months since our arrival in Israel I have acquired a sufficient facility with Hebrew to feel comfortable. These days I feel so much less the alien. I read books and newspapers in Hebrew. And I dream in Hebrew. I think less and less of our Łódź home, whose biggest comfort came after dinner when we sat as a family, green velvet drapes drawn, protecting us from the outside. Now, despite the tension building between my parents, my soul is developing invisible ties to the pulsating warm totality of Tel Aviv.

I feel its explosive energy as people scurry through the markets on Fridays and rush for the overcrowded buses before they, too, rest for the Sabbath; feel it in the way vendors shout exaggerated claims about the quality of their wares; feel it in the melodies of dozens of languages; feel it in the way groups of young people at bus stops laugh in a totally unselfconscious way and smoke with abandon. I feel it in the knowing glances of lovers huddled over Turkish coffee in outdoor cafes; in the carefree way children skip on the sidewalks, their ice creams dripping down their chins while young parents smile approvingly. I see it in the deep blue hue of the sky; in the way the foamy green waves crash onto the shore, even in the *khamsin* winds that blow from the Arabian Desert. All this energy and joy and unspoken ease of being—and every bit of it is Jewish.

Today the May air is fragrant and the weather still hasn't turned beastly hot. It's the perfect weather for *Yom Ha Atzma'ut*— Independence Day celebrations. How lucky I am to be here in time for the tenth anniversary of the founding of the Jewish state! After the atrocities of the Holocaust many people believed that the establishment of a country for Jews was inevitable. Where would *we* be if not for this young vibrant country? Stuck in our gray Łódź courtyard, enduring the bullying and trying to understand why our neighbors don't consider us one of them.

For days I've been going over in my mind what I should wear for tonight's celebration. What skirt, what shoes? Put my hair up in a ponytail, or let it flow loose, released from the braids? Going out for milk this morning, I bumped into Marina, a girl in my class. She said, "Anat, a couple of us are going out tonight. Would you like to join us?"

"I would love to," I said, immediately sorry: I sounded too enthusiastic. Now she'd think I have no friends. "Where exactly are we going?" I ask.

"Around. There will be lots going on everywhere. No matter what street we take there will be something to see, do or hear."

I burst through the door excited. "Mama, I'm going out with Marina this evening."

"We have our own plans for tonight," she says, not raising the usual objections about me staying out late. "We are going out with Esther and some old friends from Poland."

"What about Daniel?" I ask, suddenly worried he'll be alone.

"Don't worry, he's staying overnight with Uri from his class."

All day long I am breathless with the anticipation of the big night. The preparations for the anniversary celebration are in evidence everywhere. Accustomed to state-planned celebrations in Poland, like the May Day parades, I did not expect to see such personal involvement by the citizens. It seems as if all merchants are hosing and sweeping the sidewalks in front of their shops, applying fresh coats of paint. White and blue Israeli flags singly and in bunches, bloom in the most unexpected places. Men are washing windows, hanging up banners—the entire city is getting ready for a giant party. Women are baking and cooking and inviting friends and family. It is bigger than Passover, bigger than *Rosh Hashanah*, even bigger than a wedding. It is to be the crowning achievement of a dream, no longer theoretical, but a ten-year-old reality, like a gifted child who achieved way beyond the wildest expectations.

For the past ten years more than one million immigrants have thrown themselves in to remake the desert into blooming fields, to build new settlements, to learn Hebrew. With zeal and enthusiasm they—no, *we*—have knitted ourselves into the fabric of this ancient land and reclaimed age-old traditions. It is as if God has personally overseen this decade of success, a magnificent coming of age.

At last the sky is darkening. Marina knocks on my door, "Let's go, let's go, everyone is outside already," she says. Two girls I don't know, her friends, peek into my apartment. They introduce themselves: Sarah and Shoshana. "Nice to meet you," I say, feeling awkward to be spending this special night with strangers. Just for a moment I wish I were celebrating in Gvat.

We walk toward Dizengoff Street. Throngs already crowd the streets, parading with falafels in hand. The cafes are packed. Turkish coffee, baklava and pistachio ice cream are being consumed in huge quantities. The neon lights glow brighter than on other nights. Sounds of firecrackers are coming from all directions. The makeshift sound systems installed on all major streets produce a tinny facsimile of marching band sounds, compensating for their quality with volume. More music spills onto the streets through the open windows. Confetti floats down from rooftops like rainbow colored rain, settling incongruously on curbs, people's shoulders and on my hair. Periodically, fireworks burst out of the inky sky and stars descend to the ground spinning like snowflakes in slow motion.

"Hey, let's get some falafels," Marina suggests as we pass a stand whose owner is tossing the balls into the air and catching them in pita pockets. The four of us sit on a bench outside and chat. The girls are really nice and friendly. They tell me about their school and their siblings. We wipe the tahini dribbling off our chins and move on to walk other streets and meld with the crowds.

As the evening stretches into the night spontaneous dancing erupts on the streets, group *horas*, and individual couples twirling through streets closed to traffic. I feel myself being pulled into the festivities with a kind of force I have not experienced before. We stop to buy sparklers and light them, join the *horas*, and gobble up ice cream in huge crunchy cones. I want to do it all, not to miss even a drop of this joyful, once in a lifetime event. I am mesmerized by the mood, by the positive karma that seems to seep out of the sidewalks and envelop the dancers, the pedestrians, and the strolling couples. I feel buoyant and free.

On Ben Yehuda Street Sarah and Shoshana run into a cluster of boys from their school. After the introductions I can tell these boys are older than we by their smoothness and confident handshakes. These guys know how to meet girls!

Among them, a blond fellow taller and shyer than the rest, stands slightly back. He smiles as his friends banter and joke with us. It's as though he is too grown up for such silly behavior. After a while, all of us drift toward a street where dancing is already in progress on a roadway closed to traffic.

The blond fellow takes my hand after a suave bow and before I know it we are dancing. Dancing! Me dancing? "My name is *Yom Tov*," he says, his arm now firmly around my waist. I'm glad he repeats his name because it made no sense when I first heard it. It means good day in Hebrew. How strange, I think, it's a greeting—who ever heard of a boy being named so strangely?

"Anat?" he says.

"Oh, I was just wondering about your unusual name."

"My father said I was born on a good day, and anyway, my name is not so unusual among Turkish Jews."

Turkish? I look up at Yom Tov fighting my usual reticence. His looks are so incongruous with his background. Straight blond hair hangs over his high forehead. I can tell he doesn't cut it too often; he flicks it away in a gesture at once sophisticated and childish. On his upper lip a line of blond fuzz forms a nascent mustache. His eyes are exotic, green, narrow, and slanted, a twinkle in them dances in time to the music. His high cheekbones make him look like a Persian cat when he smiles. His arms feel wiry and strong as he twirls me around.

I like him and am especially charmed by his comments about my dancing. "You are such a great dancer, Anat," he whispers. At first, I think he is making fun of me. I have danced the *hora* only a few times and each time worried that I might trip over my own feet. But he squeezes my hand gently and adds, "Really, I mean it," in a way that makes me believe him.

We dance faster and faster. I see beads of sweat appear on his forehead and strands of hair stick to it, making him look vulnerable, like a young boy who has been running too fast. I worry that the perspiration I feel on my own body will show through my white blouse and spoil this magical moment.

After several more dances the boys from Yom Tov's group yell, "Get her name and address, we have got to go!" He lets go of me reluctantly and whispers in my ear, "I'll see you again soon." He walks away looking back at me a few times before he reaches his buddies.

I rejoin my girlfriends. We walk and walk intoxicated with the night air, singing at the top of our lungs about freedom, about the land of milk and honey, about the evening of roses, *erev shel shoshanim*. The celebrations continue into the wee hours. Well after midnight, we near the building in which Aunt Esther lives in her ground floor studio.

Peals of laughter reach my ears on the street before I enter Esther's apartment. Through the open window I hear my mother's giggles accompanied by Esther's gravelly voice and loud conversation of other guests. Mama's laughter is such a rare sound. It makes me wish this evening would go on forever. Tonight even my parents are behaving oddly; their celebration is far from over. What's this partying into the night? I come in for tea and cakes. Mama's cheeks are flushed and she is not annoyed that I have stayed out so late. Everyone wants to know all at once, "How did you celebrate, Anat?" But they soon forget the question and burst out laughing at another Yiddish joke. And Aunt Esther puts up a fresh pot of tea to brew. It is nearly dawn.

Usually, I am asleep as soon as my head hits the pillow, but the scrap of night that remains holds no prospect of sleep for me. I am much too excited. I replay in my mind each step of my dance with Yom Tov. How close our bodies were to one another! His strong arms encircled me. The heat between us so intense we could have melted into one. His touch has given voice to what I felt on that rooftop with Amnon. In my head the music continues to play and we are still spinning in the moonlight, the streets empty except for Yom Tov and me.

It's almost morning and I haven't yet fallen asleep. Yom Tov fills my entire brain: the exact feel of his hands on my waist, their gentle pressure at the small of my back, his warm breath so close to my neck sending chills down my spine and those unreal cat eyes!

"You are such a good dancer," he said! I repeat that to myself trying to believe it. Yom Tov's exotic Sephardic Turkish origins make me imagine sultans and veiled, bejeweled women dancing with tambourines under fig trees. Is there a chance he could become my boyfriend? The very notion thrills me. I am in love with the idea of love.

For quite some time now, I've felt something going on in my body. Not just the obvious physical changes but a growing sense of myself of being less a girl and more a woman. These emotions are confusing. I don't know exactly what goes on between men and women when they are in private. No one talks about it, but it sounds exciting and a little bit scary. I wish my mother would tell me more about the facts of life, but her mind is in our finances and other things, dark things.

I feel feverish and must do something to cool off. I flip on the bathroom light and squint. The image in the mirror surprises me: my cheeks look as if I have applied rouge, sweat glistens on my neck and breasts. I splash cool water on my face and watch it dripping down my chest. I stare at the curve of my lips. These lips must be kissed! Back in bed I notice thin morning light filtering through the curtains. A new chapter in my life has opened.

20

The doorbell rings. My heart leaps when I hear Yom Tov introducing himself to Mama at the front door. The clock at my bedside says it's four in the afternoon. I have slept far later than normal and my head is pounding. I've spent the better part of the day trying to come down to earth from the cloud onto which I climbed last night.

"Ania, your friend is here," Mama calls from the entry hall.

"I'm coming!"

I grab my brush and fix my hair then walk out to greet him, casual, as if I hadn't thought of him all night. He stands there awkwardly in the hall with a shy smile making small talk with Mama.

"Hi," I say looking at him as if he were a stranger. I've never actually seen him in daylight.

He asks, "Want to take a walk along the beach, Anat? It's not so hot today. It'll be nice."

We walk out onto the street and for the first time, I notice his slight limp. Was it there last night? Surely, I'd have noticed. He is speaking but I barely listen because now I wonder what happened to him. An accident? A birth defect? A limp would be more fitting for a war hero, like Amnon. I must not think about Amnon. Thinking about that man is crazy, I chastise myself.

We walk stiffly at first as if last night's dances had never happened, as if we hadn't been so close we could feel the perspiration of each other's bodies. After a while, he takes my hand and holds it loosely. Where is the closeness and fire of last night? We tell each other about our families, trying to make a connection that is based on something less ethereal than stars and perfumed night air. We stroll on the boardwalk nervously, tentatively, like a couple of strangers who have just been introduced by a matchmaker. We pass cafes, boutiques, falafel stalls and fishermen dipping lines into the darkening sea. "Would you like an ice cream, Anat?"

"No, thank you," I say, thinking we have to start over, retrace our way to the magic. We stand wordlessly watching the waves roll in. With each swell of the sea I am regaining my footing, though in the cold light of day it all seems less romantic than the night before. I do like him, especially his smiling cat eyes, and decide right then and there he will make a fine boyfriend—my very first one. Maybe on our next date we'll both feel more at ease. Maybe he'll even kiss me.

On the way home I wonder how I will break the news about Yom Tov to my parents. Will it bother them he is a Sephardi Jew, the kind many Ashkenazim from Eastern Europe call uncultured, illiterate, and superstitious? Of course, I have no idea what my parents might think, but I have heard such ugly sentiments voiced casually by neighbors and girls in school. Jews demeaning other Jews—revolting!

As he drops me off at my building Yom Tov says, "See you this

Saturday night? How about a movie?" There is a hopeful expression on his face.

"What movie did you have in mind?" I stall for time.

"*Vertigo*. It's a Hitchcock film starring Kim Novak."

I have no idea who either of these people are but he says, "She looks a little like you, but you are prettier, Anat."

"Okay. Let's try to see it," I say, now dying to know what this actress looks like.

When I see Mama she doesn't grill me about Yom Tov as I expected. It must be her preoccupation with the visa application. All she says, "A nice new friend, this boy who came today. Is he in your class?" And just as she asks me, Daniel strolls in, rolls his eyes and says in sing song, "Ania has a boyfriend. I saw them from the balcony."

"No, it's just a friend," Mama says. "She's not even fifteen, too young for a boyfriend."

I slip out of the room not wanting to engage in this conversation any further.

21

Chavcia, Mama's cousin, is one of the relatives who escaped death in Auschwitz and found refuge in the brand new Jewish country. Now thirty-four, she is fourteen years younger than Mama. Chavcia relates to Mama as if she were one of her elder sisters, the ones she lost in the Warsaw ghetto. Chavcia was fifteen, exactly my age now, when the Germans invaded Poland. She lost every single member of her large immediate family during the Holocaust.

A petite woman with jet-black hair and a radiant smile that makes the skin around her eyes crinkle just like Mama's, Chavcia clings to my mother as if she were a life raft. From what I have heard, prior to the war, my mother and she were not close. Their age difference was too great for a true sisterly relationship and Mama was far more emancipated, but now in a family shrunken by the war things have changed.

I'll probably never know what indescribable horrors Chavcia endured and survived, first in the Warsaw ghetto, and later in Auschwitz. I don't think I want to know. She must have a stash of nightmares locked away somewhere deep within her because outwardly she seems to be happy and is always in good spirits. Her deep red lipstick and well-fitted flouncy dresses give her tiny frame a perky look of youthfulness that make her appear even younger than she is.

For some reason Chavcia is relentless in asking my father every single time she sees him whether he has had any news of his visa to America. Knowing how much he wants it, she even gave it the kind of diminutive, loving name one would give a child. Instead of inquiring about "the visa," she calls it "*vizka*." "Did you get it yet? Did you hear anything about your *vizka*?" she asks insistently. Each time my father gives her the same response, "Not yet, maybe never."

I have no way of knowing if she is truly so interested in his visa, or whether it's just her way of relating to him, of making friendly conversation. Chavcia loves Mama, but she is tone deaf. Doesn't she realize how much she irks Mama by the constant mentions of the dreaded visa? Mama has made it quite clear by her tight-lipped expression and stiff demeanor whenever the topic comes up, that she hopes the visa for America will never come. When she's in our home, which is often, I just want to grit my teeth when Chavcia chirps about the *vizka*. Then I think of what a horrible life she's had and I know I must forgive her.

I like Chavcia best when she and I find ourselves alone in her cozy, bright apartment. After I finish babysitting for her little girl, she sits with me and tells me stories from prewar Poland. Today Chavcia is in a storytelling mood. I can tell by the way she pulls up a chair and settles in.

The baby is asleep nearby in her cradle and we sit in the little kitchen smelling of fresh challah. Chavcia reaches to rock the cradle absentmindedly from time to time. "Would you like some iced tea?" Chavcia bounces up to put on her frilly apron.

"No, but I'd like you to tell me more about my grandma Zyvia. I know you were in the Warsaw ghetto with her. Isn't that so?"

My grandmother was murdered before I could meet her, but I know so few details and thirst for more. Chavcia looks up at the ceiling. She is silent for a moment and shakes her head.

"Yes, it's true. After they all..." She stops and I don't push. We are both quiet for a while. I know this is painful for Chavcia and I'm almost sorry I asked. I move my chair closer to the cradle so I, too, can rock it when the baby stirs. I look at her tiny pouty lips and listen to her sucking sounds. Then Chavcia resumes: "So it was only she and I after a time. I was so lonely and so happy to have your grandma with me."

"Did you live in the same part of the ghetto?" I ask.

"No, but I did my best to help her, especially after she fell ill with a terrible cough that got worse daily. Maybe she had pneumonia. I don't know."

"But you had nothing. What could you do for her?"

"I brought her some of my watery soup to share... we were all so hungry... we were given no more than a couple of hundred calories a day to eat. Malnutrition was rampant in the ghetto. I had only that soup to give her. I still remember the feel of the small tin bucket swinging in my hand."

"How far did you have to walk, Chavcia?"

"Oh, it was many blocks... I rushed... I wanted it to stay warm and not to spill. There was never enough anyway..."

My eyes begin to sting and tears well in them, but I will them to stop. She was the one who suffered, not I. "I am so glad you were together with her. At least for a while."

"Look, I was young, resilient, but skinny as a skeleton... She was my favorite aunt! We huddled together in a cold dark room lit by a candle. I watched her take a few tiny sips of the soup, then she gave me the rest. She couldn't eat by then... the poor dear... She was too weak."

And I tried to picture them. What an odd pair they must have made: a skinny, dark-haired girl with deep shadows beneath her large brown eyes, lonely and frightened, the gray-haired aunt with a tattered shawl about her stooped shoulders.

Chavcia brightened, looked at me directly and said, "Your grandma always cheered me up. She often said, 'This will not go on much longer, hang on to the thought of spring. It will come, I promise.' And that thought kept me going. It's what helped me survive."

Shafts of late afternoon sun pour into the kitchen making a jarring contrast to the story. Today I wish it were raining. Traffic sounds and voices of pedestrians drift in from the street, sounds of life. The baby shifts as if she were about to wake up and begins sucking her thumb with relish.

"I know my grandma died, but I don't know how. Do you know, Chavcia?"

"Oh, Ania, you don't know?" Tears begin to make their way down Chavcia's cheeks, but she makes no crying sound and no effort to wipe them. "I am so sorry to have to tell you this. After she was deported from the ghetto in the summer of 1942, the Nazis gassed her in the Treblinka extermination camp. And not just her; there were thousands of others."

The baby fusses in her cradle but neither of us moves. We are both silent for a long time. I can hear my own blood pulsating in my temples and the ticking of the clock on the counter.

"At the time, did you know what would happen to all those people that were being deported?" I ask her.

"No, we didn't know anything. Actually, many people volunteered to go because they were promised bread and jam. They were so hungry. They thought they were just being resettled."

"And what about you? Why didn't you go with her?"

"I was young. The younger people were sent to forced labor camps if they still had some strength. The old people and children were useless to the Nazis."

I think this conversation is finished because Chavcia stands up, smooths her apron and walks into the bedroom, then returns with a small stack of diapers. "I wish I didn't have to tell you any of this, but we can't hide even the ugliest truths. That would dishonor our dead," she tells me. Then she dabs her eyes with the diaper she is holding—getting ready to change the baby—and looks right at me. "Do you understand?" she asks, and the intensity of her look touches a place somewhere deep in my gut. It frightens me.

Chavcia sees my discomfort and must want me to hear something uplifting for a change because she says with a new lightness in her voice: "Your grandmother was the wisest and kindest woman in the whole world. May she rest in peace, your grandmother was a real *tsydayke*."

"What is that word?" I ask.

"Well, it's a female *tsaddik*," she says.

"And what is a *tsaddik*?"

"Oh, it's one of thirty-six righteous people—*tsaddiks*, disguised as ordinary folk who roam the earth performing deeds of selfless kindness. The world cannot survive without them."

22

The week after my babysitting afternoon at Chavcia's, Tinek comes into the living room with a large envelope in his hand and a grin on his face. It has been such a long time since I've seen him so cheerful I immediately guess what's up. He looks as if he can't contain his excitement. "Where is Mama?" he asks.

I point to her workshop and follow him. I have to find out if I'm right.

"Dora, look, it's a letter from the American Consulate. The postman handed it to me because it couldn't fit in the mail box."

"I am not so sure I want you to open it," she says without looking up from her sewing machine.

"Ania, hand me the letter opener, please, you know how I hate to destroy envelopes." It's true. He always opens letters carefully and saves the envelopes along with the contents. "So we can always check when it was posted," he says. He opens the envelope with utmost care, absently sliding the tip of his tongue slightly between his lips in sync with the opener. He reads the letter, gasps then exclaims, "I got it, I got it! The *vizka*, it's here!" I see the blood vessels on his temples pulsating. His eyes shine and there is a barely noticeable tremble to his hands.

I knew it! Now I don't know if I should rejoice for him, or cry for Mama. It's a shock, like a bomb being thrown into the center of our lives. It's just like Mama always says, "You are most likely to be defeated by that which you fear the most." Until now I hadn't understood what she meant.

Mama accepts the news with resignation. She looks crushed. Her face looks gray, drained of blood. All she can manage to say is, "Finally, you'll get your America."

"Did someone say America?" Daniel runs in from the bedroom where he's been practicing his music. "Dad, did you get it?"

"Yes, yes, I did," Tinek says.

Daniel's mouth drops. He is speechless for a minute then asks, "Dad, will you send me a postcard of those tall skyscrapers when you get to New York?"

I leave the room to avoid saying anything. Whatever words I choose will hurt one of my parents.

I am confused and don't know how to feel. I hate the idea of losing my father. If I am ever to see him again I will have to lose Israel. What if he can't get entry visas for the rest of us? Turmoil rages in my heart; my stomach churns. I hear Tinek from the next room, "Dora, we will plan later. I am going out for a little while." His voice is flat. How disappointed he must be in our lack of enthusiasm.

From the window I can see him grabbing the bicycle. Where is he going? I look up the block and can tell he is rushing over to Chavcia's, whose apartment is just up the hill from us. I can't see him as he turns at the corner but I know what happens. He will call for her to come to the window and wave the envelope in the air.

"The *vizka*, the *vizka*, I got it!" he'll yell to her, still out of breath from the brisk ride uphill.

Daniel is back in the bedroom, at his accordion practice, playing a piece with a brisk tempo. It sounds joyous to my ears.

I think the prospect of America has made him happy. Mama is still in her workshop, glued to her machine in her little world filled to the rafters with fabric and corset making supplies. I feel the loneliest I've ever felt.

The afternoon sun floods the room, but I can only focus on the dark place inside me. Even though he hasn't yet left, I feel betrayed one minute and long to join Tinek in America the next. I can't bear the thought that we may be separated for a long, long time. How long? Who knows? Maybe *forever*. Me leaving Israel? It's unthinkable. I have come to love this place of impossible contrasts, irrational rabbinical rules and brusque sabras with hearts made of butter. Hebrew rolls off my tongue as if it had been in my brain since birth.

The front door creaks open. Tinek is back from Chavcia's. He walks in subdued, maybe even a bit deflated. "Chavcia is the only one who shares my excitement," he says to no one in particular.

"Tinek, I wish..." I don't know what I want to say.

"What do you wish, Ania?"

"I wish we'd never come to Israel..."

"I thought it would work out here. Things will be better for us in America," he says and goes back to Mama's workshop.

I hear them speaking but can't make out the words.

After a while they both come out of the small room. "Why aren't you doing your homework?" Mama asks as if nothing has happened.

I know I'm pouting but I can't stop myself. "What's the use? I may not even be here next school year."

"Not so fast," she says, "who knows if we are ever getting *our* visas?"

This gives me a tiny glimmer of hope and I get up off the sofa, go to my desk and open my books, but the thoughts keep coming. How will Mama tear herself away from her sisters and brothers? Though their warm embraces won't ever compensate for the loss of her mother and younger sisters, she has been able to smile here; a corner of the dark veil over her face has lifted since we left Poland. I know she hates that Tinek will be leaving; I just wish she wouldn't suffer in silence. When she chokes back her emotions I find it harder to comfort to her.

I vow to turn off these thoughts. I push away from the desk and begin to rummage through the bookcase frantically. If I find the atlas, I'll look up out the distance from Tel Aviv to New York.

Father's friends, Mendl and his wife Itka, are among the first to learn of Father's imminent departure for America. They and my parents are bonded because they shared a similar fate during the war. All four of them were a part of the group of refugees who traveled far south after surviving the Soviet gulags. Mendel, in fact, is the one who introduced my parents to each other after they arrived in Kyrgyzstan.

The day after the visa arrives we have a celebratory dinner with Mendl and Itka, not that we are all in a mood to rejoice. They, like my parents, know what it is like to starve, or merely subsist on a diet of boiled thorn weeds. Tonight Mendl and Itka seem envious that my father is about to depart for what they call the Promised Land.

"Ah, America," Mendl says wistfully, taking a deep drag on his cigarette. "Soon, you'll be a millionaire, Nachman. How did you manage to get the permission to enter *Gan Eyden*?"

And Itka chimes in, "The Garden of Eden, Mendl is right! Nachman will forget about us poor folks as soon as he lands on his feet."

Tinek overlooks her comment, tells them instead how hard his sister Rosa has worked in America to enlist the help of elected officials. "She has been bombarding her senators and congressmen with letters!"

"What did she say to them?" Mendl asks.

"Oy, what didn't she say?" Tinek is proud of Rosa's persistence.

"She said, 'I am a survivor. Nachman is all that's left of our large family. Please help reunite us. I will dedicate myself to raising funds for your reelection campaigns.'" How he delights in telling this story! "First, I was summoned urgently to the consular office on Allenby Street. The guards, they opened the massive gate after I explained why I was there. I felt taller, just entering the grounds of the American Consulate! On the second floor, I was ushered in very respectfully to the consul's office! Imagine! Me in the American Consul's office! 'Mr. Libeskind,' the consul said, 'You have friends in high places. I have letters here from two US senators and several congressmen requesting that we expedite your entry visa.'"

"What could I say to that? *Gurnisht*, nothing. I just hoped the consul would take my silence as respect." Itka and Mendel look at one another then back at Tinek. "I tell you, I am lucky to have a sister like Rosa." Mendl and Itka nod approvingly.

Daniel, who has been sitting and drawing a caricature of Charles de Gaulle, turns to me and sticks out his tongue when the adults aren't looking. The French general has dominated the news since the Algerian crisis in May. Daniel finds his donkey ears, bulbous shnoz, mustache and kepi hat irresistible subjects of his doodles. For a kid, Daniel has an impressive awareness of current events in the world.

"Too bad I don't have a sister in America," Mendl says, lighting another cigarette. "I'd write to her tomorrow."

"Why?" Mama asks. "You have a job." She doesn't smile.

"Ah, America, who doesn't want to live in America?"

But my mother just shakes her head and says, "Mendl, my friend, you don't know what you are talking about."

"So, Nachman, continue," Mendl says, trying to avoid an argument with Mama.

"There's not much more to say. Rosa made my visa her crusade —and it worked!"

Mendel must have noticed Mama's anguished expression

because he says, "Don't worry, Dora, I will be here for you when Nachman leaves. I am known as the world's best packer. I will help you pack up when the time comes." Maybe he thinks she'll crumple having to deal with her business, us kids, and packing. Obviously, he doesn't know Mama.

"Thank you, Mendl," she says, but she doesn't look a bit relieved.

The conversation drags into the night. Mendl's cigarette stubs overflow the ashtray and smoke fills the room. Now Itka and Mama have disappeared in the kitchen to brew another pot of tea. I have been sitting quietly listening all evening, but I begin to yawn.

Before I fall asleep I turn over in my head all the new things I discovered about America. It's not like Israel that wants all Jews, even those who never lived here, to return. America limits who can live there. And the Displaced Persons Act of 1948, passed by the US Congress, that Tinek spoke about, was meant only to admit persons fleeing persecution. Tinek wants to start a new life in America—a new start for the fourth time in his life. He is brave. But what about me? I don't want to leave Yom Tov, or Amnon, or Ruthi, and Nachum whom I haven't seen in forever, or anyone in my great new life.

23

Tinek must leave in just one week. A frenzy of preparations for his departure takes over our household, disrupting daily routines completely. I can't study for my tests. Mama has to cancel appointments with clients. Even Daniel can get away with less accordion practice. Neighbors and relatives pop in and out of our apartment with tidbits of wisdom about America—as if they had been there.

"Don't go out in the streets after dark, it's dangerous," Esther says. Then Benjamin chimes in, "Don't ever ask for time off if you do get a job. Americans say, time is money, so they never go on vacations." Daniel likes Itzhak's suggestion best, "Nachman, better learn how to drive so you can get a car and become a real American."

Mama helps Tinek pack and counsels him on how to make do on the tiny sum of money he is bringing on the voyage into the unknown. With the single exception of the day Daniel was born they have never been apart. Mama has always been the one to take care of things and I wonder how he'll survive without her. He is a very capable man, but Mama's help must be her way of letting him know that despite everything, she still loves him.

Though my parents rarely fight, I can see that these days Tinek sidesteps any topic that might turn into a landmine. Fortunately, preparations for the upcoming Purim holiday intervene and soften some of the thick tension at home. This year, Purim will take place soon after Father leaves Israel. Tinek volunteers to help Daniel create a costume for the holiday, though his mind is clearly elsewhere.

"Ania, do you want help making a costume?" he asks.

"No, I don't like costumes. I don't see what the fuss is all about," I say, unable to snap out of my misery.

"Okay. Suit yourself."

Daniel is lucky to get Dad's help. Tinek has artistic talent. Daniel's source of gift in drawing is obvious and he is a very creative thirteen-year-old. I know the costume they'll design together will be a neighborhood hit. Daniel wants to go to the Purim parade dressed as a Hussar—a cavalryman in seventeenth century Poland. The two of them work for hours making an elaborate hat topped by a feather and adorned with gold braid. They even make the saber to match and Tinek instructs Daniel on how to paint on a mustache when Purim finally arrives. When the costume is complete, Tinek, already misty eyed, says, "I won't be here to take your picture. You'll have to ask someone to take it and send it to me. I will show it off to my American friends."

"Don't worry, I will," Daniel says. "I promise to write you every day."

Now I'm sorry I rejected Tinek's offer to help with my costume.

A large group of family members accompanies all of us to the port in Haifa in a somber mood. The frowns and long faces on our relatives tell me they are angry that my father is abandoning Israel, though most say they understand that his fruitless search for work is the reason. Maybe they are more disappointed than angry. Maybe they are envious. Aunt Chava, the one who always smiles except for today, keeps repeating, "Nachman, take a good look at the trees here. You won't be seeing any in New York." I know New York has many tall buildings, but no trees? None at all? Is she saying this to discourage my mother from ever thinking of leaving? She must know how much Mama loves trees.

It is painfully clear how very different this day is from the joyous reunion on our arrival from Poland less than two years ago. My heart breaks as my father boards the SS *Israel*, the ship that will take him away. I watch him climbing the steps, holding his good brown leather suitcase from Poland, moving forward step by step behind a line of passengers. His broad back is straight, his head up as if he were already entering America with resolve. Having already bombarded him with last-minute kisses and hugs as if we were never to see him again, we now wait at the pier craning our necks watching for Tinek to appear on the deck. Uncle Benjamin taps my shoulder. "Anat, did you know that this ship was manufactured by the *Deutsche Werft* ship building company?

"No, how would I know such a thing?" I ask annoyed. I don't feel like chatting. I want to cry. "Where is this company anyway?" I try to sound more polite, conversational.

"In Hamburg, Germany."

I give Benjamin a disgusted look and he explains. "The Germans built it as part of the Reparations Payment Agreement."

"What are *reparations*?" The mention of Germans brings a creepy feel into this conversation, but I am curious. He explains the word and I am dumbfounded. This is the first time I hear that the Germans are being made to pay for their crimes. How can anyone ever compensate for the murder of millions? All I can think of is, *reparations*—it's such an ill-fitting word. Then I say out loud, "Murder isn't something you can repair." I turn to look at the hustle

221

and bustle, people scurrying in all directions and I feel a stab that Tinek won't be here among them, among us.

The irony of this whole event is not lost on me. With its on-board synagogue and 300-passenger capacity the SS *Israel* was meant to bring Jews *to* their ancient homeland. At last my father appears on deck looking small and lonely. He tries to give us hand signals because he is so high up and we can't hear him above the din. We wave frantically and call out, "Please write!" knowing he can't hear us. All too soon, the ship's horn issues a loud call and the vessel glides slowly away, leaving gray agitated surf behind it. Tinek keeps waving until we can no longer see him. The ship is just a dot in the distance. We stand there under the blue sky for a while feeling orphaned and disoriented.

24

Sweet Yom Tov comes over after my father's departure to cheer me up. I don't tell him that this is an impossible task, but he hugs me and brushes the hair off my face with such tenderness that I let him believe he succeeds. I smile and ask if he wants to go see the new musical comedy, *Gigi*. "Sure," he says enthusiastically and a broad smile erupts on his handsome face. As we exit the film he asks, "How did you like it, Anat?"

"It was fun," I say thinking that Gaston's marriage proposal to Gigi made me think of Amnon.

Mama is now fully in charge. Things are both tighter and looser. Now Mama checks if we've done all our homework, studied for tests, and if Daniel has practiced his accordion. This was always Tinek's territory. On the other hand, she lets me go on dates with Yom Tov without any hassle and Daniel can stay out with his friends much later than he used to.

In between working on her orders and fittings with customers, Mama wants us to meet as many of the people she cares about before we leave. "Who knows when that may be?" she says, when I ask. "Months? Years?" A sense of doom grips me each time I try to

223

guess how long before we are reunited with Tinek. Mama misses Tinek too and fills the void visiting her friends.

I enjoy seeing them; all interesting, self-reliant women. Guta is Mama's chain-smoking friend, a thin divorcee with an artistic upswept hairdo that ends on top in a loose bun. Her high cheekbones would be attractive if the cheeks weren't so sunken in. She coughs constantly and is always enveloped in a halo of smoke. They whisper conspiratorially and drink strong tea.

"Guta, stop smoking if you don't want your two boys to be orphaned," Mama says.

Guta just laughs her guttural laugh and says, "You can't live forever. Can you?" And they go on talking, the laughter reverberating through the sparsely furnished flat.

The next weekend we take the bus to Givat HaShlosha, a kibbutz where Mama's Zionist friends settled in Palestine before the war. Mama reminisces with Chaviva about Palestine.

Chaviva is a dark-haired, statuesque woman with lively eyes and a warm smile. She shows me a photo of Mama with a group of friends taken in Poland just before Mama departed for Palestine. How different she was from them! In the center of the 1930s sepia photo, Mama wears trousers and a tie, her hair cropped very short, falling rakishly across her forehead. Her friends look as though they belong in a different era: prim blouses with baby collars or ruffles up to their necks, their hair in demure chignons.

"Remember how you hated the mosquitoes, Dora?" Chaviva chuckles. "It was just after you arrived here, so full of idealism, but you got used to them later."

"Sure. I also remember how my hands got calloused from using the pick to break up the dry soil. And you, Chaviva, do you remember your first crazy boyfriend, the one who was so brown, you thought he was an Arab?"

Chaviva closes her eyes, as if trying to recall him, and stretches languidly in her chaise looking younger than a moment before.

"Why don't you kids go outside and get a better look at the

garden," Mama's look means she wants private time with her friend.

Daniel and I spend much of the afternoon with Motye, Chaviva's husband, who speaks to us about how he grows beautiful chrysanthemums and buttercups in the rocky soil. But all I want is to be inside, listening to Mama's time in pre-Israel Palestine.

———

Except for Thursdays when I have Amnon's tutoring sessions, I study and mope until the weekend when I can go out with Yom Tov or join Mama on a visit. Dunia is Mama's anarchist friend. She lives alone with her only daughter, Louisa, who is my age. Dunia is prematurely gray and gives a careless and carefree impression all at once. Newspapers and books are strewn about her living room in large piles on the floor, on chairs and a low hammered copper table. She runs barefoot from room to room, apologizing for the mess. The exotic aroma of Turkish coffee and a large wooden platter of dates, figs, pomegranates, and baklava on the table make up for the disorder. I like spending time with Louisa. She is worldly, like her mother. And Louisa knows things! She told me exactly how babies are made. I found it very hard to believe. I don't think I'll ever look the same way at my parents. I've been so stupid. Did all the girls know these things already? Have I been the last to find out?

After coffee, our mothers retire to the den where they chat in a tone and volume that make it clear their conversation is not meant for our ears. We overhear their voices rise with emotion. "No, Dunia, women are not meant to be baby factories," I can make out my mother's words, followed by a chuckle from Dunia.

"Dora, you are a rebel. You can still teach me a thing or two."

"Actually, Dunia, I have no mind for political talk right now. I'm just trying to make ends meet."

Louisa and I look at one another and wish we could find out

more about their beliefs. Then Louisa pumps me for information. "Do you have relatives in New York?"

"No, I have no one there."

"How about friends?'

"No."

I'm curt because I don't want to discuss leaving Tel Aviv, but she can't stop.

"Aren't you curious to see Broadway?"

"No."

On Saturday we go to meet Mama's cousins Binem and Chaim. They are brothers who settled in Palestine. Binem's daughter, Ora, comes into the house as we sit relaxing in wicker chairs on the porch. "*Shalom*, everyone," she calls out cheerfully from the hallway, then pops her head in to see who is visiting. I can hardly believe my eyes. Oh, my God, I look at the insignia on her smart military uniform. She is not just any soldier, she's a *sagan aluf*, a lieutenant colonel! I am so impressed I nearly forget how to say *shalom*.

Ora chats with me in a friendly way while I sit there trying to convince myself she is a relative. Her graceful movements, gentle and refined, have none of the brusqueness I imagined in a soldier. Later she changes into a white blouse with Yemenite embroidery and looks so regular, just a girl in shorts. Of course, I know women serve in the Israeli military, but my own cousin, an officer? I wish I could have paraded with her in front of the bullies in my Łódź courtyard.

Cousin Chaim comes in later enveloped in a cloud of smoke and apologizing profusely for his lateness. "Where is Ninel?" Binem asks. "I thought you were bringing your daughter to meet Dora, Anat and Daniel."

"Today she is at the beach with her friends," Chaim says,

flicking the ash of his smoldering cigarette over the porch railing. "Next time, she'll come."

"There may not be a next time," Mama says.

"What? You have your visas already?"

"No, but I'm bracing myself," she said.

"Oy, *Dvoyrele, Dvoyrele*, you can be so dramatic." By the look on his face I can tell their relationship goes all the way back to her time in Palestine. Chaim is an interesting man with penetrating black eyes and a mop of wavy, black hair that looks artistically disheveled. His teeth and fingers are yellow-stained from tobacco and he paces a lot. He speaks with Mama for a while but she says, "Daniel has a test tomorrow. We have got to get back early so he can review." She puts down her tea glass and stands up.

The cousins part reluctantly with a promise for another visit soon. On the way back I ask Mama, "What is that weird name of Chaim's daughter? I haven't yet met any girls here named Ninel."

Mama chuckles. "If you read her name backwards, you'll know Chaim's political affiliation."

"What?" It doesn't make sense. Then I gasp. "Mama, how can Ninel go through life with such a stupid name?"

"I don't think anyone would try reading her name backwards."

"Hmm..." It takes me a moment to absorb this notion. Then I remember all those visa application forms where Tinek had to list our relatives.

"Mama, what if some US government official figures out the anagram?"

"Then getting a visa to America may be out."

25

In his letter, posted from Naples, which we practically tore out of the mailman's hand, Tinek described his first stop:

Today our ship docked in Naples for a short while. An excursion to Pompeii is available and, amazingly, there is just enough time to sightsee and get back in time for the ship's departure from port. I can't overcome the temptation of seeing it but feel very guilty about not sharing this exciting experience with you and about spending money on it. I'll add a note when I return...

I'm back. Incredible! My guilt did not diminish my appreciation of these fascinating ruins. The place is unbelievable; I hope that one day we can go there together.

Tinek's expression of guilt made me happy at first, but a moment later I was overcome by shame. Why shouldn't he have enjoyed the beauty of antiquities. Father also wrote to us while at sea, en route to Gibraltar:

My dearest sweethearts,

At this moment my view is that of the shores of Spain. At 6:00 PM we will be in Gibraltar. This is my third letter since I got on the way. I have an idea. Why don't you save these letters for me as a souvenir of this momentous voyage.

I have to tell you about today's horrible storm. People are vomiting; it's frightful. The ship rocks so fiercely that everything flies in the air: dishes, glasses, platters of food, utensils. I heard some people even fell out of their beds. The sailors tie ropes, so we can hold on to them and stay on our feet. But me? I feel great! At this moment the sea is calm and has a golden glow from the setting sun. I have been without you two Fridays already. I miss you! Ania and Daniel, please help Mama as much as possible.

Layla Tov, goodnight, my dears.

After crossing the Atlantic, Tinek landed in the Canadian port of Halifax. Busting with excitement, he sent a three-word telegram to his sister: "*Arrived in America!*" To us he posted a letter telling all about the amazing sights of Halifax, the sleepy harbor town.

"*...You wouldn't believe the gorgeous shops here and the incredible merchandise! Dora, the brassieres here have cup sizing and you can adjust the size of the band. What an invention! Did you ever hear of such a thing? And they cost 95 cents! There are no people on the streets, only cars. And the neon lights? Unbelievable! Tel Aviv's best movie house can hide. It cannot compete with what they have here. I can't call Rosa because there are no American telephone books here. I found my friend Janek in the phone book, but a call to Toronto is $1.70 and all I have left after I bought a gift of liquor for Rosa on the ship is $2.50. I used some of it to make a souvenir medallion with my name and the date of my arrival...*"

Tinek's mention of Janek, the very one who played with me in Poland when I was three, brought a smile of recognition to my face. In a way, I envy Tinek for having friendships that go back so many years. This is something I may never have. Daniel and I pull out the atlas and mark the places where Tinek has set our family's first footsteps on the road to America.

At long last, on March 25th, 1959, Father's ship docked in the harbor of the Promised Land. The Statue of Liberty, the lady who had been his obsession since Poland had now materialized in front of him in all her copper glory. She seemed to beckon to him directly. He was mesmerized. And soon another lady whose magnetic pull was even stronger—his sister Rosa—overwhelmed all his other impressions.

In his first letter from New York he wrote:

Dearest Dora, dearest kiddies,

I am writing this in a telegraphic style. Finally, after such a long voyage, my ship arrived thirty-three hours late. We pulled into the ZIM line berth at 4:00 PM. The skyscrapers made a thunderous impression on me, as did the Statue of Liberty! Immigration officials boarded our ship when we were still far at sea to inspect documents and deal with various formalities. When we disembarked we went through duty and baggage control in a huge arrivals hall. They asked me to pay duty of $2.90 for the gift bottle I brought for Rosa. I told the official I didn't have that much money. The next minute, I heard him paging Rosa on the loud speaker.

A few moments later an elegant lady, dressed like a countess, emerged from the huge crowd. She was crying, yelling my name. I hardly recognized her; she had gotten so thin—American style! Of course, she paid. I can see already how she has been influenced by America. I told her she was too thin. There were no stick-like women in my family. Then before I knew it, I was in the arms of the rest of the contingent that came to greet me. We got into Jack's car for a 90-minute trip into the unknown, his apartment in a place called Queens...

Aunt Rosa hadn't seen my father, her baby brother, since the war. Exactly twenty years have passed since that night when the Nazis invaded Poland and she hugged him, adjusted his backpack, and said, "Run and be safe, Nachman, and watch out for the snipers near the river. Don't worry about me, I'll be fine." Neither of them had any way of knowing if the other had changed in those miserable intervening years. For now they just bathed in the glow of togetherness. His haphazard report told us that Tinek was overwhelmed and dazed, but happy. Very, very happy. He achieved his impossible dream.

My father's expectation of how America's freedoms influence people's outlook and behavior for the better are soon shattered, or so we'll find out in subsequent letters.

Though Rosa is warm enough and eager to help him, Tinek is taken aback by her changed demeanor. He writes us that the sparkle in her eyes has been extinguished by her wartime experiences. She no longer hums as she goes about her day, the way she used to. She speaks only when spoken to. There is a perpetual anguish in her eyes and in her expression. How can she pay attention to superficial things when her gut aches for her murdered child and the first husband whom she loved so much?

To make matters worse, Avram, her new husband, a very observant Jew, insists on strict religious practice, including daily attendance in the synagogue. Tinek is dismayed when his newly minted brother-in-law says, "Nachman, if you want to get a job in Harrisburg you will have to join our synagogue and attend services regularly. If you don't join, *we* will be very embarrassed, and besides, no Jewish business in this town will give you a job."

My first thought when I read this letter was: Uncle Nechemiah could teach Avram a lesson on tolerance.

I know that in America Tinek expects minds to be as wide open as opportunities in the land of plenty. I also know he'd never consider the idea of pretending to be what he is not, not even if getting a job depends on it. I can tell from his letters that what bothers him most is that his worldly sister married a man so unlike the free-thinking Bundists she used to spend time with before the war.

"Maybe as a survivor of a concentration camp Avram understands Rosa's sorrow like few others. He is a decent man and a good provider, though not someone to whom I can relate," Tinek writes.

Not wanting to offend his newly found family and feeling

suffocated by the daily religious rituals, Tinek departed for New York soon after his arrival in Harrisburg. We found this out from a letter that has been delayed by three whole days; usually Tinek sends daily missives. Mama opens the airmail envelope very slowly and carefully because he writes right up to the edges of the one-sheet aerogram, and we don't want to lose a word. She reads it silently to herself first. Daniel and I sit at the table, our soup getting cold, trying to read the contents from Mama's face.

"So what does it say, Mama?" Daniel, closest to her, cranes his neck trying to see.

"Your father is moving to New York."

"Where will he stay?" Daniel sounds alarmed, as if he were the one imminently homeless.

"With his friends."

"But how will he manage?" I jump in.

"Don't underestimate your father. He will make it, somehow."

I cannot accept her easy answer. "How will he survive without any money, without a place to live, without the language?"

"Children don't need to worry about their parents. It's the other way around."

Children? She thinks I'm still a child! I walk out of the room without another word. I feel sick with worry over Tinek's uncertain fate. From now on I hover around the mailbox every afternoon looking for the mailman.

Now when the blue envelopes arrive, each one bears a different return address. Tinek writes:

"...I live a week with one friend, then with another. I haven't seen these people since the seventh grade! I don't want to impose. They have wives, husbands, families, yet they treat me like a brother and are trying to help me find a job..."

I have visions of another frustrating job search, but then I remember—he is in America.

26

Yom Tov comes over almost daily now, except on the days I have my tutoring sessions with Amnon. He says he doesn't like Amnon, but I tell him it's absurd—he hasn't even met the man. I think he's jealous, and I am flattered. I am never as thrilled with our dates as I am every Thursday, sitting next to Amnon inhaling the fragrance of his cologne, staring at the stubble on his jaw and watching his hands as he writes out reading suggestions for me. Though officially Yom Tov is my boyfriend, we are more like kissing buddies. Yom Tov is a notch above Nachum, but he can't hope to reach Amnon's status.

Sometimes instead of going out we listen to Daniel playing his accordion. I like to imagine he is performing especially for us, but Daniel is just living up to the solemn promise he made Tinek—to practice daily. Rimsky-Korsakov's *Flight of the Bumblebee* is my favorite in Daniel's extensive classical repertoire. The way his short little fingers caress the keyboard and move with lightning speed you'd think Daniel was a whole orchestra. When he tugs at the folds of the accordion it's as if he expands its lungs and brings it to life with each breath. What amazing sounds he can coax out of his piano in a box. Its bright red-and-silver body sparkles as he tugs at it and I can only think of how impressed Tinek would be seeing him practice without the usual urging. I'll have to write him about that.

As I listen to Daniel play, I wish it were I who was drawing such heavenly music out of an inanimate object, but then I remember Tinek's music test I failed back in Poland and decide not to report on Daniel's progress. The sting of that test, so many years ago, is still with me. And Daniel has not taught me to play, which was part two of the deal.

I will write Tinek about Daniel's drawings. This afternoon, as Yom Tov and I walked out on the balcony, Daniel sat there with the newspaper spread before him. At first, I thought he was reading, but then I noticed that he'd drawn figures all over the white spaces. "Why don't you sketch Yom Tov?' I suggested, only half serious, because I've never seen him draw people we know.

"I can't."

"Why?"

"Because the exaggerated features in caricatures can offend people."

"Okay, then do me."

"I won't. You'd kill me." He began to laugh.

Daniel creates dozens of sketches in every spare minute when he is not practicing the accordion. Nothing escapes his pencil: napkins, envelopes, and like today, edges of newspapers. His caricatures of world leaders are uncanny. His incisive eye captures all their flaws: Chairman Mao's pudgy face and pouty lips, Konrad Adenauer's narrow-eyed gaze, and Khrushchev's deceptively jolly face and shiny pate. Maybe I will get him a leather-bound sketch book for his next birthday when he turns thirteen.

"Daniel, you will become an artist one day?" Yom Tov asks.

"Nah, this is not real art."

"So what is it?"

"I don't know, just doodles," Daniel says, not lifting his head from the piece he is drawing.

Lately, I find it hard to concentrate thinking about our uncertain future. I have a foreboding deep in my bones that our days in Israel are numbered. Before we leave, I must engrave it on my brain so it'll remain with me, inside me, cleaved to my cells forever. I crave the kind of deep emotional connection to Jerusalem that all Israelis have—the deeply religious and the secular. Until now, for me, Jerusalem has aroused little emotion. It has been distant like the farthest star, not in kilometers, but emotionally. I want it to become like Gvat and Tel Aviv that have taken such deep root in my heart. And a perfect opportunity to that has just arisen. My school is organizing a field trip to Jerusalem. I desperately want to go.

"Mama, please, may I have the money for the trip? We need to put down a deposit by next week."

"Let me pay the bills first, then we'll see."

"But I don't want to miss the deadline."

She sighs, stops the sewing machine and says, "Bring me my purse. It's in the living room."

I look for her bag feeling guilty. This is probably the worst time to be asking; expenses for Tinek's departure have drained all spare cash and she doesn't have many new customers right now. I bring the purse. Mama rummages through it and hands me five crumpled lira. I hesitate, but she says, "Take it. Who knows? A new client may walk in tomorrow."

Our bus arrives at the bustling main station on Jaffa Road in downtown Jerusalem. I am here at last! My classmates and I spill out of the bus like tourists, then stroll slowly through the western portion of the city that isn't occupied by the Jordanians. We look at storefronts, stop for sodas and warm pitas, but everyone is anxious to see that which is inaccessible—the Wailing Wall. During much of our bus ride the teacher discussed the tragedy of having our capital under occupation.

In this section of the city the buildings look quite modern and all are covered in blond Jerusalem stone. I know from pictures that the Old City on the Jordanian side is ancient, exotic, exciting, but we can't get there or anywhere close to the Western Wall. We call it the Wailing Wall in memory of the sorrow for the destruction of the Second temple in 516 BCE. I never knew that until we studied that period in my Tel Aviv school.

By late afternoon, tired, we climb Mount Zion, so we can see the Wall behind barbed wire, but only from a distance. Our group leader, a teacher from another class, distributes the boxed dinner: soggy sandwiches, cold hard-boiled eggs, and oranges. We eat hurriedly sitting on the ground and rock outcroppings with little conversation because everyone wants to get to the overlook before dark. As the sky pinkens we are ready.

Huge blocks of sand-colored stone form the Wall; clumps of vegetation cling to the cracks between the stones, dipping their roots into history, giving life to the barren wall.

"*Hine, hine,*" the teacher moves to a new overlook and calls us to see the Wall at a better angle as the setting sun glows golden on the stone.

"I wonder if I'll ever get to pray at the Wall," says Aryeh, a boy with soulful black eyes. He is in another class. I barely know him, but I hear such longing in his voice.

"One of these days all of Jerusalem will be ours," the teacher says, and Aryeh smiles, like he believes her. The teacher's comment makes me wonder if my cousin Ora wants to fight for our capital. Would I?

Soldiers with machine guns patrol the area. It's a disappointment not to get closer. I console myself: it's just a retaining wall, not the *actual* temple wall.

For the night, all of us, thirty students and two teachers, stay on the mountaintop in an abandoned school building. It has no facilities of any kind, except some long, worn tables too old for salvage. We spend an uneasy night here overlooking the fog-filled valley. As soon as the sun sets, it is freezing. This is the first time I shiver in the land of the sun. Not wanting to curl up on the filthy floor, or risk vermin climbing over me, I, as most of my classmates, opt to sleep on a table—if you can call it sleep. I'm so worried I'll take a tumble onto the cement floor when I turn that sleep evades me almost till dawn. The whole experience makes me think of my father and his discomfort sleeping in strangers' beds. It also brings up my ill-defined relationship to this wall that demands prayer—something in which I don't believe.

I rise to a glorious dawn: sky painted in pink streaks, the air still crisp with the chill of night and dew glistening on the grass like scattered diamonds. For a moment I feel as if I were here entirely alone, like a hermit on a mountain top, but I see Aryeh standing at the overlook. His wiry body, muscular arms and blue *kippah,* a perfect image. His hair is messy, it sticks up in the air at odd angles, but his reverent stance gives him a strange dignity. He turns as I approach. "Shh..." is all he says, putting his finger to his lips. Sunlight shines on the Wailing Wall, making it glow. The silence and light transform the whole mountaintop into a cathedral. We both stand there immersed in private thoughts. He is probably praying. I am beginning to sense a little bit of the mystery and power infused in these stones.

Today the Wall is not just a pile of old rock, a historic relic. Somehow, the stones have begun to acquire a deeper meaning for me. And I think of all the people who have poured out their hearts here over the centuries shedding oceans of tears. It is as if my forefathers are sending me a timeless message: *this is your land, treasure it always.* On this very morning I feel connected to the ancient past as I have never felt before. For a brief moment I forget that barbed wire and guns separate me from the Wall and I have an indescribable urge to touch its stones. I imagine they would feel warm, like something alive.

As the sun rises higher in the sky, one by one, bleary-eyed classmates emerge from the old school building. The teacher comes out too, her long skirt awfully creased. She smiles and yells *"Boker tov!"* Her morning greeting doesn't break the spell. Jerusalem is already mine to keep in all its golden glory. Forever.

27

My spirits lift when Mama announces cousins, Arthur and Basia, will be visiting from Paris with their mother, Mania. She is very close to Mama and has a warm place in my heart too. I haven't seen Arthur in over four years and I wonder how he looks today. He is sixteen and I'm already fifteen and a half. What will we say to each other now that we are no longer kids? I can't wait for him to arrive.

Arthur gives me an awkward hug as we meet at the airport and my cheeks redden with embarrassment. I hadn't expected him to be quite so tall, or to have the light fuzz on his face that will surely turn into a man's stubble very soon. "Ania, you look so different!" he exclaims in a voice deeper than I remember.

"You do too."

He is not the shy blond cousin I knew in Poland. Maybe it's the way he is dressed. With his well-shined shoes, and a shirt with elegant cufflinks, topped by a silky gray sweater he looks like a suave Frenchman. The next day, our mothers spend hours talking and after a while they suggest that we go to the movies. I am excited and hope my friends will see us together. I will tell them Arthur's my new boyfriend. Poor Daniel, he has to stay home keeping Basia, Arthur's little sister, company.

We take a short walk to the movie theater and I glance around corners to see if my friends are anywhere around. They aren't. Arthur buys tickets and I can't wait to enter the darkness of the theater. I don't know what I am expecting, but I can't help thinking it will be something special. It's just after noon, so the theater is nearly empty.

"Where would you like to sit?"

"Oh, it doesn't matter," I say, but I move into the back row.

We sit self-consciously until the movie starts. We lean back in the plush red velvet seats making them rock. As the coming attractions begin, he leans over and whispers to me in French, something I don't understand. At the moment I don't care what he says. It sounds exciting, like something a real French boyfriend might say. I shift in my chair and our shoulders touch in the narrow seats. I wonder if he'll take my hand, but he doesn't. The movie is *Bonjour Tristesse*—Hello Sadness. It is a perfect choice because Arthur has already read this novel by Françoise Sagan. I sneak glances at him as the plot unfolds and see him nodding in recognition at some scenes. I will ask him how the movie compares to the book.

After the movie, we walk on the beach and tell one another how we managed to get adjusted to our new countries, Israel and France. I love to hear him speak. His Polish is already accented with French. It sounds so cosmopolitan.

"Arthur, did you have trouble pronouncing French words when you first got there? Were you worried that people would laugh at your attempts to speak?"

"Not really. I spoke mostly to my Polish cousins who landed in Paris before us. Their French wasn't too good either."

"That's cheating," I say to tease him. "At least you didn't have to study the Mishnah like I did."

"What's the Mishnah?"

"Something you should read one day."

When their visit nears the end, I hope against hope the flight to Paris will be postponed so they can stay longer. No luck. After lengthy goodbyes in the terminal, we walk Arthur, his mother and sister out on the tarmac. Just before he boards the plane, Arthur turns to me and gives me a much less awkward hug this time. Our eyes lock for a moment. I have the oddest feeling of dread, but I don't know why. "Please, write me," I whisper to him. He flashes me a brilliant smile and waves as he ducks to enter the plane.

Now I wait for Tinek's letters *and* Arthur's, my trips to the mailbox that much more urgent. Tinek's letters arrive on schedule but nothing from Arthur. I'm disappointed, but at last I run into the mailman. "Do you have anything for us?"

"You have to sign for it."

"Why, what is it?"

"A telegram."

I'm puzzled, but I sign and grab it from his hands. It's from Mania! What's so urgent? Arthur's wedding? I bring it in and give it to Mama. She opens it and her face collapses.

"What's wrong, Mama? What's wrong?"

"Arthur is dead."

"What are you saying?"

"He drowned in a pool," she says, still reading, and stands up trying to hug me, but I run out and throw myself on the bed. Choking sobs shake my whole body. Snot clogs my breath. It can't be. Young people don't just die. Images of his lifeless body pulled from the water flash before me. No! No, it must be a mistake. Two hours pass and my ribs are sore from sobbing. Mama knocks on the door, but I can't speak to anyone. All I can see is Arthur's mouth, his lips forming the words, explaining the meaning of the movie's title: Hello Sadness. Did he have a premonition? For days I mourn

241

my first death, silently, drained of tears, but not of the images: us in the theater, us hugging at the airport, then thuds of earth hitting his casket. I don't want to see Yom Tov and I can't write Tinek about this. I cannot upset him. He has enough to worry about right now. I feel alone in my grief.

Sławka, an old classmate from Poland, learns of the tragedy from Mama when they bump into one another at the grocery. She comes to our place and says, "Come with me to the beach, Ania."

"I don't feel like having fun right now," I say, sitting in my pajamas amid crumpled blankets and books.

"You have got to get out of your doldrums. You can't sit home and mourn for the rest of your life," she says. "And why don't you bring Daniel too?"

"Getting close to water is just about the last thing in the world I want to do now!" I tell her. But a tiny notion begins to flicker in my gut: I have to overcome my terror of water.

Sławka stands in the doorway of my bedroom, then walks over to my bedside. She is wearing a bathing suit under her gauzy shirt, her large breasts clearly outlined as she leans over to hand me tissues. She pats my shoulder. I can see from the determined expression behind her smile that she's on a mission. "Ania, you like my parents, don't you? They specifically asked for you to join us. Please come."

In the end, I give in because I really need to lift myself out of the deep well into which I have fallen. The possibility I will have to leave Israel depressed me enough, and now a death. If I don't climb out soon I might descend to such depth that I will never emerge. Besides, I really adore Sławka's parents: her mother, Valentina, was a Russian ballerina and her father, Arkady, a musician. They are fun to be with. I force myself to go.

Daniel agrees to join though neither he nor I are swimmers. Inexplicably though, perhaps even perversely, we have an odd attraction to the sea: the sound of the waves crashing on the shore, the calls of the gulls, the azure water, and the funny shapes of people frying themselves on the beach. Maybe it's Mama's influence. She adores the sea even though she can't swim either. I pack towels and slip into my one-piece black bathing suit, glancing in the mirror on my way out of the bedroom.

Sławka and her parents wait for us outside, a taxi idles at our curb. Valentina is tall and slender, nothing like my mother or my aunts. Years of Tchaikovsky and a lifetime of plies have made her legs muscular and strong. Despite her eighth month of pregnancy she looks graceful. It's as if her belly is just a ballet prop. Arkady is very handsome, with shiny black hair slicked back neatly, and a narrow, neat mustache on his tanned face. They are always elegantly dressed and look as though they may break into a waltz or tango at any moment. Today their lively presence is especially welcome.

"Anat!" Valentina exclaims and tries to hug me, but her big belly gets in the way and we laugh. I haven't done that in a long while.

On the quieter, northern beach, we spread out our towels strategically, taking spots away from clumps of families. I cannot explain what happens next. After we sit staring at the waves for a few moments I call out to Daniel, "Hey, want to go in the water?" I need to convince myself that water—the cradle from which we once emerged—is not the enemy and that Arthur's drowning was a once-in-a-lifetime freak accident. And Daniel has to go in with me because I am responsible for him whenever our parents aren't around.

"Sure," he says, approaching with something circular, large, and dark.

"What is this?" I look suspiciously at the strange black rubber object.

"Sławka says we can hold on to this inflated tube when we go into water. It floats. You don't need to swim to use it."

"All right," I say, still dubious.

We stop at the edge where the first cool wave reaches our toes.

Daniel is holding the inner tube and looks up the sky. "Look at all those gulls," he says, but I barely hear him over the roar of the waves. We enter the water cautiously. I hold Daniel's hand and squeeze harder when he tries to get free. To my surprise, the water lapping at my white ankles feels balmy and soothing. Daniel and I grab a hold on each side of the tube as we walk in deeper.

I am surprised that it lifts us. It makes me feel almost confident. Daniel, floating now, kicks his legs pretending to swim. "Try it," he yells, but I am trying to walk on my toes, still too cautious. After a while, we both float a little farther from the shore and hang on, beginning to savor our buoyant state. The shore recedes and our nervousness dissipates bit by bit. We are in an aquatic trance. We both kick our legs and feel light, as if our bodies have grown air bladders.

Suddenly, something strange happens. I feel a powerful tug on my legs. They are being pulled and pushed against my will. Daniel calls out, "What is happening?" in a high-pitched tone, and this is when it occurs to me that an undercurrent is pulling at us. We begin to kick and flail frantically as we whirl in a circle. "Hold on tight, Daniel!" I yell at top of my lungs and can't catch my breath. The whirlpool is about to swallow us. We struggle furiously against it to no avail. We scream and scream, but the relentless sound of the surf deadens our voices.

Someone on shore must have seen us flailing because we see a figure swimming toward us as we float farther and farther away despite our panicky effort to stay in place. It's Valentina! Despite her pregnancy she is stronger than the wild current. She calls out over the din of the waves, "You just hold on tight. I have got it!" Then she wraps her slender arm around the tube between Daniel and me and uses her free arm to move through the water. She pulls us toward the shore with superhuman force. Her face is down. We can hear her breathing hard, gulping air. Her hair is wet. For an instant it looks as if we are stationary, but then she pulls forward, dragging us glued to the tube behind her. The shore is getting closer.

Exhausted, she drags us onto the beach just as lifeguards bring in a rescue boat. She is triumphant and smiling. Arkady runs toward her, but she shakes the water off her long hair, spraying him and says, "Wait," looking in our direction. We cough and spit the water we have swallowed and are too frightened to say anything. We just nod our heads when everyone around us asks, "Are you all right? Are you really all right?" My whole body trembles as Valentina wraps me in a towel and repeats over and over, "Don't worry, I am here. You will be fine."

If she hadn't saved us we might have joined Arthur. Why wasn't there a French Valentina to save him?

Somehow, I think none of these awful things would be happening if my father hadn't left. His departure set in motion a chain of misfortunes as surely as a volcanic explosion augurs the arrival of fire, putrid gasses, and black lava. I'm not telling Tinek about it. He warned us not to go near water.

I drape my towel over Daniel sitting very subdued on Slawka's blanket. "Want to go home?" I ask, rubbing his back.

At night a wave of thoughts about death assaults me. All those conversations about the murder of our family members by the Nazis lulled me into a belief death was the result of human evil. It never occurred to me that death can take many forms, can arrive on a sunny day as one splashes joyously in a pool, or swims in luxuriant ocean waves. The ubiquity of it! The fact that I and everyone I love will die one day overwhelms me. I must rip thoughts of mortality out of my mind.

28

These have been five of the longest months of my life. Daily, I snatch aerograms out of the mailbox as if they held our fate, a future as flimsy as the paper of which they are made. Another one has arrived this afternoon. I open it even before coming into the apartment.

Tinek writes:

"...I heard from my friend about a book called A Nation of Immigrants. It is written by Senator John Kennedy who is planning to run for President. Kennedy says that the limitations on immigration would even make the Statue of Liberty blush. Can you believe it? An American Senator taking the side of immigrants..."

Tinek also writes the US Congress has passed another law that gives preference for visas to individuals trying to bring their spouses or children into the country. It sure looks like our prospect for visas is improving. The realization gives me shivers.

I walk out on the balcony holding the letter. The June air is heavy with moisture. The tall pine trees bordering our building lean over the terrace spreading their green aroma into my nostrils.

Mama's favorite trees! Daniel sits there reading *Haaretz* and doodling occasionally. With the newspaper in his hands he seems older. Obsession with the news is something he inherited from Tinek. "What's this? Another letter from Dad? Let me see it," he demands and I hand him the tissue-thin envelope. He makes his way through a sea of Tinek's tiny letters.

"Wow! We may be leaving soon. I like this Kennedy guy!"

Mama hears us. "Why didn't you give me the letter first?" she asks irritated, walking onto the balcony.

Daniel hands her the letter looking smug. "We'll be leaving soon," he says.

She blanches. I can see the tremble in her hands as she reads. When she's done with the letter, Mama says, "I'll have to ask Mendl to make good on his promise."

"What promise was that?" Daniel asks.

"To help me pack."

"But we didn't get our visas yet," he says.

Mama's face darkens, she's biting her lip. "I want to be prepared the minute they come."

"Mama, I thought you weren't in such a hurry to leave," I say.

"Once the die is cast, there is no looking back," she says.

Mendl arrives full of energy. He looks dapper in his worn leather motorcycle jacket. His small wiry body smells of cigarettes and cologne. He rubs his hands and repeats assurances about his packing expertise. He points to the bag he brought with packing supplies. Mama looks at him quizzically and asks, "What did you ever have to pack? Didn't you run from Poland and from the Soviet gulag with nothing but the shirt on your back?"

Mendl waves his hand in exasperation. "Give me your most important things first, Dora."

Mama reaches into the china closet and brings out the two antique Meissen plates. Tinek, Daniel and I bought them for her one Mother's Day, long ago. I am tickled to know that she considers them to be her most valuable possessions. Remembering how she smiled one of her rare luminous smiles the day she received this gift I marvel again at the elaborate flower designs and delicate lace-like border that surrounds each plate. Mendel pulls out sheets of wrapping paper from his bag. He swaddles each plate like a frail infant and places it in the packing box.

"If these arrive in one piece, I'll send you a medal, Mendl," Mama says looking pleased, but I detect a hint of cynicism in her voice.

I arrive home in a bubbly mood after a lesson with Amnon and retrieve a letter from the hallway mailbox. After months of uncertainty and a growing stack of letters bearing discouraging news from Tinek, I always hope for something uplifting. I bring the letter into the kitchen where Mama is preparing dinner. "Look what I have." I wave the envelope in the air. Mama looks up from the counter where she is dicing an onion and I wonder if her wide-eyed expression means she knows something. Daniel sits at the kitchen table drawing. "Let me see it!" He grabs for the envelope.

"No, Mama has to read it first," I push his arm out of the way. She rinses her hands and slices the envelope with her paring knife. We watch her reading and chewing her lip. Finally she tells us the news. Like a triumphant trumpet call, Tinek announces: "Your visas are being issued as I write this!" I take the letter from her hands, wanting to see it with my own eyes, but it's there carved in black, like a commandment.

I feel deflated; my afternoon balloon has been pricked. The air is leaking out and my sense of security and stability goes with it. Mama says, "You two better go organize your things so I can finish packing. Daniel, don't forget to take your sketch pads." Daniel is flushed with excitement.

"I can buy new ones in New York. I bet they have good ones and special pencils too," he says, his eyes glistening. He is the only one here enthusiastic about the future before us. He looks as if he can already see the buildings, the cars, and bridges that Father has written about.

I can't think of America. The only thing in my mind now is how I will part with the people I love, those who are staying and fulfilling the destiny of the Jews. What will I say to Yom Tov, to Amnon, to Ruthi? Will they think I am a traitor to Israel?

When he notices my long face, Daniel asks, "Don't you want to see the skyscrapers, or the lights of Broadway? I sure do!"

"No, I don't. All I want to see is Tinek. He is the only reason to leave."

Like a stoic, Mama goes about the business of undoing our Israeli lives. I can't understand the source of her calm as she sorts our belongings, packs, settles bills, and pays goodbye calls in a kind of mechanical stupor. She has put an ad in the newspaper trying to sell our stuff: bicycles, dishes, fans, a toaster, down quilts and embroidered linens she brought from Poland.

Daniel turns out to be a major asset in dealing with people who respond to the ad. He shows them the items, talking up their quality as if he were a salesman. "No, this is the price. We cannot lower it. It's a bargain," he says to a man who showed up to look at Daniel's bike. I'm stunned at his ability to do this. He finally makes Mama smile when he says, "It's a miracle I don't have to sell my accordion."

As the final step, Mama cleans out her workshop and gives all remaining corsetry supplies to Esther to dispose of as she sees fit. The atmosphere in our home is wretched. There are no joyous parties like the ones that welcomed us two years ago. I almost start wishing to get away, anything to break this foul mood.

We are departing this week. Uncle Maxim comes for a final visit. He is not my favorite relative, but I am very touched that he brings me a parting gift—a leather-bound volume of the *Tanakh*, the Hebrew bible. I thank Uncle, and go to the other end of the living room to avoid his signature cheek pinches. He speaks with Daniel and Mama while I open the book inhaling the distinctive new book smell, then flip to page one. The inscription brings tears to my eyes: "To my introspective niece, till we meet again in Jerusalem." Between its leather covers I can take with me the Books of Moses, The Prophets, and the Writings. This is my ultimate Israeli keepsake, thousands of years of Jewish history, and my favorite prophet—Jeremiah—all packed into this tiny book. I close the Tanakh and move to sit with my uncle on the sofa. Right now I won't even mind if he pinches my cheek.

On our last Saturday, a hellishly hot, sticky day, Yom Tov comes to say goodbye. We walk on the beach, but we have little to say to one another. Our palms stick together and this time, for the first time, it starts to bother me. I hadn't noticed his sweaty palms before. He has an irritating hangdog look. Haven't I already told him that it's not my decision to leave? Why doesn't he understand? I promise to write. He promises to come to New York as soon as he completes his military service. My God, that could be three or four years from now! It's a lifetime. My brain can't project that far into the future. "Anat, promise you won't forget me in New York," he says mournfully as if he already knows that I will. As we part, Yom Tov embraces me and leans into me to give me a kiss. I can smell the *falafel* on his breath, our teeth bump awkwardly. His arms are around my waist, his hands on the small of my back. I stiffen. He just says, "Anat, you need to be more flexible." But I stand there like a wooden doll.

I pull away. "My mother wants me back early," I say, knowing full well she is not home. As I walk away, I hear Yom Tov's voice echoing in my head, "Anat, Anat, Anat, you must be more flexible," and I start to hate this moment and my name too.

The evening ends with a sorry little gathering of our neighbors. The Sapersteins, from the floor above us, come down with a basket of sabras, prickly pears, "So you'll remember *eretz halav u dvash*, the land of milk and honey," Mr. Saperstein says. He smiles a sad smile, and the tears glistening behind his thick glasses look like large raindrops. We have been saying a long goodbye to the aunts, uncles and cousins over the last few weeks, each parting more maudlin than the one before it. These goodbye visits give an unpleasant flavor to the last chapter in the land I have come to call home.

The afternoon of our departure has arrived. With one half of my brain I have hoped that this moment would never come, that I would not have to be plucked out from this sacred soil. And yet, I cannot stand to be separated from Tinek any longer. Our family has been fractured and it must be repaired before the break becomes permanent.

The excess of hugs and tears at the pier rips at my insides. I just want to board the ship and not think about if and when I might return to pick up the pieces of me I am leaving behind.

The port is as lively as ever: piles of baggage, sailors sauntering, passengers arguing. All the vendors I saw when we first arrived in Haifa are still here, permanent fixtures. They still hawk their freshly squeezed orange, carrot, and guava juices; still toss falafel balls in the air; sell the latest editions of papers, but none of it is any longer for us. All these brash sabras, Yemenites, Turks, Moroccans, Ethiopians, the whole astonishing medley of Jewish humanity will be sliced away from us as soon as the ship pulls out. We will no longer belong here.

I start thinking about Odysseus. Will there be Sirens steering us into dangerous waters, hoping we'd lose our way? Will there be

Cyclops-like people just waiting to devour us, to hurl epithets? I have but one thought: whatever trials and tribulations lie ahead of us, we must have faith in ourselves, otherwise we will not make it.

We board the SS *Constitution* and struggle with our bags down, down into the bowels of the leviathan.

PHOTOS

Ania's passport photo upon leaving Poland for Israel
in 1957 (age 13.5)

Dora's sister Chava (left), her husband Benjamin
(right) and their children: Rami, front; Ruthi behind
him; sister Zvia and Moshele, the youngest at the top

Dora's brother Nechemiah Blaustein with his two
sons, Yankel and Avreml wearing Sabbath
clothing and hats

Anat's classmates on Kibbutz Gevat. Anat, top
row, second from left. Her cousin Ruthi, center,
bottom row

Dora's advertising flyer for her bra and corset shop in
Tel Aviv, Israel

Anat and Ruthi saying goodbye at the bus stop
next to a sign for Kibbutz Gevat

PART 3
GREEN

1

I stand on the deck and stare in disbelief as the sun glints off the azure Mediterranean.

The SS *Constitution* glides into the port of Naples. Mama, Daniel, and I have completed the first leg of our voyage to America. I feel as if I have just passed the first section of a difficult exam. I can't decide if I am actually getting a bit excited. Maybe the blinding sun has burned off the miasma that descended on me as we left Haifa. Soon we'll be reunited with Tinek in New York, the place where golden coins are said to pave the streets.

At breakfast, we hear the Captain's announcement over the loud speaker: we are making a short stop, half an hour at most, as a storm is coming in. The ship must pull out as soon as a few new passengers embark. The Captain discourages passengers from disembarking, but I implore Mama, pushing away my toast, "Please let me get off, just for a few minutes."

She looks at me baffled. "What in the world...?"

"I want to find a small present for Tinek. There must be some shops in the port, like in Haifa. We can't meet him empty handed."

"He wants to see us, not presents," she frowns, but then says, "Okay, run and be quick."

I get off the ship and hurry through the Naples wharf looking for a gift shop. I am certain it must be here somewhere. Why did I leave this until the last possible moment? I turn left and right and left again, until I no longer know where I am. There are no shops here, only stacks and stacks of shipping containers waiting to be loaded. They obstruct the view in every direction, compounding my confusion. Nobody seems to be around except groups of longshoremen. They lean against the pallets smoking, chatting, and whistling as they ogle me and make lewd gestures. Tight, striped T-shirts accentuate their wiry physiques.

Too late I realize that my shorts and halter-top aren't helping matters. I am very uncomfortable, even frightened by the unwelcome attention. I glance at my watch and realize I must return to the ship immediately. I begin to run accompanied by increasingly louder catcalls. "*Ciao bella, ciao bella,*" their voices reverberate behind me. My notoriously poor sense of direction has taken me down crisscrossing alleyways far from my ship's dock. It is clear now that I am completely and utterly lost with no idea how to find my way back. My heart is pounding so fast I can feel it in my throat.

The only Italian word I think I know is "*Presto.*" Didn't I see it on an advertising poster for a pressure cooker? I look frantically at my watch and realize the ship will be pulling out in minutes. Crazed with panic, I force myself to overcome my abject embarrassment and approach a group of sailors. Gesticulating wildly, I attempt to convey that I am looking for my ship. I say, "*Presto, Presto,*" in rapid succession to get across the sense of urgency. Some of them smile, some snicker, a few just laugh out loud. I am mortified. An older man speaks in rapid fire Italian. I have no clue as to what he says and his directional arm gestures, likely meant to be helpful, are completely confusing.

As much as I am terrified at being left behind, I am even more worried about my high-strung mother. I imagine her standing on the deck now as panicked as I am, with absolutely no way to find me. As I turn this way and that, I am convinced that a huge ocean liner will not wait for one girl who will not turn sixteen for another month. My watch says that the ship will be departing in two minutes.

I make yet another turn around a stack of pallets and see sailors starting to pull up the gangway on *my* ship. Was it there all the time and I just didn't see it because I was so rattled by the longshoremen? Mama is way up on deck, clearly distraught, arguing with someone in uniform. I surmise she is trying to stall, to buy me time. She saves me. In a moment, the gangplank is back down and I ascend with my eyes downcast. With her flushed cheeks, Mama looks half angry, half relieved.

Chastened, I embark on my third voyage to a new life, and I promise myself that I won't leave important tasks until the very last moment. I must learn how to be a better planner. Mama is strangely silent about this whole incident. She doesn't mention it at all. I think her mind is taken up with trying to imagine our life in New York, just the way my mind is consumed with this question: Will I ever learn how to find my way in the giant metropolis? Mama won't always be there to rescue me.

2

The August weather is not favorable for a transatlantic crossing. Huge waves buffet this grand ship and make me walk like a drunk along the decks, my hair blown to a wild mess by the strong, balmy wind. The SS *Constitution* is a veritable city with rooms for 1,000 passengers. Daniel and I wander around the ship wide-eyed at its gleaming woods, gilded mirrors, luxurious leather banquettes in the dining room and sumptuous silver platters at the buffet. Mama meets an elderly Polish woman wearing a fox stole, sitting on the deck. It turns out that she, too, is sailing to New York. From her, we learn some amazing things about the ship, things I find difficult to comprehend or even to believe, but she must know; she lives in Paris.

Designed to the highest standards, with a sleek, upbeat American sensibility in style, the ship is still quite new. It sailed on its maiden voyage in 1951, just eight years before. It was meant to be glamorous and to appeal to rich American tourists—certainly that doesn't include us—yet.

I find out from the Polish-French lady with the fox stole that just three years ago Grace Kelly sailed on this very ship to her fairy-tale wedding with Prince Rainier. Grace Kelly may have strolled this very deck, seen these very waves foaming, heard the cries of these gulls. I am overcome with the idea that I am walking in her footsteps. Then another passenger tells us that only two years ago *An Affair to Remember* with Cary Grant and Deborah Kerr was filmed on this ship. Harry Truman, Alfred Hitchcock, and Walt Disney boarded this ship, lingered on this promenade, ate in these dining rooms. America is certainly trying to woo me in a most extravagant way.

As I wander the deck, I forget for a short time my fury at having to leave Israel. I try to envision myself as an American, but it's no use. I don't know how to be American. When I lie in my berth at night, the ache in my heart washes over me. It threatens to drown me as surely as one great wave crashing on the deck. Even the image of Grace Kelly, whose perfume I can almost smell, cannot mask my anger at being forced to leave the land of olives and palms. After a while, my agitation subsides with the gentle rocking motion of the ship. As I drift off to sleep, Cary Grant transforms into Amnon and he is the one dancing with Deborah Kerr.

The weather is getting worse each day and the rolling of the ship makes me nauseous. I am feeling lightheaded and shaky. My insides quiver in tune with the waves. I cannot even contemplate joining Mama and Daniel for meals the way my stomach is rebelling. Was Grace Kelly as bothered by seasickness? I can't picture her vomiting her guts out. We have traveled less than a week. How will I survive a two-week trip?

I decide to spend every moment while on-board studying English. If I can just manage to say one whole sentence in English I will feel better. When our cabin mates—a mother with two young children, Lonek and Lilka—aren't making noise, I study my Hebrew-English book. I repeat the words to myself silently, as if I were praying.

263

I cannot imagine going to school in America without knowing a word of English. It terrifies me to think that a new school year will start so soon after we arrive.

Learning Hebrew was tough enough, but I had Aunt Chava to help me at first, and then Ruthi and Nachum and Amnon. English is such a strange and unwieldy language. They say you need to speak it with marbles in your mouth. You don't pronounce certain letters. Why not? Why do they write them if the letters aren't needed? It was bad enough to have to divine the words in written Hebrew without the dots that denote the vowels. It was a perpetual guessing game. In English it's the stupid "th" sound. Sounds like a lisp if you ask me.

I make a promise to myself. If I learn just one sentence in English, I'll try it out on one of the American passengers. I tell Daniel, but he says, "No way. You won't do it. You'll get too nervous. Let's bet on it." Then he adds confidently, "You'll chicken out."

If I weren't so seasick, I would go out on deck to breathe in the salty sea air and watch the shimmering colors of the water. Sometimes smooth and placid like an unwrinkled brow, sometimes angry and passionate, the waters below look like a luminous mixture of liquid silver and gray silk moiré. Sometimes it harmonizes; sometimes it clashes with the sky, but where it meets the horizon you can hardly tell one from the other. Watching the ever-changing seascape feels like a salve on my frayed nerves.

In our minuscule cabin, the two young kids make an incredible racket. Their luggage was lost and never made it to the ship, so the mother is constantly taking up our tiny bathroom washing the kids' one change of clothes in a sink no bigger than a soup bowl. Even little Lonek knows this cabin is not the home he used to know. He constantly pleads in his baby voice, "I don't want this house. I want a house with a kitchen."

I can't stand it when his mother holds Lonek over the sink and lets him pee into it. It's disgusting. I know he's only three, but I can barely bring myself to use that sink afterwards, and I start wondering what the suites on the upper decks look like. Surely, everybody must have bigger quarters than ours, tucked next to the engine room. If there are any other restrooms I could use they are certainly nowhere on our deck in the bowels of this ship.

Daniel tries to make me feel better. Each morning he brings me something called "corn flakes" from the dining room after breakfast because I'm too nauseous to join him and Mama. The funny little chips in a box with a rooster make me think how different they are from the potato chips we are used to. I guess Americans eat chips that are smaller, more delicate, not as greasy. As I comment on how I think Americans eat, Mama says, "No matter how rich they are, they don't eat with two forks at once." I wish I could come up with quick retorts like hers and not get all tongue-tied. I can see from Mama's comment that she expects America to be a place where people get rich, or at least don't have to worry about putting food on the table. This doesn't seem to make her feel any better. She has left behind her family and more friends than I ever hope to have. I am sure she will be relieved to finally see Tinek, but will she ever get used to America? Will I?

I don't worry as much about Daniel, he has plenty of self-confidence. Sometimes when I look at his short chubby physique I can't understand where he gets all that bravado. He walks up and down the decks with a grin showing off his large front teeth where his baby teeth were not so long ago. It's as though he owns this ship. He is good company, especially when I'm feeling low.

When he sees me miserable curled up on my berth he says, "Want to look around the ship? I'll show you some interesting stuff."

"Like what?"

"The Grace Kelly room," he says, as if he knew her personally.

When we walk around the decks and he begins mimicking

Lonek's whining and my expressions upon hearing the little guy pee in the sink, we both burst out laughing. Daniel can be quite the comedian!

With our voyage nearing its end, I practice my one English sentence over and over. If I don't try it out on an American today, or tomorrow at the latest, I'll lose my bet with Daniel. We walk out on the deck, and I carefully observe the strolling passengers. I am trying to pick out someone sympathetic, someone who won't make fun of my pronunciation. It dawns on me it's not a good idea to stop someone who is walking or chatting with a companion. Better to find someone stationary, someone who might be interested in having a conversation. And then I see him: a tall, handsome gentleman leaning against the railing, looking straight toward me. There is just a hint of a smile on his tanned, clean-shaven face. He definitely looks like an English speaker. Yes, he must be. Like a true American, he is wearing a cowboy hat and snakeskin boots. His crisp blue shirt is unbuttoned just enough to give a hint of his hairy chest. His large silver buckle glints in the sun. I muster up all my courage and approach him with false confidence.

"Ex... Excuse me, sir," I say haltingly, my confidence draining out with each passing moment. "Do you, do you speek Ing-leesh?"

My mission is almost complete, but it strikes me that now I'll have to listen to his reply and attempt to understand it. I hadn't calculated that when Daniel and I made the bet.

The man stands up taller, towering over me now. "Young lady, I speak American," he replies in a booming voice.

I am mortified. I didn't know I should be studying American. I thought they spoke English in America. "So, so sorree," I stammer, and dash toward the closest staircase to make my escape. Daniel is right behind me laughing hysterically.

"You won," he says as he catches up to me.

"No," I say, my face still hot from the humiliation. "We have been studying the wrong language!"

For the rest of the trip I am very careful to avoid this man and luckily, I don't see him again.

Today we rise just before dawn. We will be approaching New York harbor as the sun comes up. I am not used to waking up so early, and I move like a sleepwalker. In preparation for disembarking, Mama urges us to hurry, to put our belongings in the small bags we brought on board. I slip into the little bathroom for the last time, hoping to use it before Lonek relieves himself there. I splash cold water on my face and finally fully awake, realize we'll be seeing Tinek in an hour or so. I am excited and nervous. Will he be there at the pier to meet us? Where will we go?

In a short while, Mama, Daniel, and I join the throng of passengers on the deck. It's chilly even though it's an August morning. The breeze blows off the water so hard we can hear the American flag flapping furiously. It moves so rapidly I can't even count its stripes, though I try to. We glide toward the harbor accompanied by excited cries of gulls and air horns of tugboats. And then I see it. I see its towering outline in the distance. There really is a Statue of Liberty! It's the image of America that has been engraved on my brain.

The ship moves forward and she comes into view slowly. Now I can see her majestic green robe and her seven-pointed crown. She looks like a goddess. And the torch! Its flame is really gold, just how I imagined it would be. The Statue of Liberty—it is almost the only thing I know for sure about America—that, and Coca-Cola. I didn't expect to feel this way, but suddenly I want to cheer, but I, like the rest of the people, am silent. Maybe they are all still too sleepy, or maybe they are as awed as I am. The famous New York City skyline, like a picture-perfect postcard, glides closer and closer into view. A fairy-tale city shimmers before our eyes. Mama stands near me with her hands on the railing as if she were already bracing herself for what lies ahead. I want to ask, "Is it real?" Instead, I jostle Daniel's elbow and whisper, "Isn't she beautiful?"

"Who?" he whispers back.

"Lady Liberty."

He gives me a broad smile, and I know that of the three of us, he is the happiest.

3

Tinek is at the head of the entourage waiting for us on shore. We race toward him and throw ourselves into an embrace, the four of us clinging like barnacles. We hug again and again as if we hadn't seen one another for a hundred years. Has it only been eight months?

"Let me look at you," Tinek exclaims. "Ania, you are so tanned! Daniel, how you have grown!" To Mama all he can say is, "Dora, Dora." Then he embraces her again.

When he finally lets go of Mama, he realizes he's overlooked the rest of our greeters. "Oh, I've almost forgotten to introduce everyone." And we meet his sister Rosa, her husband Avram, her two daughters, Faye and Aviva, his good friend Jack with his wife Claire and their daughter. I know these people only from my father's letters and stories. He introduces us to each one with special care, taking pride in saying our names. I feel as if I know Rosa best, but I feel awkward hugging a stranger. She takes the initiative and presses me to her saying, "So this is your beautiful Anetka."

The others just stand there smiling, not wanting to overwhelm us as if we were newly adopted children. I feel as awkward as upon our arrival in Haifa. Jack is the most animated of all, joking trying to break the ice. He's another of my father's fellow inmates from the gulag. My father loaned Jack his shoes during the winter when someone stole Jack's. Jack never forgot my father's kindness; he expressed his gratitude by sending us all those toys from Macy's when we were small kids in Poland.

The introductions done, Tinek beams and repeats over and over, "You are here, you are here. I told you I'd bring you here." He hugs and kisses each one of us in turn and then starts all over again.

The haze that settled over us when Tinek departed Israel is beginning to lift. Seeing his joy and Mama's smiling eyes I begin to believe that things may turn out fine. But Israel... my beloved Israel. I will always long for it.

Of all the people who meet us at the pier, I am most fascinated by my cousin, Faye. I stare at her bright pink lipstick making her lips puffy and luscious and wonder what she thinks of my braids and my mid-calf navy dirndl skirt. Although she's only a couple of years younger than me, she's as sophisticated as the girls and women in American movies. I can't believe we are related!

Faye wears tight turquoise pedal pushers; a low-cut blouse and lots of makeup. I recognize the pedal pushers because Grace Kelly and Audrey Hepburn made them famous. Now, everyone who is anyone in the West wears them: Marilyn Monroe, Sophia Loren, even the American teen idols Annette Funicello and Sandra Dee.

Faye carries a purse in the shape of a large wicker basket with a big gold clasp. This, too, must be the latest American fashion accessory. It dawns on me that she looks very much like the descriptions of American girls I had read in magazines when we were still in Poland. And she's so bosomy! She smiles at me, but we can't communicate. Israel—all over again!

Aunt Rosa smiles a lot too, but doesn't say very much except for a comment to my father. "You are right, Nachman, Anetka does remind me of myself at that age." I find it funny that she still calls me by my baby name. I look at Rosa and can't imagine the comparison to be right, but then I remember my father's letters about Rosa's change and feel sad for her.

As we wait for Jack and Avram to bring their cars from a nearby garage, I overhear Faye saying something to her mother. "What did she say?" I ask my aunt.

"Oh, it's silly. Faye thinks you'll need an American name, not Anetka."

I clarify, "Actually, my name is *Anat* now." I enunciate it clearly; she may not be familiar with Hebrew names.

Faye must have gotten the gist of what I said, because she laughs trying to be discrete and covers her mouth with her hand, then says something to Rosa.

"Why is she laughing?" I ask my aunt.

"Never mind, I don't know what's gotten into her. In English, your Hebrew name sounds like 'a-nut.'"

"So?" I don't get the joke.

Rosa tries to help, "The kind you eat, you know... like a walnut with a shell. Faye wants you to know that in America, a nut is someone not quite right in the head. She is not being mean. She doesn't want kids to make fun of you."

Oh, God, how embarrassing. So it means I'll have to change my name *again*? On second thought, maybe I should keep Anat. Right now, I do yearn for the protection of a hard shell around me and maybe America *will* drive me crazy.

"Look, the cars are here," Tinek says pointing at a station wagon and a large sedan. "This is America." Jack and Avram pull up to the curb and after a brief consultation it is decided that we'll ride with Jack. Rosa and the rest will follow us to someplace called the Bronx.

Jack is thin and has a shiny bald head on top of a skinny neck. He looks like a chicken. He addresses us in Polish, but it is heavily mixed with English so it sounds funny and not entirely intelligible.

Actually, I can understand him better when he speaks in Yiddish to my parents.

Jack is a typographer for the *New York Times* and tries to tell me all about his job. But why now? He natters on and on, but I am not interested in typesetting techniques at the moment. Can't he understand that I am just trying to absorb the fact that I am in New York, in America?

We head north to the sublet my father has prepared for us. As we proceed, Jack keeps saying we are going uptown and that the pier behind us is downtown. I don't know the concept of "uptown" or "downtown." As Jack tries to explain, I keep looking up and down unable to grasp this strange idea. He points in different directions, but none of it makes sense to me. He laughs, and I think he's weird. When he is done with the inexplicable explanations, Jack says, "I'll drive through Manhattan island so you can get your first glimpse of the city." What island? What is he talking about?

I am too overwhelmed to ask questions. We pass buildings taller than mountains. They go on and on and I can't see their tops from my vantage point in the car. There are so many people and everyone seems to be in such a hurry. No one seems to be strolling. And why aren't there any outdoor cafes where people just relax?

"We are not really sightseeing today," Jack says as we pull up to a complex of buildings, "but I just want you to catch a glimpse of Rockefeller Center." I can hardly believe my ears.

"Does Mr. Rockefeller live here?" I ask.

"No, but he built this place so it's named after him. Just take a look at this statue and then we have to move on," Jack says.

All our eyes turn to the golden man. His muscular body gleams in the sun. "Who is he?" I ask with my jaw agape.

"It's Prometheus."

I scramble to remember Greek mythology. "Is he the God who stole fire?"

"Oh, I'm not sure about that," Jack says, "but I know he represents the quest for scientific knowledge. Do you like science?"

"How did you know? It's my favorite subject," I say.

So in addition to Tinek, Jack, Rosa and her family, Prometheus himself welcomes us to America. Unbelievable! Jack's car pulls away and I crane my neck to steal another look at the golden figure.

We arrive at the complex of buildings where Tinek has found us a place to live for a while—another sublet! "I was so lucky to find this place," Tinek says, after he breathlessly lugs our bags five flights up. Silently I count each of the seventy-seven steps and realize right then that I should have shown more appreciation for the ease of our ground-floor sublet in Tel Aviv.

"Tinek, how long will we live in this apartment before we get one of our own?"

"I don't know yet, Ania, for now think of these stairs as good exercise."

Exercise? Does he think I am fat? I thought I had lost my baby fat in Israel. I push away the thoughts of loss and Israel instantly. That was then. This is now.

4

I wake up in the new apartment with the sun shining mercilessly into my eyes through the curtainless window. I stare at the rivulets of dirt on the glass and notice a metal staircase just behind. Why is there a staircase by the window? I lie there for several moments looking around like a recently blinded person struggling to orient myself. I am trying to make sense of a room that is clearly no longer the cabin on the SS *Constitution*. Oh, yes. It's the place Father has sublet to welcome us to America: a one-bedroom flat in the Shalom Aleichem houses in the Bronx.

Though the Bronx is as unfamiliar to me as the moon, at least I recognize the name of the housing development. Who would have thought that in America they would name buildings after one of the greatest Yiddish authors? I would have expected that more in Israel, but that would never happen. Already America is full of surprises. My father introduced me to Shalom Aleichem's stories back in Israel and explained his strange name. It means "peace be unto you" in Yiddish. Shalom Aleichem selected it himself instead of using the name he was given by his parents. Just then it dawns on me. I will have an opportunity like that myself soon. I *must* think of

274

something to replace Anat. Though by now I'm used to my Hebrew name I feel no special attachment to it.

The squeaky springs under the lumpy mattress remind me I am sleeping in someone else's bed. Not that I need reminding. Actually, I would rather not imagine its proper occupant, an elderly widow now residing in a nursing home—a warehouse for old people, is what Mama called it. All of this poor woman's things are still here: her plastic-covered pink sofa and fussy old-fashioned chairs, the closets full of coats reeking of mothballs, even her bureau drawers full of underwear smelling of lavender sachets. I was the lucky recipient of the woman's bed. Daniel got the cot and my parents are sleeping on the pullout couch in the living room.

This morning Mama seems as disoriented as I am. The first night in this strange apartment has done little to make us feel at home. "Nachman, where can I find some bath towels and a coffee pot?" Mama asks, as she wanders through the apartment in a daze, dressed in her blue robe.

"I have no idea, open the cabinets and the closet to check," he says, raising his palms in a gesture of pure puzzlement. "They must be somewhere."

Maybe I am still on Mediterranean time. Maybe I resent being plucked out of the country I have fallen in love with, but for a long while I resist getting up and facing the New York looming just outside the dirty window, cold and huge and totally alien with its uptown and downtown, wherever they are. And then some hidden voice pushes me to get up, to run down the five flights of stairs to see what New York is all about, to listen to people speaking American. Maybe I should check out if the mythic America can ever live up to Tinek's dream. If nothing else, I want to see if all American girls wear pedal pushers and makeup.

I dress and head to the courtyard. "I'll be back soon!" I shout, as I'm nearly out the door.

"Shh... don't wake Daniel," Mama says, "and come back for breakfast."

5

Reddish brick buildings surround the courtyard on all sides. They remind me of the grim textile factories in Łódź. Alongside the buildings green hedges soften the industrial appearance of the large residential houses. Neatly trimmed, the greenery gives the courtyard a slightly less off-putting appearance than yesterday, though it's still devoid of people. I look up and see the strange metal staircases reaching all the windows above the first floor, like the one I saw in front of the bedroom window. I spin around like a top trying to take in all the windows, way up to the top floors. In a short while, people begin walking in and out of the buildings, carrying groceries and laundry baskets. Kids with tricycles emerge from the wooden entry doorways. Women push strollers through the doors. The courtyard is coming to life.

A girl steps out of a building directly across from ours. She walks into the center of the courtyard and looks up at a window on the second floor. Then she yells something and an older woman comes to the window. They exchange a few words. Perhaps it's her mother. Noticing her slim figure and young face, I take the girl for a teenager, and yes, she wears pedal pushers like the ones Faye wore!

High fashion has clearly arrived in the Bronx, but not yet in Tel Aviv. The girl has short brown hair framing her animated, heart-shaped face. She is short and very slight. She approaches me with a broad smile and says something in a thin, breathy tone, but I don't know what it means.

I say, "I not speek Ameriken."

She repeats something several times and points to her chest. "Estelle, Estelle."

Finally I get it. It's her name.

She says slowly, "Not American. You want to speak English."

I only catch on to the one word—"*In-glish*" and I like her already.

Estelle gesticulates and points in the direction of the entry gate to the housing complex. I shrug my shoulders and give her hand signals that say, sorry, but I don't understand. She just keeps talking and smiling and pointing. I listen intently and suddenly realize that there are two words in her jumble of sentences that I do recognize—"Broadway" and "Coca-Cola." She can't be saying, 'Let's go to Broadway to get Coca-Cola,' can she? That sounds too improbable! Broadway is where the stars perform. And Coca-Cola—isn't that a grown-up drink? Does it make you drunk? Estelle pulls me by the hand and I decide, why not? Let me see where she is pulling me. My first decision in America.

We walk several blocks downhill, under elevated train tracks. Estelle points up and says, "subway." She seems to have realized that I can't absorb her long sentences so she speaks in single words, slower, but louder, as if the higher volume would help me understand her better. Subway? Could this be the underground train I have heard about, but why is it above ground? Everything here is crazy. I shrug my shoulders and file this odd fact with "corn flakes," "uptown," "downtown" and the metal staircases on windows. Maybe I'll decipher these imponderables one of these days. Estelle's animated face, excited tone and gestures almost make up for our inability to communicate. She is undeterred by my silence and keeps talking. I imagine she is giving me a tour of the neighborhood and I only wish I could understand it.

We pass many ordinary buildings and not so ordinary car lots with huge American automobiles adorned with shiny wings, just like the ones I've seen in the movies. As we round another corner, I look up and can hardly believe my eyes. Since Polish uses the same alphabet as English, I can read the sign. I say it out loud: *Brodvay*! Estelle claps her hands. I don't yet see any skyscrapers or neon, but I am already wide-eyed with amazement. We approach a large store with a sign that I read as *Vool-vort*, but strangely, Estelle pronounces it as *Woolworth*. Maybe she has marbles in her mouth. She guides us in. It's huge, with shelves bearing all manner of things. I have never seen a store like this!

We meander through aisles laden with merchandise as unrelated as clothing, cosmetics, foodstuffs, and bedding. What an unusual mix and how abundant the choices! I look at the shelves and can't believe my eyes: dozens of lipstick shades, pots and pans, kitchen gadgets, stationery, and toys galore! In Israel stores were devoted to one type of product and in Poland... well, back there the stores had hardly anything to sell.

We come to a counter in front of which stands a row of tall red stools. They look like mushrooms on steel stems. The counter is a sparkly green plastic. Behind it, a woman with a neat white cap on her head serves food to the few people seated on the stools. Estelle motions for me to sit down and climbs on a stool next to mine. She orders something.

The woman behind the counter places two tall glasses in front of us. They are filled with ice cubes and a brown fizzy liquid. Estelle points at them and says, "Coca-Cola." Am I dreaming?

6

A whole week has passed since our arrival and the best thing that has happened was the mail: three letters, all addressed to me! One from Yom Tov, one from Ruthi and the most amazing one of all—from Amnon. Not in a million years did I expect him to write me. But I have no time to dwell on them now. I must find a way to register for school which is to begin in just a couple of weeks.

Both Daniel and I have to register and there is no time to waste. Luckily, Paula, a friend of my mother's acquaintance, volunteers to take me to register in high school. She remembers Polish quite well and can serve as my translator. Mama is very grateful because we have no idea where to go and what documents to bring along. I have no idea who is taking Daniel.

Paula picks me up early in the morning. She is part of a small, but influential, group of former anarchists and anarchist sympathizers who live in the Bronx Amalgamated Housing complex, built by the needle trades unions. Mama knew some of these people before the war when they were still young and idealistic. Now they all seem to be quite satisfied with their lives in capitalist America, but they still stick together.

Paula looks like a healthy peasant with shiny red cheeks and hair pulled neatly into a utilitarian bun. I think she would fit in better on a collective farm somewhere in Russia instead of here in New York. She is quick to smile and speaks with what to my ears sounds like a perfect English, not accented by Polish or Yiddish like the speech of the rest of the group. She enunciates words so clearly, I can almost understand some.

As we walk out of the apartment, Tinek, who is making a sandwich to take to his job says, "I wish you luck. This day could change your future."

Maybe so, but I can't think of something so distant as my future. I just want to know how I'll survive the first day of school without knowing English.

Paula and I walk down Sedgwick Avenue, along the Jerome Park reservoir, then make a turn onto a wide street with no apartment houses, very few people and no traffic, not exactly my idea of bustling New York. It is a hot, sticky August day, more humid than Tel Aviv—something I thought impossible. I am anxious that perspiration will stain my one good blouse. I want to look respectable on this special day—my first entering an American institution.

We walk briskly and I begin to think Paula would probably just as soon get this mission done quickly. I'm not even a relative. Along the way she tells me her only child, Susan, just about my age, will be attending Walton High School. I am encouraged, because this is exactly where we were heading for registration and I'm hoping Paula might introduce me to her daughter so I'd know at least one person in the school of a thousand students.

"Paula, would it be possible for me to meet Susan before school starts?"

"Of course, you can," she says, and I feel better.

Soon we pass what looks like a brand new, three-story building on the left side of the road. Curious, I stop in my tracks and point to it. "Paula, what is this building?"

"Oh, nothing," she says quickly.

I look at her, but she stiffens and turns as if to move ahead.

"What do you mean, nothing? There must be a purpose to it," I persist.

"Well, actually it's a school," she answers dismissively in a harsh tone. A grimace makes her formerly friendly face look severe.

I don't mean to be rude, but I am getting more curious. "What kind of school?" I turn to face the front of the building and see a huge mural, a mosaic behind a glass wall. So impressive!

"Ania, we have to..." her voice trails off because I run up the steps toward the entrance plaza to get a better look at the mural.

"Please, wait a moment, Paula," I call out. As I get closer, I realize that the mosaic depicts people, larger than life. Among them, I spot Marie Curie, the Polish scientist who discovered radium. My heart leaps! She was the role model who inspired me when I was still in grade school. "Come, look, Paula!" I yell. "This building has something to do with science, I just know it. Why else would Marie Curie be here?"

Reluctantly, Paula comes closer and says, "Well, if you must know, it's a special high school for science."

"This is great! I am interested in science. Why can't I go to *this* school?" My mind churns with labs, microscopes, Bunsen burners and other science equipment; the very thought of it makes me dizzy. How I'd love to study here!

"You can't because you would have needed to pass an entrance exam last spring. We've got to get moving before it gets too late," Paula says.

I can hear the aggravation in her voice. I don't know why, but her urging only makes me dig my heels in. "Paula, won't you come in with me to find the director, maybe we can ask him if he could make an exception. After all, I wasn't here in the spring to take the exam. The sciences are my favorite subjects. *Bardzo proszę Pani Polu*," I beseech her in Polish in the most polite manner.

The yellow tiles in the mural sparkle like gold. On closer inspection it's clear all the figures are scientists whose ideas changed the world, like Marie Curie and Charles Darwin. They hold scientific instruments in their hands. That such a school exists! Long, empty corridors. A scent of fresh paint in the air. We hurry along a shiny floor, down a long corridor that leads to the director's office. Our footsteps echo through the empty hallway. Paula is brisk and silent. She's very annoyed with me.

We enter an office. My heart pounds. Paula says something to the woman behind a desk stacked with papers, and the woman, who must be the secretary, motions in the direction of a closed door. It has four words on it in large block letters: Dr. Alexander Taffel, Principal.

Paula shakes her head, knocks. A voice inside invites us in. She pushes the door open.

And there he is, the man who will decide my fate! A handsome middle-aged man sits behind an enormous desk that in contrast to the secretary's outside has practically no papers on its smooth, polished surface. He looks up and smiles. With his bow tie, crisp shirt, and wavy hair he looks almost too dapper to work in a school. As Paula says something, I watch his face carefully for any signs. He seems to have a look of amusement on his face, but he doesn't look irritated. Instead, he seems to be asking something about me. I know, because he is looking right at me.

"Dr. Taffel wants to know why you think that you belong in this school," Paula translates. She emphasizes the word *belong*.

"Please, Paula, tell him that I took one year of biology, one year of physics and one year of chemistry when I was still in school in Poland. I loved these subjects best and I was good at them too." I can't tell for sure, but Dr. Taffel seems to be smiling as Paula translates again. There is a vague look of surprise on his kind face.

After Dr. Taffel speaks again, Paula translates. "Dr. Taffel wants to know if you have any school report cards from Poland and Israel."

"Sure, I do," I say enthusiastically, knowing my grades have always been excellent.

"Dr. Taffel wants you to find those report cards right away and get them translated and notarized. Then he wants to look at them."

A panic washes over me. Who could translate them? What does "notarized" mean? Paula is so put out, there's no way she will help me. And my parents? They can't speak the language and don't know where anything is. All is lost. Paula shakes Dr. Taffel's hand and it is clear our unusual audience is over. We walk down the hall silently. I am at a total loss for words.

Paula breaks the silence as we approach the exit door. "That Dr. Taffel, he really surprised me. I don't know why he wants you to waste time translating the report cards. You still haven't passed the entrance exam."

I keep silent. What can I say? I only hope Paula is still willing to continue on the way to register me in Walton High School. What will I do if the year starts and I'm not registered in any school? I am very worried and feeling guilty that I opened a can of worms.

"So, do you have those report cards, or are they packed in some crates still on their way over to America?" Paula asks. My heart leaps. Maybe she will help me after all. The poor woman tried to do us a favor, and now she's gotten herself involved up to her ears.

"Yes, yes! I do have them. They are in my folder right on the bureau."

"Let's go get them," she says with a peeved sigh.

Paula ends up missing her other morning appointment, and we spend the afternoon getting the translations done in an office on

Jerome Avenue. A man stamps the papers and puts some kind of seal on them. Paula says they are now notarized.

Next morning, we repeat our walk to the Bronx High School of Science. This time I walk quietly and say nothing, trying not to aggravate Paula, but I'm nervous. Again, we enter Dr. Taffel's office. He stares at my report cards for a long while and seems to be deep in thought.

After a while he says something to Paula, and she has the strangest look of puzzlement on her face. She turns to me and says slowly, "You are a very lucky girl, Ania. Dr. Taffel is doing something extraordinary and not consistent with the official policy of the Board of Education. He has decided that for now you can enter the school without the entrance exam, but that in December you will take it. Of course, this assumes you'll know enough English by then to read and understand the questions. If you pass it, you will be allowed to continue. If not, you'll have to find another school."

I stand there with my mouth open, not knowing what to say. Dr. Taffel gets up and comes toward me from behind his desk. He shakes my hand, and I can feel the heat scorching my cheeks. My knees feel weak. I can't believe I will be a student at this school! The idea that I have to learn English at lightning speed hasn't yet fully registered.

As we head home, I can't stop thanking Paula for her help. "*Dziękuje*, Pola, *dziękuje!*" I want to skip but it will look immature.

When my parents learn my news, they are ecstatic and immediately share it with their friends. The news spreads and everyone who hears it clucks as if a miracle has happened. Only then do I discover that of the 20,000 students who took the entrance exam in the spring—20,000! —ninety-eight percent were *not* admitted, and Paula's daughter was among them. The school has the reputation as the best public high school in America!

I hope Dr. Taffel hasn't played a trick on me. Does he really think that a person can learn enough of a new language to pass a difficult examination in just ninety days? If only my early languages weren't Slavic I may have had more of a chance to absorb the strangeness of English words. Maybe then my tongue would be more adept at the contortions it has to make to produce sounds that require tongue, teeth, and lips to work as a team. English is nothing like Polish, in which you pronounce every letter. No, in English it is possible to ignore certain letters as if they didn't exist—ghost letters I will call them.

I resolve to study every waking moment. Wouldn't a tutor, like Amnon, be handy now! But I know there is no chance of that. My parents are barely making it on my father's meager earnings. After everyone is in bed I tiptoe to the kitchen and open my dictionary.

7

I go to bed but can't fall asleep. I toss and turn and suddenly remember I can't go to school as Anat, or A-nut! If I don't think of something right now, I'll be unable to walk into that building.

I get out of bed for a glass of water and stumble over my shoes, crashing into a chair. "What are you doing, Ania?"

Great! Now, I've woken Daniel.

"Shh... go back to sleep," I say.

His classes at the John Peter Tetard Junior High don't begin for two more days.

Back in bed, I puzzle. I wish I knew more American girl names. I start thinking of all the American movie stars I know: Elizabeth, Deborah, Doris, and Marilyn—none of them are me. Wouldn't it be ridiculous to say, "Hi, I am Elizabeth!"

As I keep making my mental inventory of names, I decide to go alphabetical. And suddenly the perfect solution strikes me— Annette—like Annette Funicello. I know American kids love her. She's a Disney Mouseketeer with a huge fan club. She sings *How Will I Know My Love*. It's been playing on the radio ever since I got here. Now it plays in my head again and again. I try not to hum it out loud.

I wake with a start to the frantic high-pitched sound of the alarm clock. Six is much earlier than I'm used to waking, but I can't take a chance on being late on the first day of school in America. I get ready extra quickly, pick up my book bag and tuck the card that was sent to me in the mail deep in my jacket pocket. I mustn't lose it. Paula translated it and told me it's my homeroom card. It says where my classroom is.

"Here, have some toast before you go. Don't start school on an empty stomach," Mama calls.

My stomach is queasy. "I just can't today, Mama."

She smiles, "I understand."

As I reach the door she calls out, "Good luck today!"

I hike along the reservoir on the route Paula showed me. The water in the reservoir shimmers in the morning sun. For an instant, it makes me think of the sea in Tel Aviv, but I push the thought out of my head. Can't do that!

There are many students walking along the Sedgwick Avenue to Goulden route but most of them are boys and the majority turn off at Clinton High School. These boys wear tight denim dungarees and short leather jackets that rest on their hips; some wear T-shirts with rolled up sleeves and cigarette packs tucked into them. Their hair, shiny with pomade is combed into what looks like a duck's behind. They look different from my Israeli classmates, tougher or angrier, as if they had something to prove.

Soon I turn left into West 205th Street. As if to denote its special status, the Bronx High School of Science stands on a lonely street, apart from the rest of the buildings in the neighborhood. As I approach it, I see many students milling in the entry plaza, standing in small groups chatting and laughing. Here, the students are more familiar types, but I notice most of the girls wear short pleated skirts and bobby socks up to their knees. My own skirt, the one I love so much, feels odd, suddenly:

287

it's too wide and too long, by a foot at least. The place suddenly looks different than on the day I came to register with Paula. It looks so vast. My stomach is now more unsettled. I'm glad I skipped breakfast.

A crowd of students streams in through the entry doors and I am swept in with them like a tiny pebble in a swiftly rushing river. No one seems to look up at the mural that still captivates me. I look up and imagine Marie Curie giving me a knowing wink, but everyone rushes down corridors and up the staircases. I must move on. I look at my homeroom card and realize that the classroom designation might as well be in Latin. I haven't a clue what the numbers and letters stand for.

I walk down the hallway looking at the numbers over the doors hoping that soon the logic of this strange numbering system will reveal itself. As I stop to check the numbers, students bump into me and give me strange looks. I have turned into a big boulder in the quickly flowing stream.

The bell rings, loud and insistent. So far, that's the only familiar thing about this school. Suddenly the halls are empty except for a couple of stragglers running at top speed. I meander up and down the corridors that veer off in unexpected directions, still searching for my classroom. In a few moments another bell rings. Now, except for me, the hallway is empty. My steps sound distressingly loud as I try to move forward. I should have asked if there is a map of this vast building. It might not have helped anyway. My horrible sense of direction gets me again. I come to a point where two corridors intersect, and I have absolutely no clue which way to go. I look desperately in each direction and dissolve into tears that soak my face, drip onto my blouse. I rummage in my pocket for tissues and stand still for a moment trying to regain my composure.

I see some people walking on the street outside and a new idea hits me. I don't have to be a prisoner here in America. I can be out there like they are, free of this school. I must find a way back to

Israel. I know there have been stowaways on ships. Why can't I do it?

As I stand there contemplating escape, I notice a tall young man approaching. He wears a tie and glasses, must be a teacher. He comes up to me and asks something. I have no idea what he says, but I imagine he wants to know what I am doing in the hallway after the bells have rung, not once, but twice. I show him my card, damp from my tears, and make a gesture to show that I don't know where to go. "*I no speek Ing-leesh,*" I say, my voice sounding small and alien to me. He looks puzzled. He asks something again. "Annette," I say trying to give it a French accent, but I feel like a complete idiot standing there so pathetic with my stupid braids, my tear-streaked face, and someone else's name.

He smiles, puts his arm on my shoulder and walks me to my classroom. We walk in together. Four neat rows of desks with boys and girls fill the brightly lit room. Everyone's eyes are now fixed on me. I want to sink under the floor, but he points to me and says something to the class in a gentle tone. He motions in the direction of a vacant desk and takes his own place behind the teacher's desk. Unbelievable! I have actually been rescued by my own homeroom teacher—Mr. Milton Kopelman. I resolve to give the stowaway idea more thought after school, but for now I am so grateful to this man I could kiss him. After a while I observe that he is quite good looking, in a boyish kind of way, especially when he smiles.

The homeroom period is very short and from there Mr. Kopelman walks me to my next class. And here a wonderful surprise awaits, he is the one teaching this class—my favorite subject—biology! He puts an anatomical model of a human torso on the desk and begins to remove its organs. I'm hooked.

8

Today I am to be a star of my very own "sweet sixteen" party. When we arrived in New York three weeks ago, I had no idea about this uniquely American ritual, but Tinek's American friends insist I celebrate it properly. "Nachman," they say, "let's make your Ania into an American teenager." I am not one for parties, especially when they don't include any of my friends. And one thing is sure: I have no friends here. But right now, parties are the furthest thing from my mind. I can't stop thinking of schemes to find my way back to Israel. I can tell from the letters that arrive regularly that everyone wants me back, even Amnon.

In my heart of hearts I know the idea is unrealistic, but I find comfort imagining there might be a way back, however insane it may be. Still, Tinek insists on today's celebration. A group of old fuddy-duddies, prewar socialist friends of my father's who live in the Bronx and some anarchist acquaintances of my mother's have been invited for coffee and cake tonight—hardly the kind of company to cheer me up. If there was at least one person my age, I'd feel better. "Daniel will provide the musical entertainment," Tinek says. "You will see, it will be fun."

The guests start arriving, most huffing and puffing after their climb to the fifth floor. Tinek takes their jackets and piles them on my bed. I am grateful that he doesn't try to hang them in the already overstuffed closets and risk releasing the poisonous mothball smell. First to arrive is Ruchcia, a busybody I met the previous week. She told me she used to be my father's girlfriend before the war and thus instantly impressed herself on my brain as the enemy. She has badly dyed hair and a false smile. I don't think Mama is so happy to see her either. Her husband, Moyshl, looks like a sweet, cowed little man with shy smiling brown eyes. They are an unlikely couple.

The next guest is Blima, my father's classmate from the first grade. It's hard to believe she knew my father when he was seven. She's tall, slim, wrinkled and very serious looking. It's equally difficult to imagine her as a seven-year-old girl. I know she took great care of my father; he lodged with her on his arrival in New York. She made him sandwiches each morning and packed them in brown bags to be sure he had something to eat as he went on his job searches. "Here, you'll eat just like an American, standing up," she'd say as she handed him the lunch sack before she herself dashed off to work. I am grateful for her kindness but think it will not be easy to make small talk with her. Her unsmiling face does not invite pleasantries.

Mordechai, her second husband, is very nice. She met him in the German Displaced Persons camp after her first husband was killed in a concentration camp. As he congratulates me, he shakes my hand vigorously, but a bit too long. His wide smile reveals crooked teeth that lean in all directions, but it seems genuine. I stare at the red pea sized growth above his eyebrow and wish I were somewhere else.

Next, Jack comes in with his wife Claire. She is the one who stands out tonight. Unlike the other women wearing nice dresses, brooches, and bracelets, she is not dressed up for the occasion. An ill-fitting navy dress with buttons running down the front envelops her thick body. Some of the buttons look as though they may pop open any minute. She has salt and pepper hair, cut very short and slicked back in a mannish style. Her meaty, florid face is sweaty, and she laughs louder than anyone. She is the only one in this group who doesn't speak Yiddish, or Polish. When I ask Jack what she is talking about, he says she's a great baseball fan and is very happy about the outcome of the Yankees game. "A real American, my Claire," says Jack. I don't know what kind of a game baseball is, but I don't want to ask Jack fearing his long-winded explanations. Anyway, I don't care much for sports.

As more people arrive, I find it hard to distinguish one from the other. They all look worn out, old. It's hard to believe that most must be my parents' age. Does America age people prematurely? After our guests have occupied every available seat, Tinek pours Schnapps. "*Le Chaim!*" he cries—to life, and they all burst out into an American "Happy Birthday" song. It makes me feel awkward and at the same time, pleasantly surprised—they all seem so sincere, except for Ruchcia. She spends the evening following my father with her eyes.

As the guests begin leaving, Mordechai grabs my hand again and says, "We'll make an American of you yet," and then adds, "May I kiss the birthday girl?" I have no chance to reply before he plants a sloppy kiss on my cheek.

When the last of the guests finally leaves I am relieved that the pathetic little party is over. Mama plops down exhausted on the beat-up sofa sending a small puff of dust into the air accompanied by a squeak of the springs.

"Nachman, your friends..." she says, hesitating.

"What about them?" he asks, as he walks around turning off the lights.

"Well, I thought they would be different. You know, it's really the first time I have met any of them."

"Different, how?" he stops and looks at her.

"It's hard to say... maybe a bit more cosmopolitan, more polished."

"Not everyone is like Guta and Dunia and the rest of your friends," he says. "My friends are like me, plain people—the proletariat. What's wrong with that?"

"Nothing."

"Not suitable for the *Engelishe koenigen?*" he pushes back in Yiddish.

"It's late, let's open up the sofa bed and get to sleep," she replies.

I toss in bed thinking my sweet sixteen was the opposite of sweet despite my parents' best intentions. I vow to promptly forget it and not write a word about it to Ruthi, or Yom Tov. I pull the sheet over my head trying not to think of what other outlandish rituals America might have in store for me.

9

When Tinek first arrived in New York all of his old school buddies sprang into action working their connections. They tracked down job leads, they drew him maps so he could get to the interviews, they taught him how to use the subway and gave him rolls of tokens, both for good luck and to save him the expense.

After a search of several months he landed a job working for A&D Photo Prints, a small printing company on Stone Street in lower Manhattan; not that he had any experience in this line of work. The reason he was hired is because his boss is a rabbi, and his shop prints lots of material in Hebrew and Yiddish. My father's knowledge of these alphabets will be enormously helpful as none of the other employees in this small shop can tell an *Aleph* from a *Beit*.

Tinek delivers printing stock to his shop. He picks it up on a metal cart from suppliers in the area and wheels it to the shop on Stone Street. Thank goodness he has the cart to help him. The reams of paper are as heavy as logs, he says.

When I first found out about his job all I could think was what a far cry it was from his position in Poland as an executive of a large firm. There are no secretaries, no fleet of chauffeur-driven cars, no meetings, no briefcase, not even a suit—just the drudgery of unskilled work.

We sit around the table finishing up supper when Daniel asks the question that has been on my mind all along, "Dad, do you hate your job?"

"No! Whatever gave you that idea? There is no shame in any work. I'd rather be in America sweeping the streets than in Poland under communist masters."

"Nachman, this is not a job for you," Mama says. "I worry about your back."

"It's helping me develop muscles," he says and winks at me.

Mama looks at him with disbelief and shakes her head.

"My boss promised to teach me layout techniques to prepare pages for printing. The special process is called photo-offset stripping," he says.

She looks puzzled and he explains, "It requires a good eye for design and a steady hand. Once I learn it, I'll get a raise."

"Always the optimist," Mama says.

She's right. His face has none of the tension I saw in it in Israel. He gets up from the table and comes around behind Mama's chair trying to give her a hug. "Let me do the dishes today," he says, makes that funny face with crossed eyes and puts on Mama's apron.

Mama's employment situation is different. In America her talents in design and craftsmanship of custom-made brassieres and corsets are of little use. Here women just buy these undergarments ready-made in department stores. No one gets them made to measure. Everyone here says it's the American way. In some ways it probably doesn't matter; there's no money for her to open a shop anyway, not even in our apartment like in Tel Aviv. What customer would seek her out in our fifth floor Bronx walk up?

Since Tinek's thirty-seven dollar a week pay can just barely pay our rent, it has become very urgent for Mama to find a job too. But where? What can she do? Her sewing machine stands forlorn as

Mama speaks to everyone she meets about job leads. It turns out that the fur industry is Mama's best hope for a job; at least that's what most of her acquaintances say. Furs are popular in America, but there aren't enough skilled machine operators and fur finishers. The trick, they say, is getting into the furrier's union.

"A union?" Mama says with a hint of suspicion in her voice. "Sounds like something in Poland. You know I don't go for this communal stuff."

"But Dora," her friend Pearl says, "in America if you can get into the union, you will probably have better wages. It's a big deal. Bosses treat workers better in union shops."

"So what's the trick for getting in?" Mama asks. I know working in a factory, answering to a boss won't appeal to her. She has always been her own boss.

"Well," Pearl hesitates. "You will... you will have to tell them you come from a long line of furriers."

"What are you saying, Pearl? You know my father was a student of the Talmud. There has never been a furrier in our family! There hasn't even been a furry pet in our family."

Pearl is exasperated. She is trying to teach her the ropes, but Mama doesn't get it.

"Look, do what you want, Dora," Pearl says. She throws her hands up in the air. "I told Mr. Greenberg to expect an applicant with experience in making fur collars. Trust me, it's not as bad as doing the whole coat."

I can just tell from her tone what she will say to her friends when she reports on this conversation with Mama. "Eh, *de greene*, they don't know anything. You have to teach them *everything*." I know, because I have heard that they call us *de greene* behind our backs, green, like apples that haven't ripened.

"So how was it, Dora?" Tinek tries to greet Mama with a kiss at the door on her first day in the fur shop.

"Ugh... I am so grimy, not now," she says.

As soon she steps inside the apartment Daniel and I run into the living room to hear all about her day.

"What is there to tell?" she says flopping into the chair, breathing heavily. "Let me first get into the bathroom to wash! It's all over me!" She grimaces, dabbing her brow with a crumpled wad of tissues, bits of fur cling to her face and neck. I look down at her stained fingernails and she says, "That's fur dye." She waves her hand in a gesture of pure disgust and sighing, gets up.

I want to cry. Her delicate hands now so grubby. "It's unbearably hot," she says and gets up to open the window, then walks into the bathroom. I follow her with my eyes thinking of her hands, delicate hands made for handling silk and lace, not leather.

"Do you want me to help you in the kitchen?" Tinek asks her, but I can already hear the bath water running.

"I'll be right out to make dinner!" she calls out.

She comes out scrubbed clean, wrapped in her robe.

"Well, now you can tell us," Tinek says. He's been waiting for her at the kitchen table he set with mismatched china.

"Wait. I forgot to wash off the ring of fur around the tub," she says.

A few minutes later she comes back, pulls a cutting board out of the cabinet and slices onions with lightning speed. I watch her deft hands making a stack of thin rings. "The boss is very crass. He curses like a longshoreman. Such a fat slob..."

The oil in the pan sizzles, like her anger.

"A Jew?" Tinek asks.

"Yes," she says, "but my shop mates are mostly Greek women. They seem nice, though we can't communicate. Anyway, who has time to talk? You have to watch out, or else the thick needle will pierce your finger," she says as she places four beef patties in the center of the skillet.

"Mama, tell us about the kind of fur you worked with," I ask.

Daniel butts in, "Who wants to wear dead animals around their neck?"

"Not now. We've got to finish supper quickly," Mama says. "Dad and I are going to enroll in Clinton High School for evening English lessons."

Classes after such a long day? I am so proud of my parents at this moment I could bust. "Okay. Maybe you'll learn English faster than me. And just remember, it's not learning American. It's English!"

Now Mama and Tinek burst out laughing and the sound calms me inside.

10

The notion that I have to learn English well enough to take the Bronx High School of Science entrance exam has finally sunk in. I mark a big X on the calendar and count the weeks, again and again. Twelve weeks! I can feel the clock ticking inside my head. Every minute is another lost word until I do nothing but study, live and breathe English. In moments like these, the words in the thick English dictionary I use to study crawl around on the tissue-thin pages like frenzied ants. The more intense my gaze, the more animated they become. The pressure in my temples keeps me awake late into the night. I study in the kitchen with only the small light on not to wake my parents. They get up too early for work as it is. They sleep on the lumpy fold out couch in the living room. I can hear Daniel breathing in the bedroom that we share and I don't want to wake him either. He might yell and wake up our parents.

He's lucky because he can take the Bronx Science entrance exam on the usual schedule, a year and a half from now, so he can sleep. In the morning, he can walk, carefree, over to his junior high only a few blocks from the Shalom Aleichem houses. On second thought, he, too, has to learn English pretty quickly to survive in an all-English school. He is chubby as a butterball; if he gets teased he will need some good English comebacks.

If I could only get Daniel interested in the stowaway idea, it would be easier to do. I know the idea is lame, but I know it has been done, though I don't know exactly by whom and how. Daniel is so clever. He could be helpful in distracting the sailors as we try to sneak onto a ship. This way we could both go to Israel where we are wanted. No, not just wanted, needed, where we know the language, where we have family and friends, where we can be our true selves, where we can help build the new country.

I catch myself in my desperate musings and realize the futility of the idea. Even Daniel would think it's childish, and he's just a kid. Better to keep it to myself until I come up with a more realistic plan to return. After all, Israel will always consider me its citizen. It's a place that will always be mine.

As I think about my brother, it dawns on me how much I like his company. Despite the two-and-a-half-year gap that separates us, I find him funny and smarter than his friends. And at thirteen he is already quite the philosopher, never at a loss for a quick quip. His sense of humor is sharp, like Mama's.

Like me, he studies English, but he does even more. He is continuing his musical education and he has started to paint in every spare minute. It seems the doodles of caricatures no longer satisfy him. "Do you plan to become an artist?" I ask.

"In America you can probably afford to be an artist," he says as a small dimple forms on his cheek, "elsewhere you'd starve." He says this often, trying to convince Mama, but she doesn't agree. She thinks each of us needs a *real* profession.

I realize how much time I have wasted pondering things this evening, so I open the dictionary and try to focus, but my eyelids are leaden. I will have to do more tomorrow.

My English teacher, Mr. Shaw, has asked me to stay after class for a moment. What could that be about? Every day I feel like an illegal alien in this school. I'm nervous, thinking I'm about to be given the boot. The class empties and I walk tentatively toward his desk waiting for him to speak. He pushes his spectacles up on his nose. "Annette, I'd be glad to help you with the crazy rules and tongue twisting pronunciation of our language... if you'd like to stay for a while after class."

"You... you would?"

"Yes, you will be my Eliza Doolittle."

"Thank you, thank you," I say, but have no idea who Eliza is.

"Okay then, we'll start next week," he says, picks up his briefcase and walks out.

I stand there, my brain in a muddle until I hear the janitor sweeping the hallway. I can't believe my luck! He is willing to stay after school and review my assignments. Everyone says this is not the way of most American teachers. "You should count your blessings," my parents say. I know it's great, but he's no Amnon.

Mr. Shaw is a silver-haired gentleman with a small, neatly trimmed mustache and wire-rimmed glasses that make his eyes look larger. When I look at him, it's as if I had him under a microscope. He wears a gray tweed jacket and smokes a pipe—very English. He must have been born in England because he speaks with what sounds like a British accent to my ears. I love listening to him even if I don't understand most of the words.

I work hard on all my assignments, even the ones that seem impossibly difficult, repetitious, and annoying. I do not want to disappoint Mr. Shaw. When I compare my American teachers to those in Poland, or in Israel, I try to be fair, but honestly, Mr. Kopelman and Mr. Shaw are so smart, so thoroughly decent, and warm, I doubt I could find another pair like them on any other continent, except for Amnon, of course.

Mr. Kopelman has become a lifesaver. Amazingly, it turns out that he knows a little Yiddish. Strange, it didn't dawn on me he could be Jewish. I had grown so accustomed to everyone being Jewish in Israel but knew that in America we would be in the minority again, so I had no expectations of meeting Jews other than my parents' friends.

Mr. Kopelman comes over to my desk during biology classes and whispers a few words of translation in Yiddish to help me with anatomical terms.

"Here, look," he points to a page in our textbook. "*Lingen*, lungs; *moyech*, brain; *mogn*, stomach." The words, heavily accented with English, sound funny, as if he is telling some sort of a joke.

"*Farshteyst?*" he then asks with a wink, do you understand?

I gather he is talking about the organs of the human body, but I have no idea what else he says. His Yiddish vocabulary is more limited than mine. Biology sounds strange in Yiddish. I don't actually know many technical terms in Yiddish, but I get the gist of the lessons because I have already taken a year of biology back in Poland. I forget for a moment how to say, "I understand," so I just nod and smile.

The course content is a breeze, and I recognize the various diagrams and drawings in the textbook, the heart with its chambers and lungs with their tree-like alveoli, the nerves emerging like wires from the spine. It's the English that kills me. Luckily, it's the same with Chemistry and Physics; they don't demand so much English vocabulary. And fortunately, the math equations are written in a universal language. My classes in these subjects in Poland have prepared me well to pass the weekly quizzes we get at Bronx Science.

My teachers have made me feel welcome, but on the other hand that also worries me. What if I don't pass the exam and have to be ejected from here like a bird being thrown out of its cozy nest? Will I land on the pavement with a big splat? I try to hypnotize myself with my own mantra: study harder, study harder, study harder.

11

We've have made it through our first two-and-a-half months in America! The American holiday of Thanksgiving will be here in just one week. I hope it's better than a sweet sixteen! Am I getting used to this place? Maybe, a little, but that hardly means that I've stopped obsessing about getting back to Israel. The more I learn, the more confused I am. America is like the Sirens who try to entice sailors into dangerous waters. On some days it is a strange, powerful beast that we need to tame, to make it work for us. On other days, it is a shimmering mirage, a beautiful oasis that recedes farther into the distance the closer I come to it. But just listening to Tinek's enchantment with New York exerts a seductive pull. Each day after work he tells us about the wondrous sights and sounds of Manhattan: the 7,000-pound bronze bull in Bowling Green Park; the Staten Island ferry; the Beaux Arts US Customs House with its lavish sculptures and Chinatown where even the phone booths are shaped like pagodas.

Mama's friend Ruth has invited us to celebrate Thanksgiving with her family. I wonder if it's anything like the holidays I discovered in Israel. Of all my parents' friends in America, I think I'll like Ruth best, she's Mama's school friend from Warsaw. Mama admires Ruth because she went to Spain in the 1930s to participate in the Spanish Civil War on the loyalist side. "Ruth sticks to her principles," Mama often says. "We need more people like her."

Before we go, Mama lets me speak to Ruth on the phone, so she can explain this holiday. Ruth's Polish is still very good. How wonderful, I think as I hang up, it's the first holiday I have heard of that has nothing to do with religion or politics, in that way, it's an American holiday through and through. I love it already, but then Ruth says, "Thanksgiving is a time for all the family to get together. Will your father invite his sister from Harrisburg? She will be very welcome in our home."

"I don't know," I say. My hand covers the microphone. "Tinek, can Rosa and her family come to New York to join us for Thanksgiving?"

"No," he laughs. And I say 'no' to Ruth, but I don't report that he laughed.

When I'm off the phone I ask him about it. "Ania, you should know by now that my sister wouldn't eat anything unless it's cooked in a strictly kosher kitchen. That certainly excludes ours and even more so, Ruth's. Ruth's husband is a Spaniard. He is not Jewish."

"But we are her only family..."

"That's the way it is with the religious..." he says.

"Not with Uncle Nechemiah," I say, and think how great it would be to celebrate Thanksgiving in Israel with my mother's two brothers, two sisters, their spouses and my many cousins.

"Nechemiah never ate in our house, if you remember," Tinek reminds me. "Our food was *treyf*, not kosher."

"But why did he leave his boys and Atara with us when Chayka went to give birth to their fourth child? They ate our food."

"Ah, Ania, it's impossible to figure out rationally the exceptions the religious make."

"Well, too bad they don't observe Thanksgiving in Israel. They have plenty to be thankful for," I sigh and it occurs to me the closest they come to it is Succoth, the fall harvest festival, but it doesn't involve a turkey, nor a pumpkin and has nothing to do with the *Mayflower*.

The winter has come early this November. It is snowing on Thanksgiving Day. Most people in New York City don't expect snow till Christmas. Though I miss the balmy Israeli weather, I like the way the snow crunches under my shoes and makes the streets look clean like a table dressed for a holiday in a starched white tablecloth. I haven't seen snow since Poland and hadn't realized I missed it. It brings to mind the snowy days in Łódź when I was five, or six, all bundled up in blankets over my wool coat and muff and the heavy felt boots with metal buckles. Father used to pull me on a sled along the street that led to the park. Then we slid down together on a small slope that felt like a giant mountain. When my hands got too cold, Father would blow warm air on them and rub them in his hands that felt like small ovens.

We approach Ruth's building on the Upper West Side. Is this uptown, or downtown? I wonder. We haven't been in Manhattan since our arrival. The buildings in this part of town are much larger than in the Bronx; not quite the skyscrapers I expected, but matronly, broad, and solid. Ruth's building is not grand on the exterior except for the small gargoyles near the entrance facade and the long green canopy extending nearly to the sidewalk; its gleaming gold supports the only hint of what's inside. The marble walled lobby is so fancy I can't imagine a friend of my mother's really lives here. It even has an elevator! The elevator exudes an aura of elegance. It is made of a dark shiny wood and has beveled mirrors all around that reflect the overhead light and scatter it into miniature rainbows.

As we exit on Ruth's floor, I can already smell a mixture of wonderful unfamiliar aromas, at once sweet and pungent. We enter her spacious foyer with its ornate Persian rug and wall sconces and immediately want to step back to take off our wet shoes. But Ruth hugs and kisses each of us in turn. "Never mind, I am so glad you are here," she says. "I wanted so much to be the first to introduce you to this wonderful American tradition."

She continues elaborating about the Pilgrims and Indians as she ushers us into the living room where a marble fireplace with a roaring fire is reflected in the huge mirror on the opposite wall. The tables are covered in festive cloths and vases full of red flowers grace the mantle.

Ruth introduces us to her son, daughter and many guests whose names I won't remember. The son is a very reserved young man with a crew cut. He seems to avoid eye contact as best he can. The daughter, a dark-haired, shy young woman makes herself scarce going in and out of the kitchen. Neither of Ruth's offspring seem interested in getting to know odd creatures like us.

We are invited into the dining room where the table is set for sixteen. In its center, a brown bird-like creature surrounded by greenery waits on a huge platter. This must be the turkey, I surmise, for I have never seen a turkey in its entirety. Around it are beautiful crystal, silver and porcelain serving pieces with foods that look unfamiliar.

Mama comments, "Ruth, this looks like a set up for a wedding. What are these exotic dishes?" Ruth names them all for our benefit: sweet potato pies, walnut-apple stuffing, cranberry sauce, pickle and watermelon relishes, roasted vegetables, and chestnuts. There are other dishes we can't name, but I guess Ruth thinks we know what those are. And that's before we even get to the desserts that look more luscious than anything I have ever coveted at a bakery: pumpkin, apple and cherry pies, Napoleons, brownies, and cookies in various shapes sprinkled in orange sugar that sparkles like diamonds. We have never seen such abundance of food. "Your table looks so lovely, it's a shame to touch anything, to disturb these works of art," Tinek says.

"Oh, Nachman, don't worry about it. We eat like this at every holiday. Eat. Eat," Ruth beams at us. "I knew you would like Thanksgiving in America."

"Where else do you have a reason to be so thankful?" Tinek asks.

"Israel," I think but keep it to myself.

Ruth's chandelier sparkles. Lovely classical music wafts through the house. Everyone is warm and friendly, especially Ruth's husband—a distinguished, silver-haired Spaniard. How did Ruth manage to marry a man of such different cultural background? I have never before met a mixed couple, very confusing.

Ruth's husband takes my hand and kisses it, just the way men of good breeding kissed ladies' hands in Poland. I blush to my ears. "Come with me, let me show you the colors in the fireplace," he says, as he picks up a thick log from a copper bin. Though I can't understand most of what he says, I like watching his lively eyes and expressive large hands, which move about him as he speaks. I wonder if he has ever fought a bull. Ruth explains that he wants to show me how they treat fire logs with various chemicals to produce beautiful color displays. In America they think of everything to enhance pleasure!

After dinner, feeling stuffed and groggy, I find a cozy velvet chair in the corner of the living room. Its arms hug me as if they were human. I feel dreamy and start thinking what it would be like if I ever had such a beautiful home of my own, filled with laughter and people I love around my own Thanksgiving table. Then I remember. In America we have so little family, probably not enough for a big Thanksgiving celebration like this one. Tinek says anything is possible in America, so maybe one day we won't be living in a sublet apartment trying to fit ourselves in between the possessions of others.

All too quickly the evening ends and Mama says, "It's time to go now." She thanks Ruth and her husband profusely. He kisses Mama's hand and says to her, "*Con mucho gusto*," in Spanish. She smiles knowing it's something nice. I shake off my daydream, and reality hits me with its hard, calloused hand—only three weeks until my high school entrance exam! I should have been home studying instead of gorging myself and daydreaming. Isn't it absurd though to take an entrance test to a school I have already been attending for three months? I feel like asking someone this question. Well... I was lucky to make it into the school. No sense complaining now.

At night I fall asleep trying to memorize the English words I learned at the dinner. *Toor-key, toor-key, Mei-floweh, Mei-floweh* I repeat hoping these words will come in handy someday.

Maybe it was one of her sleepless migraine nights that caused Mama to have such a frustrating incident shortly after Thanksgiving. She got off at the wrong subway stop. She can't remember whether she dozed off, or whether she was lost in her thoughts. In any case, as she emerged onto an unfamiliar street in Manhattan's garment district, she realized that she wasn't sure how to get to the fur factory. She was lost just like I was in Naples. She glanced at her watch and realized that she needed to punch in very soon, or else her paycheck for the holiday week would be even smaller than she already expected. Mama doesn't get any paid holidays. As she stood at a corner trying to remember how to ask for directions, she remembered something. Her sweatshop was near a restaurant called "Luncheonette." She would look for the large red letters in neon. They would be her sign that she's near her workplace.

Soon she cheered herself up because way in the distance she saw a neon sign that had exactly what she was looking for, "Luncheonette." As she approached, she looked around, but the buildings didn't look familiar in the least. She was on the wrong street! "How strange," she thought, "two restaurants with the same name in the same neighborhood." She kept walking and looking at her watch, painfully aware that she wouldn't be there to punch in on time. Now she worried more about her boss yelling, or heaven forbid, dismissing her for such lateness, than about the lost wages. A few more turns and there it was—another sign in large block letters that said, "Luncheonette."

Maybe that's near her shop building, but again, an unpleasant surprise. She was not in the right place. By then, I think, she began realizing that this English word does not stand for a particular restaurant. She told me that she had no idea how she finally found herself in front of the right building, but she was sure of one thing—it was nine-thirty, not eight. To her relief, the boss happened to be out when she walked in, punched in, hung up her coat and put on her apron. The only people who noticed her arrival were two Greek ladies who sit on either side of her sewing machine. They nodded and continued their work.

How I wish Mama had friends or family here. Surely, that would ease her loneliness. Except for Ruth, she has no one. The image of her in the long-ago photo surrounded by a pack of friends comes before me. She was a magnet. Recently I've noticed she fills her limited spare moments studying the English dictionary. "I wish I could write in English. It's such a rich language," she tells me often.

"You will one day, Mama," I try to cheer her.

But she says, "It's difficult to make a foreign language truly your own at fifty."

12

The December sun is miserly. There's barely enough of it to illuminate the day. Night falls so abruptly after I come home from school that I think someone has turned off the lights. I long for Tel Aviv's brilliant sunshine. After the excitement of Thanksgiving, we are back to our humdrum lives at the Shalom Aleichem houses in the Bronx. Somehow, our sublet apartment looks even dingier than before, the plastic covers on the chairs with their splitting seams even more unattractive.

My only and most important consolation is the steady stream of letters from Amnon. Yom Tov writes too, but compared to Amnon's, his letters are becoming tedious. When Amnon's letters first arrived in September, they were brief and filled with updates on my old school's events. "Shalom, Anat," he wrote, "we've just completed the second semester math competition..." But by the third, or fourth letter, the tone of his long missives had changed. I was downright embarrassed reading them and glad no one saw me blush. "How is my smartest and most beautiful student? I miss you desperately and look for you in every classroom..." He writes with passion as if I were a grown woman. His letters make me excited and nervous. In today's letter he enclosed a photo of himself with his baby daughter. A baby! At first, I threw the photo in the wastebasket and stashed the letter in my drawer with all the rest. Then I retrieved the picture, feeling foolish. Maybe after this one I won't open his letters.

We hardly see our parents now. They leave for work in the dark and return in the dark. I go through my school day with a single thought: I must get home as fast as possible, do my homework and study for the test. How many new English words can I learn today? Do I know how to spell them? These days I must also make sure Daniel has done his schoolwork because our parents come home too tired to be dealing with us. Anyway, they don't know enough English yet to be of much help.

"Daniel, do you have any homework today?" I ask, looking at him intently as if I haven't seen him in ages. Today he looks taller and his baby fat is nearly gone. His blondish mop hanging over his eyes and a jaw that is suddenly more angular make him look like a real teen.

"None of your business. You are not Mama to be asking me."

"Come on, I have my own work to do, don't make me mad, just tell me."

"Okay, okay, where can I find some information about American Indians for my social studies class?"

"Maybe, maybe..." I stall for time because I have no idea. "Maybe we can ask Ruth," I say quite at a loss, thinking I should have minded my own business and not acted like a parent. Then a better solution comes to me. "Daniel, do you remember when we read *The Last of the Mohicans* in Polish?"

"Oh, yes. I do."

"Well, you can start with what you remember."

As soon as he is done with his homework, Daniel usually puts his paint set on the kitchen table and begins doing what he loves most—painting. His paintings are the only way I know he misses Israel as much as I do because he doesn't like to talk about it. He paints figures like the ones we saw in Bnei Berak, Hassidim with long ear locks and black coats, toting their prayer shawls and Torahs under their arms.

But the painting I love the most, the one that pulls at my heartstrings, is his watercolor of Gvat. At first glance one can't tell what it is, perhaps a jumble of colorful triangles, but then I step back and see Gvat sitting on a hill in all its glory and I think of all the people there I miss. The only recognizable feature is the silo, way in the distance, but in my mind's eye I see the lush vineyards and the youth gathered at the *kumzits*. Daniel has also made a mosaic with tiny pieces of tile. I couldn't wait to see what image would emerge. When he was done, a rabbi's head with a skullcap and very serious-looking eyes appeared. Tinek was amazed. "Daniel, this is something," he said over and over as if he could not find the right word to express his admiration.

"Let's hang it in a place of honor," Mama said and I could see that this was the best thing that had happened to her in America so far.

Of all the worries that plague my mind the worst one is Mama's work. Although she doesn't complain, I know she hates her job. It's dirty work. She is a small cog in a sweatshop where the boss is more like a slave master than a businessman. She tells Tinek how rude her boss is to the workers, especially the women. There isn't any place to change, or to wash up. The women have to share the men's filthy toilet. And the punch clock is the worst. If you are a minute late, you get docked a half hour's pay. I hate it that Mama, the fiercely independent woman who has run her own business since she was eighteen, now has to work for someone under these wretched conditions. If Tinek would consider returning to Israel, Mama could set up her own shop once again, but I know he will never do it. He loves America already though she has not requited his love just yet. Mama never speaks about her feelings, but I just know how much she must love Tinek to put up with her miserable job and with America. She doesn't like it here, but she has no intention to go back either.

Mama's walk to and from the subway is long. She comes home tired with fur hair stuck to her skin and inky fingernails, just like on that first day. But she and Tinek rush to eat so they can get to their English classes. All over the apartment I find scraps of paper with the newest vocabulary words they learn; names of spices stuck to kitchen cabinet doors; names of bath items on the bathroom mirror attached with bits of tape. They both want to learn, but it is Mama who is most frustrated not having a full command of the language.

Tinek wants to know English too, but he isn't worried about mispronouncing words. He just plunges into conversation at every opportunity. "Don't worry so much about what people think," he says. "You will never learn that way. Americans are very forgiving, they are not like the French who hate for anyone to scar their language." He is diligent about doing his English homework with me as his tutor. I dictate a list of words and then check his spelling. He beams when I grade his paper and give him a 95, but somehow it makes me think back to the music test he gave me where I failed. I frown and he is confused. "What's wrong, Ania?" he asks. I couldn't possibly explain.

Tinek is back to his sociable self. He loves to talk with people and uses every opportunity in his small printing shop to chat with the other workers. He communicates with his boss, the rabbi, in Yiddish, but prefers to learn English from Emil, the Black press operator and from Jimmy, Emil's Chinese assistant. He likes these guys a lot.

"Hey, Nate," Emil starts a conversation with my father. Since he can't pronounce the "ch" sound in Nachman, he has decided to call him Nate. "So tell me about your job behind the Iron Curtain. Did you have to work as hard as we do here?"

"No, I vas just—how you say? Pushing da papers."

"Oh, you mean you were a paper pusher?" Emil has a broad grin on his coal-black face.

"Yes. Samting like dat."

"Did you make good money?"

"No, but my wife, she did. I had a lot of nice girls."

"What do you mean, you had girls?"

"I had secretaries in a pool."

"You swam with your secretaries? How many did you have, anyway?" Now Emil is baffled.

"You don't never heerd about secretarial pool?"

"Oh," says Emil, but Tinek realizes that Emil doesn't quite get it.

Then the usually quiet Jimmy chimes in, "Nate was a big man in Europe. That's what the boss man told me. Don't bug him."

Emil and Jimmy tell Father about their families and he retells their stories to us at dinner. I almost feel as though I know these people. It's hard for me to see my father in a blue-collar job after his powerful position in Poland, but I can't feel sad for him because he doesn't look unhappy. It seems as if just breathing in American air is enough for him. I feel he wants all of us to love America as much as he does. Anything less would mean that his struggle was for naught.

———————

With Mr. Kopelman and Mr. Shaw as my champions, I am beginning to feel a little more at ease in school until I remember that I shouldn't get too comfortable: *I haven't yet passed the admission exam.* I rarely initiate conversations with my peers for fear they won't understand me, but Susan, a girl with a halo of teased hair, and redheaded Margaret approach me and try to chat with me in the cafeteria. I bring my sandwich, they buy their lunch here. Both are friendly, yet so different from one another. Susan with her makeup is untypical of the girls in this school, but

Margaret with her tight, red kinky hairdo and owlish glasses fits right in. It turns out that Susan lives near me and invites me to visit. "I will come only after I pass my exam," I tell her. "I can't afford the time right now."

She smiles, picks up her tray and says, "At least we can walk home together."

Estelle, the girl who welcomed me to America on day one, goes to another school and I rarely see her anymore. Now that I could converse with her better, she's not around. It makes me sad. I have a feeling we could have been good friends.

13

In my homeroom, one December day, a pimply, redheaded student running an errand for the secretary, brings in a note and hands it to Mr. Kopelman, who reads it and says, "Annette, you are wanted in the principal's office."

"Me?" I always hesitate when my name is called. It takes a moment of conscious thought to connect it with the girl inside my skin, Ania, the former Anat, and before that, the little Anetka.

"Yes, go ahead," he says.

Since Poland I know that being summoned by a figure of authority is rarely good news. I go downstairs with a knot in my stomach. The secretary waves me in cordially into Dr. Taffel's office.

He looks up and smiles as I walk in timidly, stopping just past the threshold. "Come in, come in," he says, and motions for me to sit down. Why does he want me to sit? Does he have bad news for me? But he has a smile on his face. I am confused. He addresses me and I stare at his mouth as if I were lip reading.

"Annette, all your teachers have informed me you are making

excellent progress in your classes. You are keeping up with your classmates."

"Well... I try..." I have no idea what to say. "But... the test?"

"Oh, that," he chuckles. "Actually, the good news is you don't have to take it."

"What? What do... do you mean...?" I stammer. "How can I stay in the school?"

"It makes no sense for you to take the exam. You have done so well on the weekly quizzes. Mr. Shaw has seen huge progress. You belong here," he says with conviction and taps his hand on his desk.

No one gets into this school without passing the entrance exam. Is he making fun of me? Dr. Taffel couldn't be breaking the rules—for me? I sit there stupefied and he says, "Go on to class, Annette. It's fine. You are officially in."

I mumble something resembling, "Thank you."

He stands up, shakes my clammy hand and says, "Your teachers will continue to monitor your progress. Keep up the good work."

The rest of the day is a blur. I walk through the school corridors as if had just won a million-dollar lottery. I feel taller and thinner. America has smiled upon me! I feel like dancing. My cheek muscles hurt from a grin I can't wipe off. Susan and Margaret and a new friend, Carole, stare at me in disbelief as I tell them my news. They look at me as though I must have misunderstood Dr. Taffel. "But when *do you* have to take the test?" they keep asking, incredulous.

"You don't understand, I don't have to take it at all," I say, but they look at me as if I am crazy. They have an odd expression on their faces that says, "The poor thing, she didn't get it."

In the evening, when my parents learn about my improbable triumph, they look happier than on any day since our arrival. All Daniel has to say is, "Why do I have to take that test next year?"

"Because this is why I brought you to America. Here everyone gets a chance to compete, and to succeed," Tinek says tapping his finger on the table for emphasis.

My level of confidence has shot way up, but it's all on the inside. On the outside I'm still jelly when anyone, but especially a boy, tries to speak to me. Despite my newly found sense of sureness I have the overwhelming dread that Polish or Hebrew words will come springing out of my mouth like escaping convicts, and I won't even be aware of my errors.

In homeroom I sit next to Mike, a handsome, dark-haired guy. He looks like someone whose invitation to a prom I'd definitely accept. He's tall, confident, and decidedly American. Sometimes he speaks to me with a cryptic little smile on his full pouty lips, but I get so flustered I can't respond even though five minutes later I remember the right words. He must think me a mute or a total square.

In my science classes I often know the answer to questions the teacher poses and I'm dying to raise my hand with the answer. I just can't bring myself to do it. In biology class, Mr. Kopelman sometimes says, "I think Annette knows the answer, let's give her a chance." Then my cheeks burn, my hands grow ice cold as I stammer out the words.

"See, she's keeping up with the assignments," he says, more triumphant than I am.

The only class in which I truly revel is Hebrew. I'd never imagined it would be one of the language choices at Bronx Science. There's even an after-school Hebrew club that meets weekly. I've gone a few times hoping that it would remind me, at least a little, of the kibbutz *kumzits*—boys and girls gathered in common pursuit.

I couldn't have been more mistaken. Mr. Katz, the Hebrew teacher, presides, sitting there stiffly in his horned-rimmed spectacles and a tweed jacket with suede elbow patches and everyone clams up. The students prefer to chat with one another in English, except for Sheldon. He's the guy who brought up the notice from the principal's office. Try as I might, he's nothing like any Israeli boy I've known. He wants to win the citywide gold

318

medal in Hebrew so badly he can almost taste it. It's all he wants to talk about. I hate to admit it, but there's a whiff of a loser about him.

Other boys in this school belong to social and athletic squads. I see the jocks strutting the hallways in their white cardigans, with a green "S" emblazoned on the pocket, as if they owned the entire building. Usually, a trail of googly-eyed swooning girls walk behind them. The girls on the yearbook staff—the Bronx Science version of the jocks—have their noses in the air. They are the intellectuals around here. If I knew how to write in English—really write—I'd be right in there with them, but I wouldn't be snobby about it. I might even invite Sheldon because I think he has a good brain even though he is so square and needy.

At home, my parents' constant requests for help force me to use the English I have learned. To be honest, I sincerely hope my parents will get the knack of English soon because maybe then I won't have to be their assistant all the time. My own English is not great, but already they ask me to speak on their behalf to so many people. They worry no one will understand their accent, or that their limited vocabulary will be inadequate to the task. "Ania, please call the telephone company; Ania, speak to the cashier about our rent check; Ania, ask Maintenance about the washing machine repair; Ania, write this word down for me..." It gets me down sometimes to do things that adults are meant to do. I mean, I am not a baby, or anything like that, but really, I didn't expect to be the adult in this family.

14

Over the winter, Susan has become my close confidante. In some ways she is like Nachum, someone I can talk to about almost anything, but she's also unlike anyone I have known. She lives in our housing complex, so we walk home together from school, but our mile-long walk is never enough to finish our conversations.

In appearance Susan is a close match to the descriptions of the American teens I read about in Poland. She wears a lot of makeup, especially around her eyes. Dark circles of black eye pencil ring her large amber eyes. The eyelashes, sticky with mascara, shade her eyes when she looks down. Her eyelids look bruised with all the purple eye shadow. The light makeup she uses gives her a sickly pallor. Her wide lips are lined with blood-red lipstick that stands out against the pale, slightly sunken cheeks. But it's her hairdo that commands the most attention. Teased and sprayed into obedience into a tall, beehive-like structure it makes her look like a cross between a model and a scarecrow. Despite her appearance, Susan is a brilliant student, something you'd never guess by looking at her.

Usually when Susan and I do our homework in her apartment, we turn the volume on the radio way up as we listen to the latest rock and roll hits. *Mack the Knife* is our favorite because Bobby Darrin sings it and he is a Bronx Science graduate; a status we will soon attain. He has visited our school and the girls went wild, tearing his shirt to get a piece of the holy garment. Of course, I was not in that group.

But I do feel American habits rubbing off on me one song at a time, making me feel a tiny bit less foreign. Listening to such loud, crazy music would be out of the question in our apartment. "This is not music, this is noise, it ruins your ears," Mama says.

In Poland, I only heard about rock and roll and about its evil influence on young people. Such wild-sounding music never played on the radio and people even said it was like sex! Who could have guessed that not three years later I'd hum along with Paul Anka's *Put Your Head on My Shoulder?* His songs touch me and make me long for something, although I'm unsure what.

Of all her strange characteristics, I am most amazed the first time I see Susan smoking. Smoking is a taboo in our house and I have never seen a young person smoke, except for the greaser boys heading to Clinton High. Yesterday, the first school day after our midterms, as soon as we crossed the threshold to her apartment she dug the cigarette pack out of her book bag. Susan lights up her cigarettes with an unparalleled air of sophistication and exhales rings of fragrant smoke with downcast eyes and a hint of a smile. She is the essence of American cool, and I'm glad she's my friend.

I'd been thinking for a while that I should gather up the courage to discuss the letters from Amnon with Susan. I know that if I don't do it soon his unopened airmail envelopes will overflow their hiding place in my bureau drawer. Susan has a certain indefinable, worldly sensibility about her, although she's never been outside of the Bronx. I bet she can help me figure this out.

Most of the time Susan and I spend together in her apartment no one bothers us except for occasional intrusions from her little sister. So yesterday, before her mom showed up, I finally spilled the beans about the letters, hoping for Susan's enlightened opinion.

"What do you think about a married man sending me his daughter's picture and writing to me about his wife?"

"It's obvious," she said. "He doesn't seem to care about her anymore. How old is he, again?"

"I'm not sure, maybe in his mid-thirties."

"Hmm..." was all she said at first and took a deep drag of her cigarette, by then almost down to a stub, then spit out tiny bits of tobacco as she does sometimes with just the tip of her tongue showing. "He sounds as if he is courting *you* now. If his letters were written in English I could do a better job helping you figure him out. I just don't feel his tone, the subtleties of the language he uses," she said.

"I know, it's too hard to translate properly," I said, thinking I'd never consider translating his mushy love words.

Luckily, the bratty sister interrupted us, "Susan, can I have some Coke and potato chips?"

I am almost sorry I had initiated the conversation about Amnon. It feels awkward to expose something so private and weird to Susan, even if she is a font of wisdom on such matters.

"No. It's too close to dinner," Susan told her sister in a tone that sounded eerily like her mother, then turned to me and said, "Why does it make you nervous to read his letters?"

"I guess... it's better not to play with fire?"

"For Pete's sake, Annette, are all Polish girls that naive?"

"What do you mean, naive? And anyway, don't call me Polish." I was getting more embarrassed with each passing minute.

"Oh, never mind." She waved her hand as if I were a hopeless case, then proceeded to work diligently trying to rid me of my prudishness and erase my misconceptions about what men and women do in private.

Before her mother returned from work, Susan cleaned out the ashtray and waved a towel to dissipate the smoke. She didn't say so, but it looked as if she wanted to conceal the fact she'd been smoking. Susan seemed satisfied with her perfunctory cleanup, but

I could still smell the lingering aroma of tobacco and found it difficult to imagine her mother wouldn't notice it too.

When Mrs. Wright came home she greeted us in the same husky voice as Susan's. She is a hard-looking woman whose appearance is a silent testament to the burdens of her life and failed relationships. She works in a warehouse as a shipping clerk. She looked tired and changed into slippers right at the door. "It's stuffy here," she said, then opened the kitchen window and started dinner.

15

Despite the sheer impossibility of it, Mama's friends have prevailed on the manager of the Amalgamated Housing Co-ops to give us an apartment. Never mind that it's a fourth-floor walk-up. It will be ours. Finally! It has been four years since we had a place of our own. We will no longer have to wander around the objects of other people's lives in their sublet apartments, to live with their mementos as mute to us as lumps of ice.

This is even more miraculous than getting into Bronx Science without taking the entrance test. People wait for years to get into these low-cost co-ops established by the needle trade unions. Our one-bedroom apartment, facing the Jerome reservoir, is in the oldest of the low-rise brick buildings comprising the complex. Despite their age, the buildings are well maintained and face onto pleasant, landscaped courtyards. The wooden front door leading to our section is arched at the top; its heavy antique-looking hardware gives it the feel of a castle. A friend tells us these buildings were built to resemble the Tudor-style houses in the affluent community of Bronxville, which is a suburban village that's supposed to be somewhere not too far from the Bronx, but for us, it might as well be a thousand miles away.

In the new apartment my parents will sleep in the living room, as usual. Daniel and I will share the bedroom as we always have. But this will be our own piece of New York, where I won't have to smell someone's lavender sachet, or stick to plastic-covered chairs. The best feature of the compact eat-in kitchen is a window that looks out directly onto the placid waters of the Jerome reservoir. We can watch it as we sit at the table. If I sit at just the right angle, cock my head to the side to block the sidewalk across the street, I can pretend I am looking at a piece of the ocean, Tel Aviv on a calm day.

Between my parents' jobs and this apartment, we have been given a chance to lay a foundation for our lives in this country. And my frequent chats with Susan are helping too. My improved ability to express myself is like fertilizer for my fragile, hair-like American roots.

Yet as much as I am grateful for our good fortune, I can't say that getting this apartment has fully dampened my desire to return to Israel. The steady stream of letters from Amnon and from Ruthi calls me back with a power that I cannot explain. The push and pull between America and Israel makes me crazy sometimes. Should I side with Tinek and embark on a campaign to help Mama love America more, or should I take her side and make my father see how difficult America can be, despite its riches and potential?

I love having a dresser of my own and a special drawer where I can stash my box of pale green stationery and the letters I receive. I sneak out of bed late at night, or very early in the morning as the sun comes up over the reservoir, and write long letters, mostly to Ruthi, Nachum and Yom Tov and sometimes a short, polite one to Amnon and only rarely to Marysia in Poland. I have written them: 'Contrary to what I've been told, they do have trees in New York! And huge green parks and lakes!' If I write, I know they'll reply soon. I love the little jolt of excitement I get just by looking at the exotic stamps and the "air mail" stickers. They add spice to my days as I open the small metal mailbox in the lobby of our building.

Lately, Yom Tov's letters have petered out to a thin trickle, each with a tone more distant and formal, the exact reverse of Amnon's. Maybe Yom Tov has found a new girlfriend by now and I only hope that she didn't notice his limp and that her parents are not Ashkenazi Jews.

Maybe after I wrote him about my wonderful Bronx Science teachers, he concluded that the prospect of my return had diminished to zero. I suppose I must be more careful about what I write; people have a funny way of interpreting things that suits their own conception of the world. If the pace of his letters doesn't pick up and if he doesn't enclose the new photo of himself he had promised, I will forget what he looks like. Maybe that's for the best.

Despite my disappointment with Yom Tov's letters, I still charge down the stairs each day around four o'clock to check the mailbox and look for the thin blue airmail envelopes. Usually, I tear them open with relish, bounding upstairs two steps at a time and am almost done reading before I reach the door. But one letter arrived today addressed in formal looking Hebrew print. It gives me pause. It is not from anyone I know.

I run into the kitchen and rummage for a good knife to slice open the mystery envelope neatly. It is thin and blue, but longer and wider than the usual ones. The return address says Ministry of Defense. Some kind of mistake? I plop into the chair by the window to read, glad that Mama and Tinek are at work and Daniel is at his music lesson.

It's a draft notice from the Israeli military! For me! I read and reread the form letter three times. It says that as an Israeli citizen I am expected to serve in the military regardless of where I reside right now. At seventeen, I don't have to do anything just yet, but the Ministry of Defense puts me on notice that I will have to report for duty as soon as I turn eighteen, less than a year from now.

They sure don't waste any time! Already they have enclosed a list of items I must bring along when I show up—a bedroll, toothbrush, canteen and so on. The list is short and spare, but it gives me the chills. I knew that in Israel women are required to serve, but it never occurred to me that the Israeli government would find me here, in America. I didn't come here to hide, but how did they find me? It's nice to be wanted, but as much as I love Israel, serving in the military is... is preposterous. I live in America now! And besides, if the GADNA exercises, the ones I participated in with Ruthi when I first came to Gvat, were an example of what is awaiting me in the army, I am not going!

Oh, my God, that will make me a draft dodger! I bite my lip and walk around the apartment, back and forth, back, and forth... What a dreadful waste of an opportunity to return to Israel. The image of my cousin Ora in her spiffy military uniform floats before me. I could be like her, proud and courageous, defending my country, standing up to enemies.

I look out at the reservoir, the letter still in my hand. The water looks gray, nothing like the blue green of the Tel Aviv sea. I feel aggravated and confused. Israel is no longer my country, I was yanked out by my roots. Was there ever a country that was really, truly mine? And just then Roy Orbison's *Only the Lonely* comes on the radio. It seems as if he'd written it just for me. Who knows? Maybe a romance with America *is* in my future.

I put a pot of water on the stove to make some tea, then tuck the letter back into its oversized envelope and take it to my special dresser drawer, push it in deep underneath my underwear. Funny: frilly underwear and a military notice resting together. But no one will look there. I will keep the draft notice a secret; won't mention it to my parents. It'll be my last resort solution for returning to Israel if... if things don't work out here.

I try to put the idea of serving in the Israeli military out of my mind, but the draft notice keeps hounding me when I least expect it. It appears unbidden as I look at the world map hanging in class, in the basement laundry room the swooshing water in the washing machines foams like the Tel Aviv surf.

16

It's summer. My first try to do something adult and responsible is to apply for a job at Krum's, Bronx's premier ice cream parlor. Susan told me they always look for extra help in the ice cream season. I take the Grand Concourse bus at the stop on Sedgwick Avenue, feeling all grown up in my ponytail, a white plastic handbag with a gold clasp, matching pumps and a yellow shirtdress Mama bought on sale at Alexander's department store. It looks more sophisticated than the poodle skirt I got as my sweet sixteen gift.

I know Krum's from our periodic trips to the dentist on this very route—my teeth are almost as bad as Mama's—because it is right next to a bus stop. Every time the bus would stop there to discharge and take on passengers I'd crane my neck to peek through the large glass windows to see the shiny wood counters with soda fountains and high red stools. It looked so elegant: I always tried to guess how many ice cream flavors were hidden beneath the glass display cases.

I enter early in the morning. Girls in red-striped shirts are wiping the counters and filling napkin holders. Young men in silly paper hats are mopping the floor. I look around, but no one notices me. A few minutes later a pinched middle-aged woman in a black dress and a white ruffled apron appears and looks me over. "You here for the job?" She wipes her hands on the apron leaving a brown trail. Chocolate? I wonder.

"Yes," I say.

She crinkles her brow and gives me a narrow-eyed look. "Got any experience?"

"Well, I really don't, but I can learn quickly..."

She cuts me off with a wave of her hand, shuffles in a pile of papers on the counter and hands me a yellowing mimeographed sheet of paper, "Here, fill this out and leave it there." She points to the counter and walks out without another word. The girls cast glances in her direction. They seem afraid to look at her directly.

I fill out the application in my very best, neatest print and place it on the counter, then walk out feeling proud of myself and very adult.

By July of 1960, eleven months after our arrival in New York, I land my perfect summer job. A call from someone at Krum's confirms it. It's amazing that in America even young people, like me, can get jobs! I am excited to join many of my classmates in summer employment. My parents' tiny income doesn't stretch enough to make an allowance feasible. I will now earn some real money—a dollar per hour—for my own expenses, maybe even enough to buy a beautiful graduation dress.

This summer our house will be quiet and I'll have the bedroom all to myself. Daniel is going upstate to be an art counselor in a Jewish summer camp near Hunter, New York.

Though my English is quite good by now, in this job I won't have to engage in extensive conversations: What flavor would you like? A cone, or a cup? Any sprinkles? And I picture myself gorging on ice cream, tasting every flavor after work.

My first day on the job the weather is supposed to be in the high eighties, but my early-morning bus ride is still cool. The bus is packed with people going to work: men in business suits, hair slicked back, briefcases in hand; women, probably secretaries, with bright-red lipstick and nicely bobbed hair and high-heeled shoes. Everyone is looking straight ahead, avoiding the gaze of others. I feel strange, but important to be a part of this workday crowd.

I get off at my stop and walk straight toward Krum's front door, but it's locked. Through the glass I see a girl in a red-striped shirt pointing to the side. It turns out that this time I have to enter via the side door, the employees' entrance. The woman who handed me the application stands at the door as other employees approach.

"Good morning," I flash her a smile.

"Wait here," she says curtly and after speaking briefly with a girl coming in, turns back to me and says, "Follow me."

We go down uneven steps all the way to the basement. I detect a slight sour smell, or maybe it's just musty down here. There is a bank of lockers where people stow their street clothes after changing into their uniforms.

A heavy-set man with a ruddy face and a belly that must have enjoyed too many ice cream cones barks instructions. "No French vanilla today! Go easy on the nuts! Don't use the cracked glasses!"

And just before he turns to go upstairs, he yells, "All tips in this jar at the end of the shift! You'll get your share at the end of the week." He points to an enormous glass container with some dollar bills at the bottom.

I am beginning to feel apprehensive. Somehow the scene here doesn't match the friendly atmosphere of the shop.

Walking cautiously upstairs, I review the information in my mind. Rocky Road and Strawberry Cheesecake are the flavors of the day. This is my first job; I want to get it right. The store opens and I manage to dispense several scoops without incident. Okay, I'll manage this. No sooner do I think that than a well-dressed gentleman seats himself on the stool directly in front of me. He is young, attractive, surely someone who works in an office. I can tell by his elegant pinstriped suit. He looks me over appreciatively, but not rudely, and smiles. This makes me nervous. "A banana split supreme," he says, "with whipped cream, please." I freeze. I was told how to scoop and make shakes, but no one told me what this dish was. A banana? I wonder. What does fruit have to do with ice cream? How do I make the whipped cream? Does it involve eggs? Butter? My God, why did I ever take this stupid job?

As my customer smiles patiently, I work myself up into total panic. When he detects that I am having trouble, he calmly tries to suggest how to put the ingredients together. With abject embarrassment, I follow his directions lest the manager notices me. The banana is finally resting in the oval glass dish. I scoop some vanilla ice cream trying to make the balls smooth and extra large and pour gooey syrup letting it coat the three mounds. I almost manage the feat, but the whipped cream that is to be the glorious culmination turns into my ultimate defeat. How do I make this cream? A new burst of panic is about to overwhelm me, but the man points to another server as if he were reading my mind. She uses some sort of a silver canister from which a frothy white substance emerges. Ah, this must be the whipped cream, I think with relief.

I spot a similar canister on a shelf below the counter and pick it up gently. Who knows? It may explode if not handled carefully. Its coolness makes me calmer. I look at it trying to find the mechanism that will allow the whipped cream to be released. I locate a button and try to aim the canister at the banana-ice cream creation. I don't know if I needed training to use it, but to my horror, I cover the nice gentleman's suit with the whipped cream that shoots out like foam from a fire extinguisher. My cheeks aflame, my heart racing, I apologize over and over again as he dabs his suit with a pile of napkins. He isn't angry, but tears spring into my eyes and sting my ego. I excuse myself and run to the basement in shame, practically tearing off my uniform.

I vow never to return. The humiliation is just too overwhelming. I am such a klutz! The Israeli army should be grateful that I will not report for duty!

Mama is home. It's her day off. "You are back already?" She looks at my face. "What happened?"

And I tell her, but she laughs. "It's not funny, Mama," I pout. "Any idiot should have been able to do it right."

"But you are not an idiot. You need a job where you work with your brain," she says.

Jobless for the next month, I have too much time to contemplate things. I sit at the kitchen table sipping my iced tea and stare at the sweaty glass. I am trying to read, but a stew of confusing thoughts crowds out the plot of the book. Despite my admission to Bronx Science, my great teachers, our new apartment, my friend Susan, my ability to get a job—even if I can't keep it—and the rock and roll music that makes me want to sing and tap my feet, I am still not sold on America. There are still plenty of reasons why a return to Israel would be sweeter than anything else.

Then I remember Yom Tov's last letter.

Dear Anat,

This month the khamsin winds blowing from the Sahara have been so bad, I spend almost all of my time at the beach. As a result, my swimming is improving. The heat is oppressive. Remember the boardwalk we used to patrol? It's filled with strolling couples. I hate to be here by myself and might ask Sara to come with me next time. Remember her? Now I will update you on all of our team sport scores... I know you are not crazy about sports, but I want to use up all of the space on this aerogram. Write me sometime.

Yom Tov

I reread it twice and conclude this is not a letter from the type of boyfriend I want. Who is this Sara, anyway? My disappointment eats at me. I start wondering if Israel is loosening its grip on my heart just a tiny bit. I get up to pour another glass of iced tea, but first I throw the letter in the garbage. No point keeping it.

17

This is my final year at Bronx Science. I am sitting at a desk in a room outfitted with all manner of machines and tools. Mr. Belacci, our teacher, is speaking, but I feel too intimidated to absorb his words.

"Now listen, kids, pick a project that you can manage, but once you start, you must go through with it. No going back to an easier choice." He looks at us trying to hide his disdain, but the curl in his lip tells us how he feels.

"What's the matter? You think a bunch of eggheads like you can't do stuff with your hands? Try it."

I look around the room trying to make sense of it. It is unlike any laboratory I have ever seen and this class is called *scientific technical laboratory*—STL. Only this school would come up with such an exalted name for a shop class. I recognize some saws, but the rest of the machines are unfamiliar and scary looking with jagged blades and red buttons that scream "danger."

Very quickly I learn their names: table saws, jigsaws, radial arm saws, circular saws, and miter saws. Who would have imagined that there were so many species of them?

All I can think is, Oh, my God. I will have to use them. I'll never pass. This class will keep me from graduation!

The harsh fluorescent lights make the room look like some bizarre operating room in a science fiction movie. Mr. Belacci says, "Here are some safety rules. Listen carefully. I don't want to see any fingers on the floor." I'm hardly listening to him. This classroom freaks me out. I hate tools. No one in our family has one iota of technical savvy, or interest, least of all me. I stare at Mr. Belacci's fat belly and think that he looks more like a mechanic than a teacher. I can just see him under a car; his scuffed work boots and greasy overalls showing hairy ankles sticking out from under a Chevy.

In the end, I choose to make a working periscope, and Mr. Belacci bellows, "Just make sure it's not a kindergarten toy. Your graduation from this school will hinge on it." What project did Susan choose? I wish I had consulted with her before making such a serious decision.

I suppose that I could have chosen a different project, but this one seems a bit less complicated than the others that are driven by gears and shafts of all sorts. Having mostly conquered English, though still too shy to initiate any conversations, and free of the worry about taking the entrance exam, I now have to adjust to a subject I never envisioned as part of my education. This is even scarier than the Mishnah studies.

If I can manage to cut the necessary pieces of wood just so, make them square, smooth as ice and gleaming without a single bubble in the varnish and then assemble them with mirrors positioned at the precise angles, I can start thinking about a world that has always seemed out of reach—college. For someone with two left hands this will be no easy feat. Why is it that physics and chemistry are so easy for me, but a class like shop, the highest hurdle? What's wrong with me?

Tinek thinks it's hilarious that I have to go to a lumberyard and find the proper kind of wood. He is not handy either, even though his father was a carpenter, so he suggests that I speak to a neighbor for tips on my project, but ultimately, he says, "You are on your own."

"I can't do this. This is more difficult than learning a whole new language," I say, hoping for sympathy. "Why on earth do girls need to learn this stuff?" I ask.

"Because women and men must be equal," Mama says. "Just as men need to get acquainted with diapers, women need to know how to handle a hammer." She adds with a twinkle in her eye, "If I could, I'd even have men go through childbirth."

18

Mama doesn't resemble any of the moms of the new friends I have made. They are homemakers whose world revolves around the kitchen. Carole's mom spends much of her day preparing a proper Italian meal for her father; Margaret's mom rushes back from a shopping trip all out of breath just so that she'd be home the minute her husband arrives home from work. Susan's mom is the only working mother I know, besides mine.

Mama's bruised fingertips tell me all I need to know about her job. The fur collars she sews will be sold as "hand-finished" and command a higher price. It makes me so angry that her delicate fingers that sewed delicate lace undergarments have now become mere tools, roughened by fur dye and by constant punching through the leather.

By the time she drags herself home, all sweaty from her subway ride with bits of fur adhering to her, she looks like a raccoon, her furry look accentuated by dark circles under her eyes. She doesn't get much sleep. Each day she rises before dawn, hurries off to the subway with the hope it doesn't get stuck in the tunnel so she can punch her card by eight in the morning. God forbid it should be 8:01.

"Would you believe it," Mama said to Tinek shortly after we arrived and she landed the very opposite of a dream job at *Sophisticated Fashions Inc.*, "he never says hello when he sees us in the elevator. Just keeps chewing on his foul-smelling cigar. We are just furniture to him."

"Who?"

"Mr. Eisenberg, my lord and master."

"If you moved to the kibbutz, like I proposed, you wouldn't have to deal with this *putz*."

She ignores him and goes on. "If we happen to make eye contact, Eisenberg asks, 'Girls, no hello this morning?' Girls. He calls us 'girls.'"

"And what do you say to him?"

"I don't need to say anything. If he sees my expression he knows exactly what I have to say."

Now, Mama is on the warpath trying to get Mr. Eisenberg to designate a space as a women's bathroom. She's not asking for something fancy, just a place she and her coworkers can wash the fur off their arms and faces, and the black dye from under their fingernails. So far, he won't budge. He tells her they can use the men's room when it's free, but with forty men in the shop it's a rare occurrence, never mind the piss on the floor and no soap. Mama is starting to agitate for a union in this non-union shop. Having fought off communist tax inspectors in Poland, she is fearless and not as reticent as her elderly Greek and Hispanic coworkers.

Sometimes I just can't shake off the feeling that Mama has been cheated by trading Israel for America. She felt successful and competent there. She had no boss to lord over her and that made her softer, more accessible to me. Until Tinek announced his precious *vizka*, I imagined her business growing and her growing happier with it.

Tinek is content with his job. His boss, the rabbi, has finally promoted father to doing photo-offset stripping work. Surely, this is better than picking up heavy loads of printing paper from various suppliers and ferrying them on a metal cart through the streets of lower Manhattan. Since his new work requires layout skills and the ability to read the Yiddish publications this shop prints, Tinek finds the work more interesting. It perplexes me sometimes that he's not at all bothered by his loss of the high status he enjoyed in Poland. He is always satisfied with what he has at the moment. He doesn't covet the greener grass on the other side. He doesn't busy his mind figuring out schemes to do better, to go higher. He just enjoys today. Most of all, he enjoys the people around him.

Emil, from the printing shop, and Tinek have become good friends. Tinek finds Emil's stories of his southern childhood interesting and chilling. Part of Emil's family is still in Alabama where the discrimination faced by Black people is frighteningly similar to what Jews experienced before the Second World War broke out in Europe.

"The treatment of Black people is my one disappointment in America," Tinek says.

I know how much he loves America, so this statement surprises me at first. I thought that nothing about America could ever disappoint him.

19

Since the fall of 1960, my classmates have been in the frenzy of the college admissions process. Of course, for students in our school there isn't even the slimmest chance of *not* planning for college. The school library is mobbed with students vying for college catalogs. They read and talk about the features of colleges throughout the country. They bellyache about having to write essays; they fill out reams of papers and make many carbon copies. Some even go to visit the schools with their parents. Names like Harvard, Cornell, Yale, and Brandeis are bandied about like tennis balls. They don't mean a thing to me, except for the romantic notion that they are somewhere out of the city, in places with vine-covered buildings reeking of history and privilege and luxuriant lawns on which WASPy students parade in perfectly proper loafers; places my classmates can go to get away from home.

The guidance counselor's office is packed with students requesting recommendations and asking a myriad of questions. I feel left out of this process and dread running into any classmates who might bring up the subject. I avoid the possibility by making myself invisible, sliding against the walls of the hallways like a shadow. There is absolutely no chance of my parents affording college, any college. They might not even be able to afford the application fees. I listen to the entire hubbub with sadness. I have come this far in America, but now an invisible barrier—money— will keep me from going to college and later, medical school. I've dreamed of becoming a doctor. What will I do instead? I don't know. Nothing else fits me.

One January day in 1961, the guidance counselor sends a note to my homeroom: Annette, please report to my office right away. "You may be excused," the teacher says and, once again, I walk down the hall with trepidation. What now?

Mr. Marx looks up over a huge stack of papers as I enter. He looks tired, his tie is askew. "So where do you plan to send your college applications? I haven't seen you here," he says.

For a moment I don't know what to say, but I resolve not to expose my embarrassment. "Thanks for asking," I swallow hard. "Can you please tell me my options? I don't want to burden my parents with a fat college bill." I say this casually, as if my parents would pay a fat college bill if I only gave them the chance.

"Let me first look at your grades," he says shuffling through color-coded stacks of file folders. He pulls out some papers and stares at them with a puzzled expression on his face. "Aren't you the girl who came from Israel last year and got in without taking the exam?"

Oh, my God. I freeze. I think my heart will stop. He has discovered my illegal way of getting into the school. Who knows? He might get Dr. Taffel fired for letting me in.

After a moment that stretches into eternity he lifts his eyes and says with a smile, "How did you manage such good grades? Hmm, I see you even aced the regents exams. What's your secret for learning English so quickly?"

My whole body exhales, though my palms are still damp.

"With your grades you should have no trouble getting admitted into City College. It's considered a scholarship school, one of the best in the country. Those with a very high grade point average, like yours, can attend for free."

Free? Now it's my turn to be stunned. "You mean my parents won't have to pay anything?"

"That's right, but you'll have to earn some money to pay for your books."

I leave the office elated. I am floating through the hallways in slow motion undisturbed by the torrent of students rushing in all directions at once. I know I will get in because my grades exceed the requirements for admission. *I* have chosen my college. Isn't that so much better than waiting and praying and holding your breath for a college to pick *you?*

Carole passes me on my way down the hall and for a change I initiate college talk. "I have made a decision on where to go," I say confidently. "I want to stay in New York, it's more exciting than a rural area."

"So to which schools are you applying?" she asks, eyebrows raised.

"I am applying only to City College." Then I add casually, "Why waste my time on others?" and a faint smile rises spontaneously to my lips. I can't hold it back even though I try to. America—this is why my father wanted us to be here. Where else could I even think of going to college?

When my parents learn of my college decision they are very pleased, especially Tinek who always says under good circumstances, "Ah, America! *Di goldene medine.*" America, the golden land. When he learns from his friends that City College is known as the "Harvard for the proletariat" he beams in double satisfaction.

Just as I absorb the idea that I will be attending college, a wave of blues envelops me. Does this mean I am not going back to Israel? What about the draft notice? Adult life is looming like a pregnant cloud. You don't know if it'll bring welcome rain or a torrential flood. Life is so complicated and full of contradictions. And this is

342

where something else, quite paradoxical, strikes me for the first time: why do I say 'Oh, my God,' so often? I am not a believer, after all. I am simultaneously sad and happy and I don't know how to resolve the confusion churning inside me.

I call Susan to see if she's home.

20

School is out for spring break. It is almost noon and I am sitting at the kitchen window in my bathrobe and curlers, looking out at the reservoir across Sedgwick Avenue. It isn't the Mediterranean, but today it will do.

One minute I'm relieved that I have gotten into college, another minute I agonize because that probably means I'm never going back to Israel. What use is it to speak enough English to ace my exams when Susan is my only real friend. And other than my parents and Daniel, with no family here, it's lonely. New York feels like a carnival at the end of a long day when you have had enough of the raucous atmosphere, flashing lights, nerve-wracking rides and hollow calls of the hawkers. All the noise only makes you feel more alone.

I hide my feelings with a standard-size smile, like someone in a toothpaste commercial. On the outside I may look more American than when I first stepped off the boat. But who am I on the inside? I don't know, certainly not American, Israeli, Polish or Russian. I may have lived in all those places but I am not of them.

Though there's no school, my mind is still on all the hurdles I must jump before graduation—the periscope is one of them. I pick up my half-completed instrument, turn it in all directions, inspecting the alignment of the mirrors. Maybe I should hop over to Susan's to see what she thinks of the honey-color stain I've selected for it.

With no homework or exams to study for, I treat myself to a late wake up. Mama and Tinek are at work. Daniel is visiting a friend so I have these rare quiet moments alone. Since he practices on his accordion for hours on end, I rarely have total quiet.

I get up and put on a pot of water for tea, then pick up a copy of Tinek's *New York Post* from the counter. He can't start his day without the news. First, he reads the English paper as best he can, then he completes his understanding by reading *The Forward* in Yiddish. I browse through the headlines while I wait for the water to boil. It's funny how the turmoil in the world—Pakistan, Cuba, Russia—matches what's going on inside me.

In the meantime, noises downstairs get my attention. I stand up to see who is shouting in the courtyard below our fourth-floor window. It's only a bunch of kids. That is when I notice the swollen buds on the bushes. Remnants of soot-covered snow still cling to the sides of our front steps, but the buds get me thinking about Passover. This year, we will be celebrating with Aunt Rosa and her family in Harrisburg, Pennsylvania. I wonder how Americans conduct a Seder.

I am looking forward to the trip though I remember well the disappointment my father suffered on his arrival in Harrisburg. Rosa's time in the Łódź ghetto and later, in Auschwitz, had changed her. She turned from a bubbly, free-thinking young woman into someone he hardly recognizes. But I'm eager to get to know my cousin, Faye. She's my image of the real American girl. Faye is younger than I am, but I suspect she can clue me into things about America I can't learn from anyone else. Now that I can manage a conversation with her in English she won't think me as strange as she did when I got off the SS *Constitution* in the stupid dirndl skirt and braids like Heidi's.

We arrive at the cavernous Penn Station where sounds of people and trains echo. The pace is frenetic. The nervous jostling of passengers, porters and vendors makes me anxious. Soon we are off on a four-hour ride through the American countryside to Harrisburg. The fields don't differ very much from rural areas in Poland. Familiar crisp greens, ochres, and rich browns flash through the dusty windows, yet I don't see any horses hitched to plows. Instead, large tractors, grain silos and stately farmhouses catch my eye. Soon the monotony gets to me. The rhythmic revolution of the wheels makes me close my eyes and my mind wanders to Israel.

Nothing on this journey reminds me of Israel's Jezreel Valley farms. There is no cotton with its creamy white blossoms, no fragrant orange groves, no vineyards laden with luscious grapes. The memory of my grape-picking job makes my mouth water. I am suddenly overwhelmed by a desire to get to the Passover Seder hoping it might remind me of the glorious kibbutz Seder.

The train's whistle, sudden and sharp, announces our arrival. The train slows to a stop. "Ania, Ania, wake up. Mama and Daniel have already gotten off," my father says tapping my shoulder.

"I wasn't asleep," I say, gather my purse and jacket and reach for my small bag overhead.

Rosa's entire family awaits us at the train station.

"Dora, Nachman! I am so glad you are finally here together," Rosa exclaims and squeezes my parents, one after the other.

"Anetka, come here." She pulls me to her and hugs me tightly, but her second husband, Avram, stands to the side looking down at his feet, unsure how to behave.

Cousin Faye is busting with excitement. "We never have

overnight guests," she says with an ear-to-ear smile and picks up my bag.

I can't take my eyes off her red nail polish and lipstick. "Really?" I ask.

"No, never," Faye says. "And you can sleep in my room. I will sleep with Aviva."

"You have your own room?"

"Sure. Who doesn't?" she looks at me and rolls her eyes.

Faye's little sister Aviva jumps up and down until my father scoops her up and admires her pink straw hat. He is the only relative on her mother's side still living. She isn't old enough yet to know they were all murdered.

From the station we ride in their roomy blue Rambler station wagon to the house on Green Street. I can't believe they own a car. Very few of the people we knew back in Israel had a vehicle. Well... Tinek's friend Mendel had a motorcycle and Edek had a car. No one we knew in Poland had a car either though they weren't exactly poor, but Americans just can't get along without wheels. Aunt Rosa and her husband also own a house—a whole house for one family! That and the car surely mean that even regular people can become rich in this country.

We park in a driveway lined with flowering dogwoods; some buds have already popped open. The moist lawn emits a fresh oniony scent—a whiff of spring and promise. A curving brick walkway brings us to a wide wooden door with glass panels.

"Come in, come in," Avram welcomes us.

We enter the hallway. It's like in the movies. All of us stop for a moment looking up. There is a curving staircase with a polished banister. Wine-colored roses wind their way up the carpet that rises up the stairs. It looks grand.

"Faye, show the guests to their rooms," Rosa calls out. "I have to do something in the kitchen."

"Let me help you," Mama says, and follows her.

"We scrubbed the whole house clean of *hametz*. I am

347

exhausted," Faye tells me as we make our way upstairs. "Did you clean out your *hametz*?"

I try to avoid this conversation, but she thinks I don't know what *hametz* is and launches into an explanation. "Orthodox Jews have to clean out all leavened-bread products from every corner of the house. They are banned on Passover."

"I don't think they did that on the kibbutz," I tell her. "Who makes the rules for Jewish celebrations anyway?"

"I will ask the rabbi," she says.

A rabbi? Oh, no, are they as religious as our Hassidic family in Bnei Berak?

I walk into the kitchen where my father is already chatting with his sister. I glance at Rosa every so often trying to discern why Tinek told me that I look like her. She wears an apron over a fancy dress with a lace collar and silver buttons down its front. There is no sparkle in her eyes. It's as if a flame in them has been extinguished.

I inhale the enticing aroma of chicken soup that hangs in the air and watch Rosa boil the matzo balls she's preparing for tonight. "If you made them like our mother, they will be light and fluffy," Tinek says.

"Oy, Nachman, that was a lifetime ago. Who can remember?"

Since it looks as if I won't get any tidbits of information about my grandmother, or her cooking, I move on to the dining room.

The table is set with fancy porcelain dishes whose silver scrollwork around the edges matches the ornate silver candlesticks and an elaborately carved goblet for Elijah's wine. An embroidered matzo cover lies over a large platter. My cousins are dressed up. Their black patent leather shoes shine as bright as the crystal tableware. I get the sense that this evening, the first *Seder*, is not an ordinary one in this home. Yet despite all these holiday trappings, the jubilant atmosphere of a kibbutz Seder is missing.

Avram glances toward my father, who is not wearing a *kippah* but makes no comment.

After dark, Uncle mumbles the *Haggadah* in an Ashkenazi variant of Hebrew that sounds nothing like the Israeli Hebrew I know. Daniel sits at the other end of the table. The way he looks around the room and shifts in his seat I can tell he's bored. Tinek's eyes look as if they will close any minute. Mama gives him a nudge and he turns to her mouthing, "What?"

Where is the excitement? Where is the inspirational retelling of how we were freed from slavery in Egypt? Rosa leans over to Tinek and whispers. "We'll be eating soon." He winks at her as if in agreement to get the ceremony over with.

Next comes the recitation of the ten plagues. Avram dips a pinky into his wine glass and flicks a drop of wine with each... blood... frogs... lice... until I cringe at the violence of it. The beautiful symbolism of this Seder is lost on me this year.

Since Aviva is still too young, the job of asking the traditional four questions falls to Daniel. He looks pleased to play a part and recites them in a clear, loud Hebrew, his voice at least an octave deeper than just a few months ago. Next month he will be fifteen.

"How is this night different from all the other nights? Why do we eat matzo on Passover?" Avram looks astonished. He is wondering how a child of Nachman could possibly know the contents of the *Haggadah*.

By the end of the evening, the four glasses of wine make me sleepy and I can't wait for this service to be over. But it cannot end until the *afikomen*, a hidden piece of matzo symbolizing hope for the future, has been found. Its secret location is what has kept little Aviva awake. She races around the living room and dining room to find it and brings it, victorious, for a prize. Avram distributes small pieces of this matzo to all of us, and his off-key rendition of *Had Gadya*, the traditional Passover song, follows. This service is nothing like the one that transported me to another dimension at the kibbutz Seder and yet, I can see Avram and Rosa's commitment to our traditions. It pleases me that after all they'd been through they are able to muster the energy for Jewish rituals.

Rosa gets up from the table and begins cleaning up. She looks worn out. Her skin is sallow and the numbers tattooed on her forearm stand out. She doesn't smile, her shoulders are stooped, and I can almost see her in her striped Auschwitz garb. Avram continues to murmur prayers under his breath.

At last, we retire to our rooms. I stop by my parents' bedroom to say good night. Tinek says, "Ania, Rosa is not the same woman I've described to you all these years. Every last note of song has been squeezed out of her."

Mama asks, "Nachman, what will you do tomorrow morning when Avram asks you to join him in the synagogue?"

"I am not going to pretend. I won't go. I don't care if people practice their religion, but I don't want them to force it upon me."

"But what about Rosa? She will be hurt."

"She knows me, Dora. She accepts me as I am and if you noticed, even Avram didn't hassle me about wearing a *kippah*."

I can't wait for the morning. I pull the covers over my head, inhaling the smell of Rosa's laundry soap.

21

I am glad to be back in New York. Its bustling atmosphere is so refreshing after the small-town monotony of Harrisburg with its unsettling quiet. Here the music of dozens of languages, faces of many colors, shouts of messengers, police sirens, luxurious department stores, all fuse into a splendid whole, pulsating with excitement. We experience all this only when we venture outside our small, mostly Jewish enclave in the Bronx. In Manhattan we only eat at Horn & Hardart automats. They are fun. We pull out our sandwiches from under the little glass doors, wondering whose hands have placed them there.

Soon after our return, our home is in a flurry of excitement. Two wonderful things have happened: Daniel has passed the entrance exam to the Bronx High School of Science *and* been invited to play at the luxurious Barbizon Plaza in Manhattan—one of New York's top performance venues. Sponsored by the American-Israeli Cultural Foundation, the evening at the Barbizon will feature outstanding young musicians who were supported in their music studies in Israel by the foundation. My brother will share the stage with the promising violinist Itzhak Perlman, the mezzo-soprano Malka Efrat and the cellist Michael Rudiakov. Mrs. Serge Koussevitzky, the widow of the renowned Boston Symphony Orchestra conductor, will host the elegant event.

Tinek's excitement is contagious. He whistles non-stop and tells every neighbor he meets about Daniel's impending stage debut and his admittance to *my* high school. Mama is happy too, but she is much more reserved. Both of them make time to sit and listen as Daniel practices the pieces he will perform. Mama sits with her eyes closed and listens, a barely perceptible smile on her lips. Tinek listens too and sometimes turns the music pages, but he seems tense, expecting a perfect rendition. Each time Daniel plays a classical piece flawlessly, Tinek claps furiously. It proves to him that his choice of which child to enroll in music lessons was right.

On the night of the performance we dress up, not that it's saying much. Daniel, the star, is wearing a white short-sleeved shirt that Tinek dressed up with a bow tie. A bow tie? Where did he get it? He never uses a bow tie and only wears a tie for extraordinary occasions. I do wish Daniel had a jacket for this evening. It would make him look more his age.

Tinek is decked out in his one suit—brown sharkskin—and a blue striped tie. Mama puts on her wool navy dress that buttons down the front and clips on a pin that looks like gold if you don't look too closely. "Ania, can you do something with my hair?" she calls out to me. "It's such mess."

"Sure, I will as soon as I finish fixing mine," I shout from the bathroom, struggling to curl my eyelashes. It was Faye who showed me an eyelash curler, a lethal looking device, like a surgical implement.

As I work on her hair, I ask Mama, "Does Daniel's debut surpass my admittance to the Bronx High School of Science?"

"Why are you asking such a silly question, Ania? You got in

without even taking the entrance exam! And now you are an "A" student."

I am embarrassed. My competitive spirit is rearing its head. Maybe it's jealousy. This *is* a triumph for Daniel, but I wonder: will his head be visible behind his huge accordion? He is still very short. One would never guess he is almost fifteen. Eleven or twelve maybe, but fifteen—never.

It turns out that during the concert my little brother is totally in command. The classical piece he plays fills the concert hall as if it were played on a powerful piano. The audience goes wild with applause, but I clap louder than everyone. Tinek has tears in his eyes; he claps furiously and yells, "Bravo! Bravo!" Mama smiles her mysterious Mona Lisa smile.

After the excitement of the concert and the celebration of Daniel's high school admittance, life goes back to normal. I complete my periscope after sanding and varnishing, time and again to avoid any bubbles in the varnish and to get a mirror smooth finish. I must say, it looks professional. I hope Mr. Belacci will agree.

Another letter from Amnon arrives but I am reluctant to open it because I think I have forgotten how to read Hebrew. I know that's hardly possible, bizarre in fact, but when I tried to read some of his recent letters, the Hebrew characters turned into undecipherable hieroglyphics dancing on the page, teasing me to decipher the message with each pirouette. Maybe I'm not quite ready for what he writes.

Daniel's recital was a welcome and uplifting interlude in our lives after our trip to Harrisburg. But as I have already learned, something good is almost always followed by something bad. Now Tinek is laid up with an undiagnosed back pain and cannot even stand up, much less go to work at his print shop.

It makes all three of us feel helpless the way he just lays there not saying much. He is a stoic and doesn't complain, but the pain is written on his face. The stairs are the worst obstacle of all. How can he hike up and down four flights of stairs in our building and then another huge staircase at the elevated subway stop on Jerome Avenue when he can barely make his way to the bathroom? Going to work is out of the question and he gets no sick pay.

In the evening, Mama cooks Tinek's favorite potato soup and sets it before him. He is too miserable to eat; not like him at all. She hands him his pain pills and a glass of water. He swallows, looking ashen. Then she takes his elbow and tries to help him up from the kitchen chair. "What are you doing?" He is embarrassed at the trouble he has standing up.

"Nachman, you have to lie down. I'll help you back to bed," she says gently. He shuffles slowly, bent like an old man. Not long after I hear him snoring.

"Mama, what will we do without Tinek's paycheck?"

"Shh, let's not worry about that now. We have to focus on helping your father get better. We have survived tough times before. We'll be okay."

"But we just barely make it to payday on *both* your wages."

"This is not your business," she says and gives me an annoyed look. "Don't worry, you won't starve. No one starves in America."

"What about the people in the South?"

"Look, I don't have the head to discuss it now." She is exasperated.

I get ready for the night, sleeping on the living room sofa with Mama. Since Tinek began having this back trouble I have given him my bed, the one with a better mattress. As I lie in the dark watching the shadows on the ceiling I think back to Poland where we planned vacations in the mountains and spa resorts without a shred of concern about money.

All I want now is for Tinek to recover so he can come to my graduation. Without him there I won't even feel like going.

Father continues to suffer and the doctor's bills are mounting: we have no insurance. One of the doctors finally says that medicines won't help. He needs to put my father in traction at Mount Sinai Hospital. "What is traction?" I ask Mama.

"They sort of stretch you using some newfangled machines."

"Machines and stretching, that sounds like a medieval torture," I say lightly to cheer Mama up, but inside I am terrified for Tinek.

"Maybe while he is in the hospital they will find out exactly what is wrong with him," Mama says.

Tinek goes into the hospital reluctantly. By turns, he is resigned and hopeful.

Mama visits him there every day after work, week after week, but Daniel and I can't. We go only on weekends. Mama is more tired than ever and sick with worry, but my ever-practical mother has started to think about how we can find an apartment in a building with an elevator. She worries most about the stairs. She thinks Tinek will not be able to manage them on his return home. Each evening she talks to various acquaintances on the telephone in hushed tones. Most of them have lived in America for a long time. I think they are hatching a plan.

It has been three months now and Father will be released from the hospital shortly because the traction seems to have done him no good at all. On some days he's actually worse than before. "We must remember to hide the hospital bills from your father when he returns," Mama says.

"He won't even look, you are our finance minister," I remind her.

She smiles. "But he's the one who writes out the checks," she says. "Money management is a joint project in a marriage. I won't keep the bills from him forever, just until he feels better."

"When will that be?" I ask, but she's already in the kitchen, marinating the chicken for next day's dinner.

What bothers me most is that the best doctors in the world—American specialists—can't figure out how to cure my father. This makes me resolve with more conviction than ever that I will find a cure when I get to medical school.

Eventually, Mama's friends do come up with an idea, but the problem is that their scheme involves *me*. They think I should write a petition to Mr. S., the President of the Amalgamated Housing Corporation, and then visit him in person to plead for a different apartment in our housing complex. A president? They want me to see the man responsible for thousands of apartments.

Only the newer buildings in the Amalgamated housing complex have elevators and the waiting lists are a mile long. People wait for years and years to get these low rental apartments and that's *with* connections.

I can't imagine myself doing what Mama's friends suggest. I am annoyed and can't stand the humiliation of pleading for anything. "Why can't you go see Mr. S., yourself, Mama?" I ask even though I already know the answer.

"I don't speak enough English to express myself properly," she says. She entreats me with her eyes. This look is so uncharacteristic of her. "He may be more receptive to a young girl."

"I don't know how to do this, Mama," I say, knowing full well I will give in. "Please, please don't make me do it. This is a job for grown-ups. I can't handle this."

As soon as the words leave my mouth I am ashamed. I compose a letter that very evening and open by saying, "Dear Mr. S., You will probably throw this request into the wastebasket as soon as you read it..." and then I tell him all about my father's condition. I seal the envelope. Mama doesn't even bother to ask what I wrote. She mails the letter.

Before the week is out we get a call from Mr. S.'s office. His secretary wants to set up an appointment for me to see him. I ask her to make it after three in the afternoon. I am still in school, I explain. She doesn't respond for a moment, then she says, "I didn't know Mr. S. made appointments with children." She sounds so superior, I am terrified. I have cooked my goose and offended him with my stupid letter. She must have read it too. How will I face him? Mother's hopeful look stops me from saying anything, but my insides are roiling. I'd do anything to avoid this meeting.

On the day of the appointment Mama is still at work so I go by myself. I sit outside Mr. S.'s office suite nervously twisting my fingers and watch the large clock on the waiting room wall. Its hands move ever so slowly, but all of a sudden it's three-thirty. A pinched-looking secretary summons me in. She points to her boss's door without so much as raising her head.

I enter and find him sitting behind an impressively carved desk. The arch of his bushy eyebrows gives him a look of polite surprise. He is large and sits perfectly erect, dressed in a gray suit. His deeply lined face, an impressive nose and fleshy lips make him look like a wood carving. Definitely the look of a president, I think to myself, someone with a power to affect people's lives. Then he speaks with a deep booming voice that comes from the depths of his belly. "I have read your letter, but I'd like to hear from you in person, now that you are here."

I swallow hard and launch into my request. I know if I don't start now, I'll run out of here. My cheeks are on fire. I can feel my lips moving and I know I am speaking, but I am not sure even I know what I am saying. He listens intently, his deep-set, intelligent eyes fixed on my face. After a moment of silence he leans back in his chair, runs his hand through his silver hair and says, "Annette, you have explained your family's situation quite well. Our waiting lists are long, but I will see what can be done."

I am startled when he utters my American name. For a moment I don't know whom he is addressing. But I know the meeting is over because he stands up and shakes my sweaty hand lost in the grip of his huge palm. I think I detect a hint of a smile on his face, though I can't be sure. I am just so relieved to be done. "Thank you for listening, Mr. S.," I say and make my exit.

If it weren't for the acceptance letter to City College that just arrived, I'd have been obsessing about the outcome of my meeting with Mr. S. But now I'm in the thrall of the college. Me an American college student? It sounds impossible to my ears even though it's right here before me in black and white. I have no clear idea of what my major will be, but I know I'll study medicine someday. There must be a cure for Tinek and others like him.

As with my and Daniel's admission to high school, my parents are euphoric. "Ania, you will be the first college graduate in our family," Mama says proudly. "That's something!"

"Wait, I haven't yet graduated from high school," I laugh, and inside I feel good that I've given her something to be happy about.

In less than a week, we get a call from the Amalgamated Housing Corporation's management office. We have been assigned a one-bedroom apartment in the eighth building on the twelfth floor. It not only has an elevator, but an expansive view of Van Cortlandt Park. Mother hugs me so tightly I think she might crack my ribs. "This will be the best medicine for your father," she says. "Just one look out the window at the emerald vista is all anyone needs."

"Will you and Tinek finally move into the bedroom?" My question sounds more like an instruction.

"No!"

"But why, Mama?"

"You and Daniel need a quiet place to study. You will share the bedroom as you always have. Your father and I will be fine on a pullout couch in the living room."

We start packing even before Tinek returns from the hospital. The task is child's play. We have so little to pack. Nothing as special as the Meissen plates that Mendl wrapped so carefully before we left Israel. As Mama predicted, her most treasured gift arrived smashed into a thousand pieces. She looked more sad than angry when she unwrapped them and said under her breath, "What's another casualty? We can never replace what we have lost."

To me, making my mother happy is a bigger achievement than

getting the new apartment. Usually her deep sadness is just below the surface. It seems as if the grief of losing so many of her family members seeped into her brain, skin, and bones. She hasn't gotten over having to leave her sisters behind in Israel either. Maybe my graduation will make her see not only me, but America in a new light, the golden light Tinek wrote about when we were still in Israel.

Tinek will be coming home in just a couple of weeks. What wonderful surprises we will have for him, a new apartment with an elevator *and* a grand view—just the way he imagined our new American lives. All we need to get now is that electric vacuum cleaner!

22

Late one afternoon, as I am changing from my school clothes, the phone rings. I am tired, having stayed up till dawn studying for the finals, and do not pick it up quickly. After several rings it sounds so insistent that I lift the receiver wearily. A familiar deep voice says, "Anat?" It jolts me out of my skin. It can't be. I must have misheard. "Anat, Anat can you hear me?" The insistent voice of the caller is getting louder.

"Who is calling?" I ask knowing in the pit of my stomach but refusing to believe my own ears.

"Don't you recognize my voice, Anat?"

"Yes... yes I do." I answer inaudibly, thinking how could it be Amnon? He lives across the ocean. Normal people don't make expensive overseas calls unless someone is dying. After a moment of silence in which my heart beats so fast I think he can hear its thumping, I whisper, "Amnon? Is it really you? Where are you?"

He laughs and I see him in my mind's eye: the black curl dangling over his forehead, the long eyelashes, the mischievous boy look. "Yes, it's me. Didn't you get my letters?"

My mind races to the stack of his unopened blue envelopes in my dresser. I begin to perspire. With the letters tucked away, their content sat in the farthest reaches of my brain.

"Anat? I wrote you that I was coming to New York. Didn't you get my letter?"

"Where are you?" I ask again, unable to absorb his words.

"I am in a hotel in Manhattan. Can you come to see me? I have got to talk to you." There is a tension in his voice, a kind of pleading.

My knees feel weak and my heart races faster. I stand there stupefied. "All right," I say tentatively. "Give me the address." I scribble it on a napkin but have no idea what I'll do with it. I'm too overwhelmed to think rationally.

He laughs again and says, "Anat, your Hebrew has a bit of an American accent already." I imagine his broad smile and the stubble along his rugged jaw. I push the image away though his voice calls forth emotions I had long buried. "I have school tomorrow. I will see you on Saturday." I hang up the receiver quickly as if it were made of hot metal.

I must talk to Susan immediately; she is the only person who can advise me how to handle this bombshell. How did it come to this? What did he say in all those unopened letters?

I think about our meeting at the hotel and I feel feverish, though my hands are ice cold as if I were about to get sick. There is a kind of queasiness in my stomach I have rarely experienced. It's the kind of feeling that presages something big, something difficult to absorb, like Tinek's departure for America.

I head over to Susan's to discuss my dilemma. Her mother is not at home. Great! We can talk. We sit at her kitchen table where the ashtray is already overflowing. "Go ahead, spill the beans," she says and lights another cigarette.

I tell her about Amnon's call. The ever-worldly Susan says immediately and confidently, "It's obvious; he is in love with you. That's why he came."

"You must be nuts," I say. "He is at least twenty years older; he is a married man with a child for goodness sake!" She laughs her throaty, cigarette-infused laugh. As soon as I say this I remember the last line of the last letter I dared open "...with love, Amnon." I feel funny telling Susan about it, but I begin to have a vague sense of what she means.

"What other reason would he have to come all the way from another continent and spend ten days on an ocean voyage?" asks Susan.

"Oh, I don't know... maybe he got a job offer here... maybe he is doing some business for the Israeli military?"

"Okay, I suppose that is possible, but if I were you, Annette, I'd read all those letters. They'd have a clue."

For a moment, I contemplate telling Susan about the strange thing that began to happen when the trickle of Amnon's letters turned into a flood. I decide not to tell her because it sounds impossible, though it's true. Really true and weird. I began to forget how to read Hebrew script. The harder I tried to read them, the more impossible it became. It was as if my brain rebelled at being forcibly extracted from Israel. If you aren't there where you belong, I won't spit out the right information, it seemed to say. I knew the words were still among my brain cells somewhere, but they started fading, hiding so deeply among my neurons that I couldn't access them. I felt awful and wondered if I was losing my mind.

Susan moves on to a different subject. "We have got to do something about your hair, Annette. You can't go to see him in your —pardon me—freaky braids. I'm taking you for a haircut at my hairdresser's."

"Haircut?" I say it as if I don't know what it means. "Why?"

"So you look a little more mature," Susan laughs again and flicks the ash off the end of the cigarette.

"But... my mother will—"

She stops me midsentence. "It's about you, not your mother. Come on, you are not a baby." I am apprehensive. What will upset my mother more: that I am going to some Manhattan hotel to see a man, or that I am about to cut off my braids, the ones she's loved and combed and braided with pleasure my entire childhood?

Saturday morning I sit in the beautician's chair on the Grand Concourse as Susan explains to her how to style my hair. She thinks I will look good in a Jackie Kennedy hairdo. I see the braids flop to the floor in slow motion and I am seized with momentary regret. All the years of effort Mama has invested in my hair are now on the floor, waiting to be swept up. Garbage. I cringe and look up into the mirror.

I do not recognize the face staring back at me. It's someone else, a girl with tousled hair suddenly given free rein, unrestrained by daily plaiting and ribbons. I turn my head this way and that, to see if the face resembles Jackie, or starlets I have seen in magazines, or me. Holy smoke, dare I say it? I am actually pretty. But how will I face Mama?

As we leave, Susan announces with panache, "I'm paying; it's my treat. You are now ready to visit lover boy. No, wait. Let's go to your house and let me give you some advice on what to wear."

"Okay, Susan, but I have a special favor to ask of you."

"What is it? You know you can ask me anything."

"Susan, would you come with me and wait in the hotel lobby, just... in case."

"In case of what?" she asks with a smirk.

"I don't know."

"Sure, what are friends for?" Susan says with a mischievous look.

The hotel seems modest by what I imagine American standards to be, though I've never seen any New York hotels. The simple lobby seems cramped with just a smallish sofa showing imprints of former guests and a couple of leather chairs with cracks at the seats and arms, small curlicues forming along the tears. A few guests sit smoking. A hapless clerk stands behind a cluttered wooden counter.

Susan says, "Good luck. I'll be here waiting for you."

"If I'm not here in half an hour come look for me," I say with a nervous titter. Then I glance toward the clerk, but he appears to ignore our cryptic exchange.

I ride up the small elevator wishing it had a mirror. Is my lipstick smudged? I tug at my skirt suddenly wishing it were longer. The door slides open with a groan and I'm there. My heart thumps furiously. I walk down the long corridor to room 306, glad that despite its worn look the carpeting muffles my steps. I knock cautiously.

Amnon opens the door immediately. It's as if he were standing at attention just behind it, waiting for me. He steps back into the room as I enter, looking entirely too large for the space. He looks at me with a huge grin and says, "You have certainly grown up since I last saw you."

I become very conscious of my hair, my tight skirt, my high-heeled shoes. What am I doing here? I feel a hot blush spread over my face.

"No, I take it back. On second thought, you are still a kid," he says winking.

I don't know if I should be offended or calmed.

Then he approaches me and embraces me ever so gently, wrapping his muscular arms around me. I stand there struck by lightning and just for an instant I melt into his embrace, then just as quickly I stiffen and he lets go of me, stepping backward. In a voice filled with gravity and emotion he asks me to sit down. My heart pounds like a drum. I half stagger into the chair by the window. I sit down crossing my legs and throwing my head back casually, trying to appear relaxed while my insides are churning.

He leans against the window frame and stands there quietly, backlit like an image on a television screen. Right now he is all of Israel: strong, rugged, vulnerable. He breathes audibly and I notice him fumbling with his fingers. His face is serious. I could have never imagined this war hero being nervous, but I can see that I am not the only one here in a state of turmoil.

"It wouldn't have been right to say it in a letter," he says.

"What did you want to say?" I ask gently because it embarrasses me to see him in such a muddle.

"To propose," he says, his brown eyes fixed on my face.

For a moment I have no idea what he is talking about. Propose? Propose what? What is he talking about? Then it dawns on me. The letters I did read, months ago, plus all the unopened ones begin to add up, begin to make sense.

"Anat, do you remember my wife?"

"Yes."

Her beautiful Yemeni face and her jangling earrings appear in my head though I'd rather not remember.

"I wrote you that we divorced. Do you know why?"

"No." The words that come out of my mouth feel foreign. They would fall on the floor with a thud if it were not for the carpet. I am not even sure I am speaking Hebrew.

"Anat, my beautiful Anat, you must know. I can't live without you. I want you... I want you to marry me."

Marriage? I feel as if I have been hit by a great boulder. I start shaking and my hands feel clammy. Tears fill my eyes. "But what about your little girl?" I try a weak diversionary tactic, but one I know instinctively will not work with a man who has fought and won a war.

"She will be fine with her mother. Children are resilient," he says looking at me as if I hold the key to his life.

No, I wasn't prepared for this. What was I thinking? I am an unsophisticated boob. This man has been declaring his feelings for me all this time and I didn't have the sense to put a stop to his written advances. Now, what do I do? This may be my only realistic chance to return to Israel. Should I grasp it?

There is an expectant look on his handsome bronzed face. Despite everything, he looks vulnerable, exposed and more boyish than his age. "Amnon, I am sorry, I'm, I'm... not ready for this," I stammer. I don't want to hurt him. I begin to realize the full extent of my stupidity. I have been irresponsible in hoarding his unopened letters filled with declarations of love. He looks indescribably grief stricken.

"I was afraid you might say that when you stopped answering my letters. Still, I hoped. You must think I'm an old fool."

I avoid his penetrating gaze. The room is dim and stuffy. A cheap-looking floral bedspread is the brightest thing in the claustrophobic space.

Old? Only if you can call Charlton Heston in *Ben-Hur* old. I stare out the window at the blinking neon light on the building across the street and feel the wetness on my face.

He walks over wearily to my chair and faces me. He stands there for a moment looking like a supplicant, studying me intently, as if I were a painting. Then he bends down, grasps my shoulders with his large hands and plants a passionate kiss on my mouth. His lips are firm and warm. I can feel the stubble on his cheek. I smell his cologne. And against my better judgment I kiss him back. I have never been kissed like this before. How can a man be so huge and so tender? From my scalp to my toes, my whole body is electrified. He pulls me up from the chair and wraps me in his arms. We stay locked in an embrace and kiss like people who have hungered for love for years.

Suddenly Amnon lets go of me. He sits on the edge of the bed with his shoulders sloping, eyes half closed and says, "I'll give you time, Anat. Don't worry."

"Amnon, I... I..." My attempt to say something, anything, fails.

Still unable to absorb what has just transpired I decide this is my time to make a dignified exit from this most undignified situation. My body is so tense I could break if he touches me again. This is so bittersweet. Why hadn't he asked me when I was still in Israel? What would I have said then? I don't know, but my life could have taken a different path.

I pick up my purse from the floor and walk stiffly out of the room without so much as saying goodbye. I do not want to turn around and see his face. If I do, I might stay forever. I am so shaken I don't even know if I can tell Susan about it, but she is cool.

When she sees my face in the lobby, she keeps quiet and knows instinctively that this is not a time for one of our chats or for a smart mouth remark. Instead, she hands me a lit cigarette. For lack of a better response I put it awkwardly in my mouth and not knowing exactly how to use it I suck on it like the baby I feel I am. A fit of coughing and choking on the smoke brings me back to my senses and we both burst out laughing, laughing like hysterical ninnies.

On my return home Mama's reaction to my shockingly short hair is as startling as the rest of this day. She just gives me one of her tight-lipped looks that say more than words and sighs gut deep. Her mute anger is worse than yelling. I actually wish she would yell.

"Go wash your face," she says.

I walk toward the bathroom quickly hoping she won't smell the cigarette odor that must be clinging to me like the overwhelming sense of my own naiveté. I go into the bedroom that Daniel and I share, glad that he is out for a while. My eyes still red from crying or from the cigarette smoke land on the calendar held by the Statue of Liberty, sitting on the desk. The statue is tiny, but she looms very large in my mind. I can almost see a smile on her little plastic face. It seems to be saying, "Give yourself time, America will love you back one day. It was a good decision to stay here." My thoughts revolve in circles and I keep coming around to the same questions: Do I love him? Could this be *it*? I have no idea. I don't know what love is yet. My mind races faster than my heart. I feel as if I've slammed the door to Israel shut permanently.

I hear Daniel at the front door. In a minute he bursts into our room like a whirlwind, then stops dead in his tracks and stares at me. "You cut your hair!"

"So what?" I say, unable to interpret his intense look.

"It's nice," he says and stacks his sketchpads on the desk.

23

We are en route to my graduation. Mama and Tinek have taken the day off work, something they have never done in America. Even Daniel is cutting school. Instead of our usual chitchat we're uncharacteristically quiet, immersed in private thoughts as the bus rolls along the Grand Concourse on this sunny June day in 1961.

My mind is already racing to college. I wonder if my parents are thinking that all they have been through since we left Poland has been worth it. Tinek is sure to think so. America opened to his children and the generations to come. I look at my little family group, grateful they are all here today.

Mama wears her best navy linen dress with a long row of gold buttons down its front and carries her one fancy beaded dress bag. Tinek sports a brown suit with a white shirt, his collar open. I hardly ever see him so formal. Daniel in a crisply starched white shirt seems taller than last year. He must be feeling proud he passed the entrance exam and got into Bronx Science by the normal route. His hair is long and hangs over his eyes. The way he brushes it to the side with a suave gesture tells me he is no longer a little boy.

But Mama is harder to figure out. There is no doubt she's very pleased with my and Daniel's successes, but on a personal level there is a void in her life not filled by any of us. She and Tinek are sitting on the bench across from us and I see her serene, yet inscrutable face in profile. Tinek holds her hand and winks at me when I catch his eye. I know she came to America only because Israel would have lost all of its charm without him.

We are just past Bedford Park Boulevard, heading south. Behind us, the bells of the St. Philip Neri church ring joyously as if all of the Bronx were celebrating this day. The bus moves past Alexander's department store. Near it, a line of shoppers with bulging bags stands at the bus stop. Only a few of them manage to board our packed bus. The Grand Concourse pulsates with life; it is different from Tel Aviv yet reminds me of it.

The bus stops near Loew's Paradise Theater. As we get ready to exit, I grab Mama's hand to calm myself. She gives me a little squeeze and the warmth of her palm feels at once pleasing and surprising. Have I made her even a little bit happier? If I did, I'd feel a little less guilty about being excited.

We walk with a throng of dressed-up students, parents, and grandparents, all advancing toward the Bronx icon with its romantic, ornate gray baroque facade; a two-story grand building topped by an antique clock.

Under the graduation gown my elegant navy taffeta dress rustles as I walk. With its snug embroidered bodice it is very chic and the high heels complete the look I've planned for weeks. My hair is styled in a wavy bob and for once behaves as it should. I'm nothing but another American girl primped and ready for her big day, anyone can see that. My interior is a whole other story; it still isn't so sure where this girl belongs. But the sky, the bluest I've seen in days, tells me today is not made for brooding. There is something indefinably grand in the air. Maybe it's the waves and smiles of the classmates who I recognize. Maybe it's my parents' constant questions: "Who is this?" "Who is that?"

"You have so many new friends," Mama says, and suddenly I realize that though I had many in Gvat, in Tel Aviv there were few classmates who were as close to me as Susan. I hear cheering on the crowded sidewalk and a group of pedestrians is applauding our procession: women with shopping bags and strollers in tow, men in workaday clothes. I give them a smile and wave as if I know them.

Through an enormous bronze gate we enter the opulent gilded inner lobby of the Paradise theater. Tinek says this is one of the great theaters built in 1929. It amazes me the things he knows. The lobby is packed with family groups and students, teachers and ushers trying to create order out of chaos. Like an unstoppable stream we flow into the main theater. Here I notice that some students are accompanied by huge contingents of family members: wrinkled, dignified grandmothers and grandfathers with silver hair, leaning on carved canes; little boys in pants with suspenders and seemingly countless brothers and sisters.

The main auditorium is an extravagant depiction of a baroque Italian garden. Around me I see marble, cherubs, gargoyles, delicate vines snaking around massive pillars, but it's the ceiling that catches my attention. It has a sky with twinkling stars and softly gliding clouds. Paradise! For a split second I'm sorry I don't believe, because such a heaven would be a lovely place in which to spend eternity.

In a noisy scramble for seats I bump into Susan, her mom and sister. She and I take our places and our families end up in the row behind us.

An expectant hush falls over the theater. All eyes are on the stage where Dr. Taffel and the faculty sit smiling, savoring all the effort they've put into us. Mr. Belacci is there, Mr. Katz whose Hebrew club I'll miss, Mr. Shaw who called me his Eliza, Mr. Rensin, our music teacher, Mrs. Tsaggos, the history teacher who gave me an A on my first American essay, so many others and, of course, my all-time favorite, Mr. Kopelman who rescued me on day one. He is far away on the stage but I can swear he's looking right at me.

Dr. Taffel introduces the commencement speakers, including a small man wearing a white military dress uniform. He's a dignitary from the Philippines. What is he doing here? I am a ball of nerves and can hardly hear the many speeches or absorb what the speakers are saying. They speak about our youth, our opportunities, our bright future, our chance to grasp our dreams. And it is that dream part that resonates most: medical school, a real American boyfriend, a home where I'll have my own private space and something special to bring Mama more joy. Well, maybe not in that order. The speakers' voices can't drown out the dueling thoughts in my brain. No, my list of dreams is wrong. It's too prosaic. To have given up Israel I must achieve something grander in my future, but what that is... I still don't know. I am anxiously waiting for my name to be called, to step up onto the giant stage dressed in my cap and gown to receive the piece of paper that'll prove I belong.

The speeches over, the students' names are called. I recognize all of them by their faces, even know the names of many by now, but I clap loudest when Susan, then Margaret go up on stage, followed by Sheldon and Carole. In the volley of applause that follows each recipient's turn there's a brief pause. That's when Tinek points to Dr. Taffel on the stage and whispers, "This is the man who made it all possible for Ania." And his comment makes me think that none of the friends I left behind in Gvat, or even Yom Tov, will ever have the kind of prospects that are now open to me. Tinek's fateful decision to emigrate, to take a chance at a new start no matter the obstacles, has set something miraculous in motion. It will be up to Daniel and me not to let it go to waste.

I half hear Dr. Taffel calling, "Lauder, Ronald please step forward." It's as if I have been elsewhere for a moment. Susan, sitting next to me clutching her diploma, touches my shoulder. "Annette, listen, they are already calling the L's."

"Libeskind, Annette, please come forward." Dr. Taffel

enunciates my name clearly and I hear it broadcast throughout the entire theater all the way up to the rafters. And this time, maybe for the first time, Annette sounds completely right, like a name I have always owned.

Slowly, I ascend the steps to the stage, savoring my moment of glory, trying not to trip in my high-heeled shoes.

Dr. Taffel hands me my diploma tied with a pink satin ribbon. "Congratulations, Annette," he says, shaking my hand vigorously and giving me a knowing wink.

The applause is thunderous. I think I can pick out my parents and Daniel clapping amid all the other hands. Finally, the diplomas all having found their proud owners, the class of 1961 bursts into the Alma Mater song written by Mr. Rensin, our math and music teacher:

"Science High our school whose towers reach for truth and light;
all for thee our hearts and powers solemnly unite."

And at that instant, as has become customary ever since Bobby Darrin was graduated from our school, we sneak in *"Oh baby!"* just before the chorus. We do it on cue, in an unspoken sliver of rebellion and approaching adulthood. The crowd laughs and I know Daniel and Tinek and Mama are laughing, and I am at last, one with my class, my all-American class, joining the song at the top of my voice, *"Oh baby!"*

PHOTOS

Foreground: Annette and her mother Dora aboard
the SS Constitution; Daniel on his mother's left

Annette and her parents visiting aunt Rosa in
Harrisburg, PA. Rosa (Nachman's sister;
Auschwitz survivor) and her husband Avreml
on the left

Nachman and Dora shortly after arrival in New
York; The Bronx

Annette (age 16) and her parents on a bench near
the Jerome Reservoir in The Bronx, 1959

Nachman and Dora after several years in America

Annette's graduation photo from The Bronx High
School of Science, 1961

Annette (age 19) visiting her brother, Daniel at Camp
Hemshekh in Hunter, New York, 1963

EPILOGUE

Nachman's faith in America paid off richly in the years that followed.

Annette married David, a first-generation American, and a Bronx High School of Science classmate whom she met during their first semester at City College. She'd been so reticent that she never ran into the gregarious young man who hung out with a pack of the most popular students at the Bronx High School of Science.

Both Annette and David pursued the study of sciences in graduate school. David became a chemist and a materials engineer who founded the first Environmental Testing Laboratory at the Port Authority of New York and New Jersey.

Annette began her professional life in cancer research at the Memorial Sloan Kettering Cancer Institute where she worked in the laboratory of the pioneering HIV/AIDS researcher Dr. Mathilde Krim. Later, Annette switched to work in wildlife conservation. She retired from the Wildlife Conservation Society as its first Senior Vice President in Environmental Education. Annette and David have been together for 60 years.

Dora turned to fiber arts, mixed media collages and writing during her eight-year struggle with cancer.

Nachman continued working at A&D Photo Prints into his seventies, until he resigned to take care of Dora. Something remarkable happened on her death bed: she extracted a promise from him to undertake painting after her passing. Nachman drowned his sorrow at her passing by plunging into art with a zeal usually attributed to young men.

You can read more about him in Annette's memoir, *In the Unlikeliest of Places: How Nachman Libeskind Survived the Nazis, Gulags and Soviet Communism.*

Daniel became a world-famous architect whose buildings, theaters and museums span more than two dozen countries.

Today, new generations of Libeskinds put their imprint on America and the world.

Please visit **annetteberkovits.com**
for more information

AMSTERDAM PUBLISHERS HOLOCAUST LIBRARY

The series **Holocaust Survivor Memoirs World War II** consists of the following autobiographies of survivors:

Outcry. Holocaust Memoirs, by Manny Steinberg

Hank Brodt Holocaust Memoirs. A Candle and a Promise, by Deborah Donnelly

The Dead Years. Holocaust Memoirs, by Joseph Schupack

Rescued from the Ashes. The Diary of Leokadia Schmidt, Survivor of the Warsaw Ghetto, by Leokadia Schmidt

My Lvov. Holocaust Memoir of a twelve-year-old Girl, by Janina Hescheles

Remembering Ravensbrück. From Holocaust to Healing, by Natalie Hess

Wolf. A Story of Hate, by Zeev Scheinwald with Ella Scheinwald

Save my Children. An Astonishing Tale of Survival and its Unlikely Hero, by Leon Kleiner with Edwin Stepp

Holocaust Memoirs of a Bergen-Belsen Survivor & Classmate of Anne Frank, by Nanette Blitz Konig

Defiant German - Defiant Jew. A Holocaust Memoir from inside the Third Reich, by Walter Leopold with Les Leopold

In a Land of Forest and Darkness. The Holocaust Story of two Jewish Partisans, by Sara Lustigman Omelinski

Holocaust Memories. Annihilation and Survival in Slovakia, by Paul Davidovits

From Auschwitz with Love. The Inspiring Memoir of Two Sisters' Survival, Devotion and Triumph Told by Manci Grunberger Beran & Ruth Grunberger Mermelstein, by Daniel Seymour

Remetz. Resistance Fighter and Survivor of the Warsaw Ghetto, by Jan Yohay Remetz

My March Through Hell. A Young Girl's Terrifying Journey to Survival, by Halina Kleiner with Edwin Stepp

---

The series **Holocaust Survivor True Stories WWII** consists of the following biographies:

Among the Reeds. The true story of how a family survived the Holocaust, by Tammy Bottner

A Holocaust Memoir of Love & Resilience. Mama's Survival from Lithuania to America, by Ettie Zilber

Living among the Dead. My Grandmother's Holocaust Survival Story of Love and Strength, by Adena Bernstein Astrowsky

Heart Songs. A Holocaust Memoir, by Barbara Gilford

Shoes of the Shoah. The Tomorrow of Yesterday, by Dorothy Pierce

Hidden in Berlin. A Holocaust Memoir, by Evelyn Joseph Grossman

Separated Together. The Incredible True WWII Story of Soulmates Stranded an Ocean Apart, by Kenneth P. Price, Ph.D.

The Man Across the River. The incredible story of one man's will to survive the Holocaust, by Zvi Wiesenfeld

If Anyone Calls, Tell Them I Died. A Memoir, by Emanuel (Manu) Rosen

The House on Thrömerstrasse. A Story of Rebirth and Renewal in the Wake of the Holocaust, by Ron Vincent

Dancing with my Father. His hidden past. Her quest for truth. How Nazi Vienna shaped a family's identity, by Jo Sorochinsky

The Story Keeper. Weaving the Threads of Time and Memory - A Memoir, by Fred Feldman

Krisia's Silence. The Girl who was not on Schindler's List, by Ronny Hein

Defying Death on the Danube. A Holocaust Survival Story, by Debbie J. Callahan with Henry Stern

A Doorway to Heroism. A decorated German-Jewish Soldier who became an American Hero, by Rabbi W. Jack Romberg

The Shoemaker's Son. The Life of a Holocaust Resister, by Laura Beth Bakst

The Redhead of Auschwitz. A True Story, by Nechama Birnbaum

Land of Many Bridges. My Father's Story, by Bela Ruth Samuel Tenenholtz

Creating Beauty from the Abyss. The Amazing Story of Sam Herciger, Auschwitz Survivor and Artist, by Lesley Ann Richardson

On Sunny Days We Sang. A Holocaust Story of Survival and Resilience, by Jeannette Grunhaus de Gelman

Painful Joy. A Holocaust Family Memoir, by Max J. Friedman

I Give You My Heart. A True Story of Courage and Survival, by Wendy Holden

In the Time of Madmen, by Mark A. Prelas

Monsters and Miracles. Horror, Heroes and the Holocaust, by Ira Wesley Kitmacher

Flower of Vlora. Growing up Jewish in Communist Albania, by Anna Kohen

Aftermath: Coming of Age on Three Continents. A Memoir, by Annette Libeskind Berkovits

Not a real Enemy. The True Story of a Hungarian Jewish Man's Fight for Freedom, by Robert Wolf

The Glassmaker's Son. Looking for the World my Father left behind in Nazi Germany, by Peter Kupfer

Zaidy's War, by Martin Bodek

The Apprentice of Buchenwald. The True Story of the Teenage Boy Who Sabotaged Hitler's War Machine, by Oren Schneider

———

The series **Jewish Children in the Holocaust** consists of the following autobiographies of Jewish children hidden during WWII in the Netherlands:

Searching for Home. The Impact of WWII on a Hidden Child, by Joseph Gosler

See You Tonight and Promise to be a Good Boy! War memories, by Salo Muller

Sounds from Silence. Reflections of a Child Holocaust Survivor, Psychiatrist and Teacher, by Robert Krell

Sabine's Odyssey. A Hidden Child and her Dutch Rescuers, by Agnes Schipper

The Journey of a Hidden Child, by Harry Pila with Robin Black

---

The series **New Jewish Fiction** consists of the following novels, written by Jewish authors. All novels are set in the time during or after the Holocaust.

The Corset Maker. A Novel, by Annette Libeskind Berkovits

Escaping the Whale. The Holocaust is over. But is it ever over for the next generation? by Ruth Rotkowitz

When the Music Stopped. Willy Rosen's Holocaust, by Casey Hayes

Hands of Gold. One Man's Quest to Find the Silver Lining in Misfortune, by Roni Robbins

The Girl Who Counted Numbers. A Novel, by Roslyn Bernstein

There was a garden in Nuremberg. A Novel, by Navina Michal Clemerson

The Butterfly and the Axe, by Omer Bartov

Good For a Single Journey, by Helen Joyce

The series **Holocaust Books for Young Adults** consists of the following novels, based on true stories:

The Boy behind the Door. How Salomon Kool Escaped the Nazis. Inspired by a True Story, by David Tabatsky

Running for Shelter. A True Story, by Suzette Sheft

The Precious Few. An Inspirational Saga of Courage based on True Stories, by David Twain with Art Twain

Jacob's Courage: A Holocaust Love Story, by Charles S. Weinblatt

The series **WW2 Historical Fiction** consists of the following novels, some of which are based on true stories:

Mendelevski's Box. A Heartwarming and Heartbreaking Jewish Survivor's Story, by Roger Swindells

A Quiet Genocide. The Untold Holocaust of Disabled Children WW2 Germany, by Glenn Bryant

The Knife-Edge Path, by Patrick T. Leahy

Want to be an AP book reviewer?

Reviews are very important in a world dominated by the social media and social proof. Please drop us a line if you want to join the *AP review team*. We will then add you to our list of advance reviewers. No strings attached, and we promise that we will not be spamming you.

info@amsterdampublishers.com

CPSIA information can be obtained
at www.ICGtesting.com
Printed in the USA
JSHW062024160822
29345JS00003B/12